Burden of Proof:
An Introduction to Argumentation and Guide to Parliamentary Debate

Mark R. Crossman

THOMSON
™

Australia · Canada · Mexico · Singapore · Spain · United Kingdom · United States

THOMSON
™

Burden of Proof
Mark R. Crossman

Executive Editors:
Michele Baird, Maureen Staudt &
Michael Stranz

Project Development Manager:
Linda de Stefano

Marketing Coordinators:
Lindsay Annett and Sara Mercurio

Production/Manufacturing Supervisor:
Donna M. Brown

Pre-Media Services Supervisor:
Dan Plofchan

Rights and Permissions Specialists:
Kalina Hintz and Bahman Naraghi

Cover Image
Getty Images*

The Adaptable Courseware Program consists of products and additions to existing Thomson products that are produced from camera-ready copy. Peer review, class testing, and accuracy are primarily the responsibility of the author(s).

Burden of Proof / Mark R. Crossman
p. 225
ISBN 0-759-36391-9

International Divisions List

Asia (Including India):
Thomson Learning
(a division of Thomson Asia Pte Ltd)
5 Shenton Way #01-01
UIC Building
Singapore 068808
Tel: (65) 6410-1200
Fax: (65) 6410-1208

Australia/New Zealand:
Thomson Learning Australia
102 Dodds Street
Southbank, Victoria 3006
Australia

Latin America:
Thomson Learning
Seneca 53
Colonia Polano
11560 Mexico, D.F., Mexico
Tel (525) 281-2906
Fax (525) 281-2656

Canada:
Thomson Nelson
1120 Birchmount Road
Toronto, Ontario
Canada M1K 5G4
Tel (416) 752-9100
Fax (416) 752-8102

UK/Europe/Middle East/Africa:
Thomson Learning
High Holborn House
50-51 Bedford Row
London, WC1R 4L$
United Kingdom
Tel 44 (020) 7067-2500
Fax 44 (020) 7067-2600

Spain (Includes Portugal):
Thomson Paraninfo
Calle Magallanes 25
28015 Madrid
España
Tel 34 (0)91 446-3350
Fax 34 (0)91 445-6218

Preface

In the mid-1990's, I converted the El Camino Forensics program to Parliamentary Debate. We had been blessed with success in CEDA, but I had grown to feel that CEDA had evolved to a place where it was no longer a good fit with our student body. Parliamentary Debate has opened the doors to debate competition to students that may not have been able to bridge the access barriers associated with CEDA. In the Pacific Northwest and California, "Parli" has supplanted CEDA as the dominant style of debate.

Despite the rapid growth of Parliamentary Debate, there are very few textbooks that provide, in my estimation, an adequate balance between discussing concepts that are accessible to all students, while providing more challenging theories that will be of interest to potential debate team members. I believe that *Burden of Proof* offers a valuable introduction to argumentation theory and Parliamentary Debate, while covering enough detail to interest students who have already been introduced to Parli.

I think that instructors will agree with most of what I have to say in this book. I am confident, however, that there will be points of disagreement. It was difficult, for example, to assert categorically the "stock issues" for the various propositions. I understand that there is no real consensus on issues such as criteria, topicality, etc. There is even some movement (I think in the wrong direction) to ignore any distinctions between proposition types. In constructing the theories, I have tried to strike a balance between what is practiced, and what is consistent with valid argumentation theory. Clearly, my background in CEDA and NDT has influenced my approach to Parliamentary Debate. Many of the theories associated with CEDA and NDT have shaped, and will continue to have an influence on the evolution of Parliamentary Debate. This phenomenon is natural as the core theories of value and policy debate reflect reasonable methods for testing propositions of fact, value, and policy. I think that *Burden of Proof* accurately reflects the evolution of Parliamentary Debate. I view the book as an ongoing process. I intend to regularly rewrite and update sections of the text and eagerly solicit constructive criticism.

FEATURES OF THE TEXT

Reasoning behind the Structure

The first three chapters of the text discuss general theories of argumentation, fallacies, and the Toulmin model. I think it is important that students understand the fundamentals of analyzing arguments before they tackle the game of debate. Chapter 4 provides an overview of Parliamentary Debate and introduces argumentation theories that are regularly discussed in the context of debate rounds. Chapter 4 may be used to quickly prepare students for a debate. Chapter 5 describes research strategies appropriate for both in-class debates and tournament competition. Chapters 6 and 7 detail burdens on propositions of fact/value and policy. Chapter 8 describes strategic issues associated with structure and refutation. Instructors may wish to assign the delivery chapter (Chapter 9) concurrently with the debate chapters. Chapter 10 can be used to prepare students to observe a forensics tournament. Chapter 11 is intended to be used only after students have mastered the basics.

Chapter on Advanced Theory

Chapter 11 is new to the third edition and it samples advanced debate theories. The goal of the chapter is to provide tournament debaters with some background into the more advanced theories and strategies which they may encountered as they progress in their debate careers. Because many of the theories are controversial, the intended tone of the chapter is more descriptive than prescriptive. The chapter will be particularly useful for coaches who have been looking for accessible theory readings to use as starting points for squad room discussions.

Special Section on Speech Anxiety

While research shows that speech anxiety is a common problem, it is one of the least discussed issues in argumentation texts. Authors have assumed that students who take argumentation courses are not anxious about doing debates. My experience indicates that this is a faulty assumption and that nervousness can impact both the speaker's enjoyment of the process and his/her ability to effectively deliver arguments. Consequently, I have included a section on speech anxiety as part of the discussion on delivery that is found in Chapter 9.

Introductory Chapter on Forensics

I have found it useful to send argumentation students to forensics tournaments to observe debates and individual events. Even students who will not be competing benefit by watching their peers perform. Out of concern for unintended interruptions and to give students an idea of what to expect when they arrive at a forensics tournament, I have included a chapter (Chapter 10) that describes tournament procedures and introduces the events.

Suggestion Concerning Incorporation of Research

Though written evidence is not allowed in Parliamentary Debate rounds at tournaments, I believe that Parliamentary debaters, like students who compete in Extemporaneous Speech, should be encouraged to defer to authorities. I have found that allowing students in argumentation courses to use written evidence in the context of Parliamentary Debate encourages the utilization of arguments from authority and promotes understanding of the tests of those arguments. This practice underscores the importance of using excellent research to support arguments, and helps foster the habit of quoting sources among would-be tournament debaters.

MANY THANKS

I begin by thanking the Creator for guiding me to a career that I love. Thanks also to my parents, Ray and Shirley, for supporting my efforts in debate through high school, college, and beyond; to my wife, Professor Diana Crossman, for proofing my thoughts in the delivery and forensics chapters (and for picking up the slack around the house while I was busy at the computer), and an especially big thank you to Professor Francesca Bishop for her tireless proofreading of the manuscript. I owe a great deal to my coaches: Robert Laskey (Sacramento High School), Chris Iwata, and Ken Lynch (Los Rios Colleges). I must pay tribute to the finest debate coach that I have known, Dr. T.C. Winebrenner (Cal Poly, San Luis Obispo), as the greatest influence on my choice of careers and primary contributor to what I know about debate. His knowledge, integrity, and dedication to debate and debaters has inspired me throughout my career. Finally, this text represents a small payback to the community of colleagues and competitors that I have learned so much from.

Mark R. Crossman

PREFACE

To Claire and Sara,
who numbered their arguments before they could read.

CONTENTS

Chapter 4   51

An Overview of Parliamentary Debate 51

Chapter 5   69

Research: Discovering and Supporting the Issues 69

Chapter 6   85

Arguing Propositions of Fact and Value.. 85

Chapter 7   111

Arguing Propositions of Policy 111

CONTENTS

CONTENTS

An Invitation to Argue

Well you can stake that claim, good work is the key to good fortune. Winners take that praise, losers seldom take that blame (Peart).

Everyone, every breathing person can make the winning argument. Many are forced into the mire and mud of the stagnant, immutable past. Locked in their psychic closets, many do not argue. And many who dare fail in their arguments and are frustrated or silenced. Many more argue, almost blindly, like those who have never held a bat in their hands who strike at the ball, strike and strike until finally, and by sheer chance, the ball collides with the bat (Spence, 5).

WHY YOU MUST CARE ABOUT ARGUMENTATION

Students new to virtually any discipline must certainly ponder its relevance to their lives. If you take the fast track, you will spend at least four years working on your undergraduate degree. If you are like the typical undergraduate, coping with work, perhaps a family, or other obligations, you will be spending considerably longer mastering "general education requirements." While the utility of many courses may not be readily apparent, you probably already have some sense of the importance of argument in your life.

Your Career

First, argumentation skills are necessary for career success. Taught within the context of a Speech Communication course, the study of argument will help you to become more verbally assertive and confident. Even a cursory review of journal and magazine articles aimed at the career conscious adult learner produces the very clear impression that public speaking skills are perhaps the most important factor in determining personal and corporate success. And while any forum that promotes public speaking confidence is useful, argumentation provides a particularly relevant context in which to work on public speaking abilities because it generally assumes an adversarial relationship between participants in the communication situation. Where a student participating in a basic public speaking course might be satisfied with having delivered his or her message well, a student of argumentation must be concerned with how to adapt arguments in response to a verbal challenge.

Having the ability and the courage to invent, deliver, and defend your ideas is key to career success in virtually all fields of endeavor. It is clearly not enough to be a gifted speaker. Eventually, lack of content will catch up to you. Nor is it enough to have great arguments and ideas, yet lacking the ability to communicate those ideas to the decision makers and audiences that may influence your career. Too many bright people will not realize their career and financial potentials because they lacked the courage or ability to communicate their message. Argumentation offers the potential to help you develop both a strong and logical message, and a compelling and effective delivery.

Your Public Life

A second benefit of the study of argumentation is its impact on the learner in public life. Particularly in a democracy, the ability to reason and to argue well is critical. Consider, for example, the 2004 presidential election. As parties and MTV scrambled to "turn out the vote," how many messages did you hear aimed at getting those voters informed? There are those who mourn the relatively low percentage of voters who participate in the electoral process. But voting can be worse than useless if the voter is not informed. Consider the fact that in many states, laws are actually made at the ballot box in the form of propositions. The average voter, however, may be basing his or her vote on the political advertisements broadcast on T.V. Students of argument learn to critically evaluate the arguments of candidates and the issues involved in propositions. A healthy democracy requires not simply an electorate, but an informed electorate. Those not willing to take the time to understand the issues and the process are not meeting the responsibility that comes with the right to vote.

Consider also the many other public forums in which argumentation skills are required. We live in a country that is home to three quarters of the world's lawyers. The result has been an increasingly litigious society. Depending on jurisdiction, you can be brought before a judge in a small claims court and sued for approximately $5000.00. If you fail to appear, a judgment can be issued against you. If you show up, but cannot defend yourself or support your argument, you may lose a case that you could have won, had you been prepared. There are, of course, countless other areas of public life that require argumentation. You might have to argue before your children's school board, or in front of a zoning commission to modify your property. You might even have to present an oral argument to determine whether or not you will be admitted into the university of your dreams. It is hard to imagine a venue in which public business occurs that does not require the use of argumentation.

Your Personal Development

Arguing is almost always thought of in the pejorative. We think of the overbearing attorney, or perhaps even the obnoxious friend who always has to assert his or her opinion (regardless of the evidence to the contrary). Like any tool, argument can be misused. When used correctly, however, it has the potential to change the way that you see your world. Today you may find yourself opposed to the death penalty, supportive of abortion rights, and a strong proponent of the legalization of marijuana. Careful study of the other side of those issues might change your opinion. People who study argument are forced to look at both sides of any issue they are supporting. Keep in mind that the best way to support your position is to know what your opponent is likely to argue. This process of examining both sides of issues frequently leads to personal change and growth. We all know people who have become too set in their ways of thinking. Perhaps they have become obsessed with some cause or issue. Passion for the position that one is advocating is noble, but if it blinds us to possible truths held by the other side, then we argue both weakly and incorrectly.

It is important to view debates and arguments as opportunities to refine perspectives until the best possible outcome is reached. Unfortunately, people grow to view conflict as personal. Instead of arguing ideas, some arguers will make personal attacks on their opponents. Some potential arguers are so sensitive to the possibility that they may be challenged, they run away from arguments. Both perspectives are obviously problematic.

Conflict within the context of debate is a good thing. At the heart of freedom of speech is the concept of the marketplace of ideas. Left unchallenged, arguments can shape beliefs. It is only through the introduction of contrary opinions that weaker ideas can be exposed. Being a good arguer assumes your willingness to be open to the possibility that you are not always right. To be able to find and acknowledge truths, even small ones, in your opponent's position will make you a more reasonable advocate and, ultimately, a more mature human being. You might, for example, disagree with much of the agenda of contemporary feminism. While you would probably oppose the idea that fathers are not important, or that marriage is tantamount to slavery, you would probably agree that women should be paid the same as men when performing the same job.

3

Finally, there is no evidence that being a competent student of argumentation and debate will enhance your personal relationships. If anything, within this context, the desire to prove oneself right usually comes at the expense of being happy. It has been my experience that couples who argue are rarely objective enough to recognize when their partner has defeated them. This text focuses on arguments that are made in front of relatively objective third parties who can evaluate the merits of the competing positions. Courses in Interpersonal Communication offer strategies for handling conflict within relationships.

While any one semester course can only promise to do so much, the study of argumentation and debate offers you many potential advantages. The goal of this textbook is to introduce you to a sampling of basic argumentation theories. Parliamentary debate will provide the framework for understanding the application of many of these theories. Debate provides an invaluable laboratory for exploring argument because it encourages participants to support their arguments and clash with the ideas of their opponents while being evaluated by a judge. But before we can proceed with our exploration of contemporary argumentation and debate, we must first pay homage to history.

HISTORICAL ANTECEDENTS OF ARGUMENTATION AND DEBATE

Initially, it is important to note that what follows is not history for the sake of history—sometimes the past is just the past, and sometimes it matters. It is difficult to imagine, however, how the study of argument would have evolved without the influence of the Greeks. We begin our analysis of the historical antecedents of argumentation with Plato.

Plato

You may know that Plato (429-347 B.C.) is widely viewed as the father of Western Philosophy (Golden, Berquist, Colman, 1984). You may not know that he had a great deal of influence on the development of theories that formed the basis of contemporary argumentation. Plato believed that the well-lived life was spent pursuing truth. Keep in mind that truth was an obsession for Plato. He thought that it originated with the gods and was, therefore, divine.

Plato's search for truth found itself at odds with developments in ancient Greece around the time of the founding of his Academy (387 B.C.). As Greek society became increasingly more democratic, the need for formal instruction in public speaking grew. The study of methods of oratory was referred to as rhetoric. Plato was concerned that, through the use of what he called a "false rhetoric," speakers would dupe their audience into believing something other than the truth. We can all think of contemporary examples that support his concern. Politicians are widely assumed to use trickery to fool voters into electing them. One could argue that voters have become so numb to the probability of politicians being deceitful that lying to the public is no longer even considered to be particularly offensive. Polls taken during the Clinton scandals indicated that Americans did not trust the President but generally thought he was doing a good job. Similarly, our judicial system is regularly criticized for allowing innocent people to be convicted and the guilty to be released. Juries are frequently the targets of ridicule. Following the decision in the Michael Jackson case, for example, pendants on both sides had critical things to say about the jury. Lawyers are also viewed with suspicion, but retain a great deal of public respect. One great irony of American life is that lawyers are disdained to the extent that vicious jokes are frequently told about them (Q: What do you call 1000 lawyers at the bottom of the ocean? A: A good start), yet law remains a more prestigious career than teaching.

Plato was highly suspicious of common people and their ability to know when they were being duped. Keep in mind that his teacher and mentor, Socrates, was put on trial on a bogus charge of corrupting the youth, and by a vote of 360-141, was put to death (Kennedy, 1980). Given this miscarriage of justice, how can the average person be trusted to fend off the power of rhetoric?

Plato's call was for a rhetoric motivated by truth. Plato is known for making his arguments in the form of play-like stories known as dialogues. In the dialogues, he would use contemporary philosophers to voice, sometimes using allegory, their opinions on specific issues. In one of his most famous dialogues, *The Phaedrus*, Plato uses the character of Socrates to argue for a noble form of rhetoric. In this view, the speaker worthy of social praise would be one who ignored self-interest, who sought not to mislead, but to reveal the truth.

Aristotle

Aristotle (384-322 B.C.), a student of Plato's, forwarded a systematic theory of rhetoric that attempted to address many of Plato's concerns. In his work, *The Rhetoric*, Aristotle developed what many consider to be the single most important text on the subject of persuasion ever written. It is safe to say that most textbooks that address either argumentation or public speaking have as their genesis Aristotle's *Rhetoric*. It is important to understand that Aristotle was a great classifier of things. He studied extensively all aspects of Greek life. Consequently, his analysis of rhetoric is quite comprehensive. For our purposes, however, we will examine only a few key areas.

5

Aristotle devotes some time to justifying the study of rhetoric. He first defines rhetoric as "the faculty of observing in any given case the available means of persuasion." He then argues that there are four primary benefits to the study of rhetoric. The first benefit is that rhetoric is necessary to uphold truth and justice. Here, Aristotle argues that truth and justice are naturally stronger than their opposites. If a speaker fails to persuade the audience and the truth loses, it is the fault of the speaker. Realize that this is really the basis behind our adversarial system of justice—two attorneys, each prepared, arguing in front of a jury. This theory would hold that the jury would be able to determine the truth because it is naturally stronger.

Questions to Ponder

Is the truth really stronger and can juries generally tell a lie from the truth? If the truth loses, whose fault is it?

Second, Aristotle argues that rhetoric is beneficial because it aids in teaching in a way suitable for a popular audience. Clearly the truth cannot be blamed if an advocate does a poor job of presenting his case. But legal arguments today are more complicated than they were. Recall the O.J. Simpson trial and the huge quantities of evidence associated with DNA and the various tests used to identify DNA. In a trial that lasts not weeks, but months, it is amazingly difficult to craft arguments that the average person can understand. Throw in the complexities associated with contemporary forensic evidence, and the odds of confusing a jury are high. Good advocates must analyze their audiences carefully, to determine the methods best suited for explaining their arguments. As Aristotle said, the advocate must look for all the available means of persuasion. Do not, however, take that statement to mean Aristotle would support the use of trickery or deceit. He held speakers to the highest ethical standards.

The third benefit of rhetoric that Aristotle articulates is that it compels the advocate to examine both sides of the issue. As I indicated earlier, strategically speaking, it is important to know what the other side will argue. As a debater, you should prepare a list of your main arguments and consider what the other side might say in response. Then think about what you will say back. Look for areas of agreement; these are issues that you need not argue. Being able to agree with small points that your opponent makes will make you sound more reasonable. A great debate coach once noted that arguers come into an argument with a sum total of credibility and, each time you argue, you lose a bit of it (this same philosophy can be applied to life and the total number of arguments you make). It is important, therefore, to choose your positions wisely and understanding the other side's positions is a great place to start.

The fourth and final benefit that Aristotle articulates is that rhetoric is necessary for self-defense. It is ironic that students will receive countless hours of instruction in physical education, they will be enrolled in a variety of extra-curricular sports, their universities will spend hundreds of thousands of dollars on athletics, but most schools will oblige you to take only one course in public speaking or argumentation. Someday, you may have to run away from a mugger, so a background in track and field may prove useful. But know that you will need to defend your ideas throughout your career. You may even find yourself in a career in which you are paid to argue. While it is important to remain physically fit, Aristotle would have you think of your work in argument and debate as a kind of verbal self-defense training.

Having laid out the benefits of rhetoric, Aristotle turns his attention to developing a comprehensive study of the methods by which a speaker might best persuade an audience. Perhaps the mostly widely discussed of these are the three artistic proofs. He argues that proof in a speech is either artistic (created by the speaker) or inartistic (things like documents that the speaker need simply compile). We turn our attention now to the three artistic proofs. These are probably the three most important concepts ever articulated with regard to persuasion. The artistic proofs are ethos, pathos, and logos.

Ethos is the proof that concerns itself with the credibility of the speaker. Credibility can be thought of as the extent to which the audience finds the speaker believable. Aristotle held that character, intelligence, and goodwill were necessary to establish a speaker's credibility. And while his belief was that character was established during the speech, as opposed to it being based on prior experience with the speaker, contemporary theorists have expanded the definition of credibility to include the credibility that you have prior to a speech (initial credibility), the credibility which you generate during the speech (derived credibility), and the credibility that you leave the room with (terminal credibility).

Questions to Ponder

What is character? Should the character of the speaker matter?

It is incorrect to suggest that credibility resides in a speaker. Credibility exists in the minds of the audience with regard to the speaker. This distinction is important because argumentation, unlike formal logic, is an audience-centered activity. A speaker may have a great deal of credibility in front of one audience, but entirely lack credibility in front of another. But make no mistake, credibility is critical for the persuasive message to be effective.

Consider the impact of ethos in the strange saga that was the Clinton Presidency. For some, the lies told under oath, coupled with adultery compromised the President's credibility. For others, Bill Clinton remained a champion of the working class. His speeches during and subsequent to his impeachment were filled with language attempting to establish his desire to return to the work of the American people. For this group, the speaker's goodwill was sufficient to establish his credibility. While a gross oversimplification of the complexities associated with Bill Clinton's public image, the example illustrates that credibility is both complicated and audience-centered.

Pathos is the proof associated with the emotions. Aristotle goes to great lengths to describe the emotions that might motivate audiences. Among the emotions he examined were anger and calmness, friendship and enmity, fear and confidence, shame and shamelessness, kindness and unkindness, pity, and envy. Each of these emotions has the potential to add to the persuasiveness of the speaker's message.

The use of emotional appeals in argument is quite common. Think of virtually any television campaign and emotional appeals will come to mind. Consider the anti-smoking advertisements that have become so prevalent. In one such advertisement a woman who had a hole placed in her throat as a result of cancer speaks to the audience about her addiction to cigarettes. At the end of the ad, she takes a drag through the hole in her throat. The underlying argument of the ad is that smoking is so addictive that even someone who has nearly died as a result cannot give it up. The pathos of the ad is clearly based on fear.

Fear appeals are quite common in television advertisements. Perhaps you've seen the advertisements for Brinks home security systems. A woman and two small children are home alone, an intruder tries to break in, and the woman uses the Brinks alarm to frighten the would-be intruder away. The narrator of the ad indicates the fee is just $24.95 a month and asks how much your security is worth.

Another commonly used emotional appeal is pity. We have probably all seen the Sally Struthers advertisements that ask us to adopt a child for just "pennies a day." Animal rights advocates have used a mixture of pity and shame to attach a stigma to the use of fur in fashion. Considering that the fur industry has lost millions in sales, it is not a stretch to say that their efforts have been effective.

Questions to Ponder

Think of advertisements that use emotional appeals.
Do you think that emotional appeals are overused?

As Aristotle knew, emotions are an inherent part of the human experience. While it is not entirely prudent to reason from our emotions (unemployed teens ought not get married simply because they "love" each other), emotions do play a part in our decision-making. They both influence and indicate our reactions to messages. Think about the undeniable influence on donations caused by the vivid imagery provided by television coverage of disasters such as the tidal waves in South East Asia and the hurricanes in Louisiana. Those images were viewed by people all over the world, and unprecedented levels of giving followed.

An ethical arguer can certainly use emotions to make a point. A well-balanced argument should include, however, evidence and proof which help to explain the reasoning behind the argument. When an advocate for a cause shows you a picture of something really disgusting, you might feel sad; it might enrage you to the point that you feel inspired to act. Imagine that the same image was suddenly made to look attractive. Think, for example, of animal experimentation. Clearly rats getting tumors for cancer experimentation is not a pretty thing to look at, but what if the rats looked really happy and content? Is the practice of animal experimentation still wrong if it looks like the animals enjoy it? Consider the opposite situation. What if someone showed you a picture of brain surgery and demanded that it stop because it looks really painful? The point here is the look of the thing is part of the message, but the argument is incomplete without the reasoning necessary to develop the underlying ethical and practical ramifications of the act. The reasoning involved in the argument can be found primarily in the logos employed by the speaker.

Logos is the development of the logic of arguments in the speech. Under logos, Aristotle develops the framework for two systems of logical thought: deductive and inductive reasoning. Deductive reasoning utilizes a model of argument known as the syllogism. The focus of the deductive argument is on the structure of the premises relative to the conclusion. Deduction, then, is concerned with whether or not the argument adheres to the rules of formal logic; whether or not it is valid.

A deductive argument reasons from general claims to a specific conclusion and the relationship between the conclusion and the premises is one of certainty. That is to say, if the premises adhere to the rules of formal logic (are valid) the conclusion must follow with certainty. The basic categorical syllogism has three parts:

Major Premise: A generalization which takes the form all X's are Y.

Minor Premise: Applies a particular example to the generalization expressed in the major premise (Z is an X).

Conclusion: The result of the application, which follows with certainty (therefore Z is a Y).

Major Premise: You must be at least 35 to be President of the United States.

Minor Premise: George W. Bush is President of the United States.

Conclusion: George W. Bush is at least 35 years old.

Deductive reasoning is a significant part of any formal logic course because it offers a rigorous framework from which to test the validity of argument. What it lacks, however, is flexibility. Because its focus is on the rules of logic, deduction ignores the interpretive interactive dynamic that occurs between an audience and an argument. A deductive argument, therefore, can be valid (adhere to the rules of formal logic) but simply inconsistent with the audience's experience. Consider the following twist on a famous categorical syllogism:

Major Premise: All men are fish.

Minor Premise: Aristotle is a man.

Conclusion: Aristotle is a fish.

The formal nature of the structure of the deductive argument also makes it challenging to utilize in debate situations. Aristotle's enthymeme is a type of syllogistic argument that makes more use of audience adaptation. The enthymeme is a truncated syllogism. The arguer will leave out either a premise or the conclusion and allow the audience to fill in the missing part based upon their experience. This strategy both includes the audience in the argument and reduces the risk of stating the obvious. An example of an enthymeme would be as follows:

Major Premise: Everyone who drives in Los Angeles needs auto insurance.

Minor Premise: You drive in Los Angeles.

Conclusion: If left unstated, the audience fills in the answer.

While deductive argument reasons from general premises to specific conclusion and the relationship between premises and conclusion is certainty, the inductive argument involves the use of specific observations and examples to support the probable truth of a claim. Many inductive arguments assume that the future will resemble the past:

Claim: I will not get a speeding ticket on Main Street today.

Support: I have sped down Main Street every day this week and have not received a ticket.

Like many arguments from induction, this argument is based upon experience, and you can clearly see that the relationship between the support and the claim is simply probability (the future does not always resemble the past).

People regularly use inductive reasoning. When you choose to fly on an airplane, you are basing your decision on past experience—the probability that you will land safely at your destination. Because of the probable nature of the relationship between support and claim (there is no guarantee that you will land safely) the comparatively good safety record of flying versus driving will not be persuasive to those who fear flying. Your experiences with studying have undoubtedly demonstrated a relationship between studying and getting good grades on examinations. Your past experiences with disclosure in relationships impact the manner in which you disclose in future relationships.

Questions to Ponder

How frequently do you base future decisions on past experience?
Is it wise?

While Aristotle recommended that an arguer should use an enthymeme first and examples merely as support, most modern audiences demand less formal and rigid methods of argument. Inductive argument, with its focus on examples and experience, is more commonly used today and will be the focus of much of our discussion throughout this text.

A CONTEMPORARY DEFINITION OF ARGUMENTATION

Having discussed some of the roots of argumentation, we now turn to a contemporary definition. *Argumentation is the process of formulating, presenting, and defending claims.* The formulation of claims involves understanding the proposition being debated, researching and gathering relevant support materials, and developing cases. The presentation of argument involves analyzing your audience and understanding the dynamics of both nonverbal and verbal communication. The defense of claims includes the ability to respond to attacks on your position and the ability to launch successful attacks on your opponent's arguments. Argumentation is not purely about logic, nor is it only an exercise in persuasion. Logical arguments which lack audience analysis will not be effective, and desperate attempts to win over the audience with nothing but emotional appeals are likely to fail, as well. A student of argument must understand how to best adapt logical arguments to win his or her case.

SUMMARY

It is unlikely that you will escape the need to engage in argument throughout your life and career. The study of argumentation promises to enhance your critical thinking, as well as your public speaking abilities. It is not enough to merely have good arguments. A competent arguer knows how to adapt those arguments to his or her audience. Ultimately, your academic and career success will be impacted by your ability to argue well.

The roots of modern argumentation can be found in ancient Greece. While many rhetoricians of the time impacted the manner in which we study argument today, Plato, and especially Aristotle, played particularly significant roles. Aristotle developed the notion that the most persuasive argument involved ethos, pathos, and logos.

Argumentation is the process of formulating, presenting, and defending claims. Effective arguers learn to adapt their arguments so that logic need not be abandoned for the sake of persuasion.

REFERENCES

Aristotle. *The Rhetoric and the Poetics of Aristotle*. Ed. Friedrich Solmsen. Modern Library, 1954.

Golden, James, Berquist, Goodwin, Coleman, William). *The Rhetoric of Western Thought*. Kendall/Hunt, 1984.

Kennedy, George. *Classical Rhetoric and its Christian and Secular Tradition*. Chapel Hill, 1980.

Peart, Neil. *Rush: Roll the Bones*. Atlantic, 1991.

Plato. *The Phaedrus*. Trans. W.C. Helmbold and W.G. Rabinowitz. New York: Macmillian, 1956.

Spence, Gerry. *How to Argue and Win Every Time*. St. Martin's Press, 1995.

EXERCISES

Chapter One: Invitation to Argue

1. List ten examples of careers that require expertise in argumentation. List ten examples of circumstances in your non-professional life that might require argumentation skills.

2. Watch either a live or televised speech. Describe the speaker's use of ethos, pathos, and logos.

3. Describe the emotional appeals in five television advertisements.

4. Write five deductive arguments. Clearly identify the major premise, minor premise, and conclusion of each argument.

5. Using InfoTrac, research an article on Aristotle's Rhetoric. Provide the source citation and a description of the central thesis of the article.

CHAPTER 1

Chapter 2

Identifying and Testing Inductive Arguments

FIELD DEPENDENCY

As was mentioned in the preceding chapter, scholars involved in the study of deductive reasoning analyze syllogisms and apply a variety of rules to determine whether or not they are valid. While the syllogism provided an excellent model for analyzing the deductive argument, for many years, methods for analyzing the inductive argument were not so clear. In 1958, a British rhetorician named Stephen Toulmin published a seminal book: *The Uses of Argument*. In it, he developed the notion that various fields of endeavor (law, medicine, academia, sports, etc.) may have language and issues that are unique to their specific fields. Arguments unique to a particular field are *field dependent*. However, perhaps more importantly, he pointed out that there exists a basic structure for all inductive arguments that can be outlined and analyzed. These parts of the argument are called *field invariant*; they do not vary as a result of the specific content of the field being discussed. The field invariant nature of these core building blocks enabled Toulmin to develop a model that allows us to break inductive arguments down into their primary parts.

TOULMIN MODEL

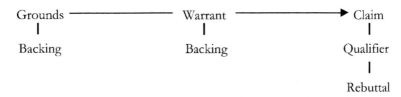

15

Claim

The claim is a single statement, advanced with support, which seeks to gain the adherence of an audience. A well-stated claim is very important. Too many arguers like to hear themselves argue; consequently, they develop claims that are paragraphs rather than sentences. To effectively communicate your claim, you must understand what the central point of your argument is and then phrase it as a single statement. Which of the following is easier to understand?

> "The ultimate goal is to find a way to cause a necessary termination
> of the activities associated with the putting to death of prisoners
> who have been convicted of murder."

> "The death penalty should be abolished."

When formulating your arguments, then keep your claims simple. The goal of argument is not to impress an audience with the quantity of words used. As you get more comfortable and skilled with making arguments, you will be able to make better use of your time by making better use of your word choice. If all else fails, keep it simple.

Claims are statements that are supported. Argument is an activity that requires that you justify your position. Argument is about providing adequate reasons to support claims. An arguer who cannot support his/her claim has an obligation to simply retract it. An arguer, then, always has a certain burden of proof (a concept that we shall discuss in greater detail later). A single statement that is offered without support is referred to as an *assertion*. Claims and assertions are alike in that both attempt to gain an audience's adherence or belief. Arguers making assertions, however, have failed to provide the requisite support necessary to adequately prove their claim. Because the person who brings the claim has a burden to support it, we would always presume against assertions. That is not to imply that merely providing a reason will be enough to guarantee an audience's support. But claims and their necessary support make the first step towards gaining adherence. After we have scrutinized the claim and its support, we may find the support inadequate. But, where real proof is needed to decide the truth of a claim, we should not accept a mere assertion, no matter how strenuously it is presented.

Questions to Ponder

Which of the following are assertions and which are claims?

"Gun control will reduce the number of handgun deaths."

"Limiting abortions will cause an increase in dangerous illegal abortions."

"Ideally, both a mother and a father will parent a child. Consider statistics that show the high rate of teen pregnancy among girls who had no father in their lives."

Grounds

When you refer back to the illustration of the Toulmin model you will note that an arrow points from the *Grounds* through the *Warrant* to the *Claim*. This is to suggest that the arguer is reasoning from the examples, analysis, and evidence that he/she is providing to the claim being made. Another way of thinking about it is that the grounds or support lead to the claim.

The grounds can take a variety of forms. In some circumstances, it is best to use a quotation from an expert (argument from authority). When an arguer uses a series of past examples to prove a claim they are arguing from example or generalization. Arguers who compare the attributes of similar examples argue from analogy. Arguments that suggest that the presence of one event predicts the existence of another are referred to as sign arguments. Arguments from cause contend that one event is contributory, sufficient, or necessary to cause another event.

Warrant

The *warrant* is the reason or logic behind using the grounds to support the claim. An arguer who provides grounds for a claim gets his/her argumentative foot into the door but, if under scrutiny, we find that the grounds provided do not support the claim, we are not warranted in using the grounds as support. Sometimes, the warrant is explicit. If, when arguing from authority, the debater presents the credentials of the source, those qualifications represent an explicit warrant to use the grounds (the quote) to support the claim. If the source is well-known to the audience, the source's credentials may not need to be articulated. In this circumstance, the warrant is implied.

Backing, Qualifier, and Rebuttal

Backing comes in the form of additional support for the grounds or warrant. An arguer might, for example, defer to authority by reading a quotation. Thinking that the audience could reject her initial source, he/she might include a second quotation as backing. *Qualifiers* are words that modify the claim, requiring more or less support. Claims all have relative argumentative strength. A claim that is qualified with words, such as may, might, could, possibly, etc., is not as powerful as a claim without qualifying language. Consider the following two claims:

> "There may be a connection between second hand smoke and cancer."

> "Second hand smoke causes cancer."

The first claim obviously seems more tentative. The result of the qualification is that the first claim requires less support. To argue that something may be true is not saying a lot. While the first claim does require less support, it also has less argumentative significance. Winning this claim does not do much for someone debating the need to implement smoking laws. The second claim, however, is quite certain. It carries a great deal of argumentative power. Accordingly, it is a difficult claim to support. The evidence supporting such a claim must be very strong. To be consistent with the language of the claim, the evidence must not be overly qualified. It must prove that second hand smoke causes cancer.

The *rebuttal* relates to the qualifier in that it defends the conditions requiring qualification. If, for example, it could be proven that second hand smoke caused cancer only in those people who carried a gene which made them susceptible to the disease, that circumstance would be the rebuttal to the claim that second hand smoke may cause cancer. That is, it both provides the reason that the claim must be qualified and explains the circumstances under which the claim is false. When faced with arguing a claim that has qualifiers in it, you should point out the qualifying language in the claim and ask under what circumstances the claim isn't true.

Questions to Ponder

Under what circumstances would the following claims not be true?

"The death penalty may deter crime."

"Smoking marijuana may not be hazardous to your health."

"Freedom of speech may be the most important right."

It is important that you be able to identify the various types of arguments. Once you can identify the type of argument, you can apply a test designed to analyze a specific argument type. We now turn to a closer examination of argument types and their specific tests.

IDENTIFYING ARGUMENTS FROM AUTHORITY

> School uniforms will reduce violence in our public schools. Steven Schultz—Former Superintendent of Public Schools—noted last year in Education Weekly that "Research conducted by the Long Beach City Unified School District showed a significant decrease in a number of crimes after school uniforms were adopted."

The preceding is an argument from authority. The type of argument is extremely common, not only in academic debate, but in virtually any context in which complex issues are argued. To quote authorities to support our arguments is to defer to authority. We defer to authority when we have reason to believe that the audience is not sufficiently expert in the subject matter of the claim. Keep in mind that the audience has to decide which arguer has the more correct interpretation of the facts. Obviously, the debaters have a vested interest in the outcome of the argument. Their opinions, therefore, are biased. Using a quotation from an authority is a way of introducing a third party into the debate so that the audience might defer to that authority when adjudicating the claim. Where an assertion is common knowledge, no evidence is necessary. But in a contested area in which the audience has little background, authority provides an appropriate means of supporting your claim.

The grounds in an argument from authority are the opinion of the source being quoted (the text of the quotation). The warrant is the qualification of the source—some sign that the source is a relatively unbiased expert in the field of the claim. Unlike other argument types in which the warrant may be implicit (not stated), the qualifications of the source should almost always be explicit. The exception to this rule is when the source is well known to the audience. Backing may come in the form of additional biographical information on the source or additional reasoning in the text of the quotation.

Recall again the argument concerning public schools. Using the Toulmin framework, we would break the argument into its key parts:

> *Claim*: School uniforms will reduce violence
> *Grounds*: Research conducted....showed a significant....adopted.
> *Warrant*: Steven Schultz is former Superintendent of Public Schools

Backing. Schultz's opinion was published in *Education Weekly* and he uses analysis from a study conducted by the Long Beach City Unified School District

TESTING THE ARGUMENT FROM AUTHORITY

Having identified an argument as an argument from authority, we can then apply a series of tests that will help us determine how strong the argument is. These tests are useful; both for constructing strong arguments, and enabling you to more effectively analyze and attack an opponent's arguments.

1) *Is the source an authority in the field of the claim?* This test probes the qualifications of the source. Recall that claims frequently involve certain fields of expertise. If you are making a claim involving law, the source you use should be an expert in law. Because expertise is really a subjective and relative attribute, an arguer is actually burdened to show a sign of expertise. Signs of expertise attempt to demonstrate that a person has a strong background in an area. A sign of expertise might be a degree in a field, or authorship of a book, or years of experience working in a particular field. The requisite sign is relative to the field. If you want a great plumber, you don't need a Ph.D., but a person with experience and training. You want to make certain, however, that sources do not cross fields of expertise. Recall during the 2004 presidential election that celebrities such as Barbara Streisand and Sandra Bullock argued vehemently for their candidate. Newspapers endorsed specific candidates. Actors are experts (sometimes) on acting. Newspapers are qualified (generally) to report facts. Neither is qualified to tell you for whom you should vote.

Consider also the amount of air time dedicated to celebrity opinion on the war in Iraq. Laura Ingraham (2003) writes,

> Whenever a top entertainer has a political bone to pick, he or she has an instant platform...So for the months leading up to the war in Iraq, it was Susan Sarandon, Tim Robbins, Martin Sheen, Janeane Garofalo, and Mike Farrell, in an ensemble anti-Bush performance. The media gobbled it up. They were everywhere. Susan at an antiwar rally in D.C. Mike in Los Angeles debating Sean Hannity. They are given the platform because they are celebrities. Period.

Clearly celebrities have a right to express their opinions. One has to question, though whether democratic decision making is enabled when, given the finite amount of time available on the national news media, celebrity opinion is being substituted for expert opinion. News organizations have an obligation to provide the best possible sources on both sides of an issue. Particularly on issues as important as when a nation should go to war, critical thinking audiences need access to qualified sources.

Being able to analyze the source's qualifications assumes that you know them. These qualifications provide credibility (ethos), which helps to provide the reason (warrant), that the quotation (grounds) supports the claim. The arguer should almost always present the qualifications of the source, typically before reading the quotation. Arguments from authority that lack the source's qualifications are invalid because there is no reason to use the grounds to support the claim. The exception to that rule is if the source is well known or a recognized institution. It would be redundant to qualify a well-known source to an audience (e.g., the President). Like the enthymeme, the warrant in that circumstance is filled in by the audience.

When deferring to an institution (a magazine, newspaper, journal, etc.), you might not verbally cite the name of the author of the quotation. In this circumstance, you are seeking to derive credibility by deferring to the authority implicit in the institution. *Time* magazine, for example, has an implicit institutional credibility. When quoting *Time*, you might choose to only cite that the quotation was from *Time* and provide the date the article was published. The fact that a particular staff writer wrote the quotation is not what provides the sign of authority. The editorial reputation of *Time* provides the sign that the quotation is accurate.

2) *Is the source relatively unbiased?* A source is biased when he/she is unduly influenced to take a position. Bias tends to be caused either by personal interest or ideology. Personal interest usually takes the form of money. One of Washington's on-going controversies concerns whether or not to impose limits on campaign contributions. When tobacco companies provide enormous campaign contributions to members of congress, many voters are left wondering whether that will influence those members' votes on anti-tobacco legislation. Bias caused by personal interest is often an issue in court, as well. The so-called expert witness is frequently paid for his services. Juries have to decide if they are testifying in a way that will please the side that hired them, or if they are legitimately trying to present the truth, the whole truth, and nothing but the truth.

Like personal interest, ideology is also a potential cause of source bias. At one end of this spectrum, we think of people who are overly obsessed with a cause as fanatics. The opinions of extremist are usually dismissed as overly biased. This issue gets tricky, however, when we think of people who are not clearly extremists, but are simply assertive advocates of their causes. Like a double-edged sword, no one will be more expert than a person who dedicates his or her life to a particular pursuit. The question here is whether that dedication has caused an obsession that stops him/her from recognizing the truth of opposing perspectives. High-ranking members of a political party are probably expert on the key issues of their party. When arguing, however, will they attempt to present the most objective perspective on a particular issue, or will they argue in a way that will ensure the stability of the party? Of course, bias, like many principles of argumentation, is relative to the audience's perspective of the source. A group of true believers in a cause will not reject as biased a quotation from someone who holds their perspective, no matter how extreme.

Bias, then, is clearly a relative concept. All sources are biased to some degree. Newspapers and television newscast are biased when they choose stories that will increase their marketability. Critics contend that many members of the news media are also ideologically biased. In their book, *The Media Elite*, Lichter, Lichter, and Rothman (1990) report that approximately 80% of reporters vote as democrats. Their positions on key social issues are quite liberal. A poll of reporters, published in *The Media Elite*, found that 90% of reporters believe in abortion rights, 19% believe environmental problems are overstated, and 80% support affirmative action. Regardless of your position on those issues, it is important to recognize that such an overwhelming liberal emphasis among reporters may have an influence on the "spin" given to stories on political issues. As a student of argument, it is important that you not take for granted that all things published in a newspaper are necessarily accurately reported.

The 2003 California Governor's election drew national attention. In the final week of the election, the *Los Angeles Times* ran a cover story reporting that candidate Arnold Schwarzenegger had groped a number of women. The timing of the article, and the fact that no similarly critical pieces on other candidates had appeared, raised questions about the paper's objectivity. Jill Stewart, a former *Los Angeles Times* columnist wrote,

> The overriding issue is the out-the-gate bias with which the paper conducted its coverage. The *Times* ultimately created a huge team dedicated to digging dirt, of any kind, from any decade, on rumored and reported personal behavior by Schwarzenegger. Yet while the newspaper poured massive resources into this effort, it did not create a similar team, or even seriously discuss a team, to dig dirt on rumored and reported personal behavior by Davis (Stewart, 2003).

But the influence of bias is not limited to newspapers. Everyone who works for a company or a cause has some financial interest in his or her employer. Advocacy written for that employer, therefore, may reflect the author's financial stake in the impact of his/her words. It may be impossible to find an entirely unbiased source.

As a critical thinker and a participant in the electoral process, you should read a variety of newspapers and news magazines. Ideally, those sources should reflect a range of political opinion. As an arguer, the best that you can do is to try to eliminate sources that seem overly biased and, if necessary, admit any important biases to your audience. It is better that revelations harmful to your sources come from you.

3) *Is the source's opinion recent?* Facts, opinions, and statistics may change over time. An author, who might support one opinion at one point in time, could change his or her mind completely at some distant later date. Consider the recent marriage of Gloria Steinem, contrasted with her statement made in the 70s that "a woman needs a man like a fish needs a bicycle."

The date associated with a quotation is not always relevant. Quotations involving history or philosophy may be timeless. The key question is, do we have reason to believe that the facts have changed? Be especially careful to scrutinize the dates on studies and statistics. New findings in research regularly replace their predecessors. When comparing the credibility of two quotations, the most recent source may reflect the more contemporary understanding of the facts and may, therefore, give an arguer a competitive advantage.

4) *Does the source provide any reasons for his or her opinion?* The primary warrant in an argument from authority is the source's qualifications. When the grounds/quotation are exceptionally short, there may not be enough of the source's reasoning present to provide adequate backing for the authoritative warrant. In our example concerning school uniforms, you'll note that in addition to the source's qualifications (warrant from authority), there is backing in the form of a study (a second authority warrant). Unless some of the author's reasons are present in the quotation, we have to rely strictly on the credentials of the author. Given that audiences may doubt those credentials, it is risky to omit at least some of the author's reasons.

On the other hand, debate is a timed activity. You do not have time to cite extremely long quotations. When you are in a forum in which there is an expectation that you will read quotations to an audience, make sure that quotations are short enough to keep the audience's attention, yet have enough information for the audience to gather how the authorities reached their conclusions. When constructing the quotation, it is acceptable to omit unnecessary material from the original text, so long as the resulting quotation accurately reflects the original intentions of the author as reflected in the article.

5) *Is the source's opinion consistent with the opinion of other experts in the field?* Experts can be wrong. When two sources are on opposite sides of a claim, one of those sources is

probably wrong. Something has to explain that difference in opinion. One sign that an expert is correct is that his or her opinion is consistent with those expressed by other experts. We live in a time of easy access to large amounts of information. Arguers today can access thousands of relevant opinions on most issues simply by doing a search on the computer. What you'll find if you do much research is that you can find someone who will say virtually anything, regarding virtually any topic. It is easy, therefore, to find a source with reasonable credentials who expresses an opinion entirely opposite to that which the majority of experts believe to be true. If an arguer can present only one or two sources to support a claim, it may weaken the credibility of that claim.

On the other hand, sometimes the one source arguing against the crowd is correct. There was a time when people thought the world was flat and that those advocating a round earth theory were crazy. Having multiple sources that support a claim does not prove conclusively that the claim is true; it just makes it more probable. In terms of the Toulmin model, using additional sources to support an argument from authority provides *backing* for that argument. Arguers who defend a claim with only one source need to be able to explain why that source's opinion may differ from those of their colleagues.

6) *Where statistical evidence is concerned, have qualified authorities gathered the statistics?* Statistical evidence provides context to our arguments by giving our audience the "big picture." They quantify a problem or a situation. Statistics are either *descriptive* and measure data from an entire population or are *inferential* and base their description of the characteristics of a population upon data gathered from a subset of the population referred to as a sample. Statistics can be powerful tools for an arguer. Where an emotional illustration may stir the audience through pathos, a statistic can help the audience know how frequently that emotional example actually occurs (logos).

Those who gather statistics (or statisticians) must be careful not to introduce variables into the process that bias the outcome of their research. Consider, for example, research on human sexuality. How honest do you think most people are when responding to surveys in this area? Researchers find that the mere presence of a researcher can influence the outcome of a study. People may be much more likely to respond truthfully in private, because they are not attempting to create an impression through their answers. Many people will attempt to impress the researchers or to appear socially responsible. People who indicate that they will vote oftentimes don't or will indicate that they are voting for the less controversial side of an issue when, in fact, they are voting the opposite way. Prior to the passage of California's controversial Proposition 187 (a measure which attempted to cut back aid to illegal immigrants), surveys indicated that the proposition carried only a narrow lead. The actual vote demonstrated a substantially larger margin of victory than was predicted.

*Are **you** more likely to be honest in response to a written survey or a verbal survey?*

Another factor that impacts the outcome of statistical research involves the question of *randomness*. In inferential statistics, researchers infer something about a large group (the population) based upon the responses of a subset of that group (the sample). Inferential reasoning is necessary because populations can be too large to question everyone. If the sample is to accurately represent the characteristics of the population, every participant in the population must have an equal chance of being included in the sample. This is tricky to accomplish. When conducting polls, researchers must be very careful not only about whom they call, but when. Polls conducted during the day may unfairly skew the sample towards the unemployed or stay-at-home parents. Surveys taken on weekend evenings may skew the sample in favor of groups of people less likely to go out. The importance of randomness grows as the sample size decreases. Researchers attempting to predict the outcome of Presidential elections may utilize sample sizes of a few thousand. One need only look to the fact that the pollsters are frequently wrong to note how prone to error small samples may be.

As an arguer, you should be familiar with at least the basic manner in which your statistical evidence was compiled (the methodology of the poll or research). You should be able to question your opponents about the methodology involved with their statistical evidence, as well. Few audiences have the ability to accurately scrutinize statistical evidence. Because of the complexities associated with gathering statistical evidence, you may defer to the credibility of the source of the statistic. Polls conducted by organizations like Roper and Gallop are generally well-trusted. In addition to looking for expert sources for statistics, avoid research conducted by organizations that may have a vested interest in the outcome of the research. Research conducted by the tobacco industry is likely to be supportive of their products. Studies conducted by government bureaucracies to monitor and report on their efficacy are less likely to be critical than those conducted by independent researchers.

IDENTIFYING THE ARGUMENT FROM SIGN

When arguing from sign, arguers suggest that the presence or absence of one event is predictive of the presence or absence of a second event. Argument from sign involves correlation, not causation. The arguer is saying that A accompanies B, not that A causes B. Consider the following sign argument:

> "John is very good at making frugal financial choices. He is going to a community college, and we all know how much cheaper than four year universities they are."

In terms of the Toulmin model, the *claim* made here is that John is frugal. The *grounds* are that John is going to a community college. The *warrant* is the implicit association that going to a community college is a sign of being wise about managing money. Clearly, many students do attend a community college for financial reasons, but others may well be there for other reasons. The example points to the potential fallibility of sign reasoning. Remember that sign reasoning assumes that because two things have gone together in the past with regularity, they will continue to do so in the future.

In some circumstances, sign reasoning can be very useful. Consider that medical diagnoses are often based upon reasoning from sign. If you have been vomiting and have a high fever, the doctor may conclude (by sign reasoning) that you have the flu. Because sign reasoning is not an exact science, there are some questions we can ask when faced with analyzing arguments from sign.

TESTING THE ARGUMENT FROM SIGN

1) *How regularly do the two observed events accompany each other?* When analyzing an argument from sign, you are attempting to determine whether or not the presence of one event is a reliable predictor of the presence of another event. One method for analyzing sign arguments, therefore, is to examine the history of the relationship between the two events and determine if there are a sufficient number of examples that establish the truth of the warrant and to determine if there are examples to the contrary.

> "Dr. Laura must be an expert on relationships. She has written many books on relationships, has her own radio show, and, after all, she is a Ph.D."

The arguer here is contending that having written many books on relationships, hosting a radio show, and having a Ph.D. are all signs of being an expert on relationships. When analyzing this argument, we would first ask how often people who have these credentials have been considered expert. We would also ask if there are many circumstances in which people who are not relationship experts have their own radio shows. Are there circumstances in which people with a Ph.D. are not relationship experts? Are there people who write "many books" on a subject who are not expert in their area of publication? To be able to effectively analyze this argument, you have to be able to rely on your knowledge and experience with these issues. A good arguer has the ability to draw upon his/her experiences and knowledge and apply them to an argument. It would help, for example, if you knew that Dr. Laura Schlesinger's doctorate is not in a field related to relationships, it is in physiology. You might also note that there is a difference between writing one book and writing "many books." Authoring several books could be viewed as a stronger sign of expertise.

2) *Could other factors have confused the relationship?* Keep in mind that sign reasoning is a form of circumstantial evidence. Many factors can be involved that will weaken the predictability of the sign relationship. Without an eyewitness to a murder, we are forced to rely on physical evidence (such as blood left at the scene) as a sign of the guilt of defendant. It is possible, however, that the blood left at the scene was the same type as the accused, but not actually his blood. Advertisers would have you reason from sign when they suggest that owning expensive cars, and other status symbols, are indicators (signs) of financial success. If you believe the advertisements, happiness can easily be achieved if you can afford to purchase their products. While it is true that wealthy people often own expensive toys, many wealthy people are financial stable because they do not choose to spend their money frivolously. Additionally, the man or woman behind the wheel of the luxury car may be deeply in debt.

IDENTIFYING THE ARGUMENT FROM CAUSE

In sign argument, the contention is that A correlates with B. In argument from cause the arguer is taking on the more challenging task of contending that A causes B. Causal argument is very common, but also easily prone to error. When trying to make sense of some causal relationship, it is difficult to be able to isolate what is actually producing the effect. Environmentalists have contended, for example, that industrialization has caused the phenomenon known as global warming. There is, however, a substantial body of evidence on the other side of that issue that indicates that global warming may simply be temporary and reflect the natural increases and decreases that have occurred over the lifetime of the planet.

A cause is sufficient, necessary, or contributory to the production of an effect. A *sufficient cause* is one that is enough to produce the effect, but not the only possible cause of an effect. Jumping out of an airplane without a parachute is a sufficient cause of dying, but obviously not the only way of doing it. A *necessary cause* is a causal factor that must be present for the effect to occur, but may not be sufficient to produce the effect. Researchers have long struggled with the cause of cancer. We know that many people who smoke get cancer, but most don't. Smoking, therefore, cannot be a sufficient cause of cancer or everyone who smoked would get cancer. Gene researchers have been looking into what they believe are necessary causes of diseases like lung cancer. They would argue that the necessary cause of cancer might be a genetic predisposition to the disease. According to this theory, if you have the genes that predispose you to a cancer risk and you smoke, you get cancer. The genetic predisposition, therefore, is the necessary cause of cancer.

A *contributory cause* is a factor that is significant in the causal environment, yet is neither sufficient nor necessary to produce an effect. Because of the complex nature of causal relationships, it is often difficult to isolate a necessary or sufficient cause. Education, intelligence, motivation, parental involvement, and the impact of mentors all may contribute to career success. It would be difficult to isolate any one factor as a sufficient or necessary cause. Arguers may define a relationship as contributory to avoid the rigorous burdens associated with necessary and sufficient causes. An arguer could contend that just about anything contributed to an outcome. To argue that something is a contributory cause compels a substantially reduced burden when compared to sufficient or necessary causes because the contributory cause is not being isolated as the unique cause of an effect. It is much easier, for example, to argue that violent lyrics play a role in teen violence than it is to argue that violent lyrics alone cause teen violence.

Argument from cause can take the form of cause to effect reasoning or effect to cause reasoning. In effect to cause reasoning, the claim will be the cause, and the grounds will be the effect:

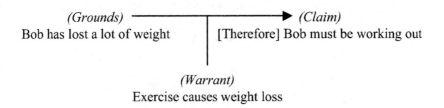

(Grounds)
Bob has lost a lot of weight

(Claim)
[Therefore] Bob must be working out

(Warrant)
Exercise causes weight loss

In cause to effect reasoning, the claim will be the effect and grounds will be the cause:

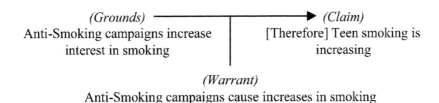

(Grounds) ────────────────► *(Claim)*
Anti-Smoking campaigns increase | [Therefore] Teen smoking is
interest in smoking | increasing

(Warrant)
Anti-Smoking campaigns cause increases in smoking

TESTING THE ARGUMENT FROM CAUSE

When evaluating the argument from cause, it is important to consider the following questions.

1) *Is there any reason to believe that the relationship between the claim and grounds is coincidental rather than causal?* A common error in reasoning occurs when an arguer reasons that because one event precedes a second event, it must be the cause of the second event. To reason this way is to commit the *Post Hoc Ergo Propter Hoc* (after the fact, therefore because of the fact) fallacy. This is the basis of superstitions. There are those who think black cats cause bad luck or that breaking a mirror causes bad luck. If they do these things and something negative happens, they reason that the first event must have caused the second event.

2) *If the cause is sufficient, is it present in any case in which the effect is absent?* There are those who argue that the key to solving crime is to rid the country of poverty. Few would argue that a poverty-free society would not be a noble goal. But to contend that poverty is a sufficient cause of crime, one would have to argue that all poor people commit crimes. Any example of poor people who do not commit crimes (that would be the vast majority of poor people) would disprove the causal relationship.

3) *If the cause is necessary, is it absent in any case in which the effect is present?* Looking again to the argument that poverty causes crime, we can prove that poverty is not a necessary cause of crime by listing cases of wealthy people who have committed crimes. If poverty were a necessary cause of crime, it would be present whenever crime (the effect) was present.

4) *If the cause is contributory, what conditions must be present for the effect to occur?* Because contributory causes are generally vague, they are difficult to test. Those who argue that a cause is contributory are implying that some percentage of the entire causal formula can be explained by a particular cause. You should press them to articulate that percentage. Can, for example, poverty explain 80% of crime? Additionally,

those who would argue that a cause is contributory should be pressed to demonstrate what other causes must be present for the effect to occur. You can then point to instances where that combination of causes was present, but the effect was absent. Both of these questions would be extremely difficult, if not impossible to answer. It is important to try to find the real causes of effects, particularly when dealing with serious social problems. For solutions to be effectively crafted, arguers must first isolate the true cause, or their solutions will be doomed to failure.

IDENTIFYING THE ARGUMENT FROM EXAMPLE (GENERALIZATION)

When arguing from example, arguers attempt to establish the truth of some general principle by using examples. The argument from example uses examples drawn from a class of subjects and attempts to make conclusions about that class based upon the examples provided.

Argument from example is extremely common. We base many of our daily decisions on generalizations that we have formed based upon our experiences (Adler and Towne, 1996). In some instances, faulty use of generalizations can lead to stereotyping. Our fears of Americans of Middle Eastern decent should not increase as a result of the evil actions of fanatics who are not even American. We should not use a few examples of radical Muslims to create a generalization about all Muslims.

Consider how many decisions you make based upon your experiences with companies. If you regularly receive good service at a particular bank, you are more likely to continue to bank there. If a particular make of car has served you and people you know well, you may purchase another one someday. Because our lives are filled with so many decisions, it is difficult to evaluate each circumstance independently. Further, the risk associated with a decision may influence the number of examples that we require to make that decision. This is not always rational thought, but risk plays an enormous role in decision-making.

Questions to Ponder

How many examples are required to adequately support an argument?

Following the President's speech before Congress that rallied the nation for war against terrorism, CNSNEWS.COM (a conservative on-line news source) argued that most news organizations supported the President's speech. In support of their argument they listed examples from several prominent news organizations. Using the Toulmin model, we could diagram their argument as follows:

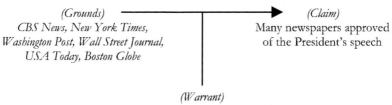

(Grounds)
CBS News, New York Times,
Washington Post, Wall Street Journal,
USA Today, Boston Globe

(Claim)
Many newspapers approved
of the President's speech

(Warrant)
These newspapers are representative of most newspapers.

Qualifiers play an important role in argument from example. The argument above uses the word "many" to qualify the claim. There are two types of claims involved in this argument type: *limited generalizations* and *universal generalizations*. *Limited Generalizations* propose that something is true more often than not, and the claims advancing these arguments will include qualifiers like many, most, and often. "This house believes that, more often than not, national security is more important than privacy" is a limited generalization. The burden when arguing that something is more true than false is great, but not as challenging as proving that something is always true. The second type of generalization is the universal generalization. A *universal generalization* is an argument that contends that what is true of some of the members of a class is true of the entire class of subjects. "National security is always more important than privacy" is a universal generalization. Claims intended to be universal in orientation might include words, such as all or always, to indicate that the arguer intends to describe the entire population of subjects, rather than a more limited group. If the intent of the argument is unclear, be sure to ask. Failure to ask questions or to determine in some other manner what the arguer intends to support will make the argument very difficult to defeat as you attempt to show examples to the contrary and your opponent responds that he/she never intended to show that all X's are Y, just that most are. A good rule of thumb in debate is to find out what it is you are arguing before you formulate your attack.

TESTING THE ARGUMENT FROM EXAMPLE

1) *Have a sufficient number of examples been provided?* When an arguer is supporting a universal generalization, he must be able to support that all members of the population in question conform to the claim. Where a more limited generalization is claimed, the exact number of examples required becomes less clear. Ultimately, the audience becomes the final arbitrator of the argument and will determine if enough examples are provided.

2) *Are the examples provided in the grounds representative of the population involved in the claim?* If we are arguing about the attitudes of men on the issue of feminism, simply polling male college students is probably not sufficiently representative of men in general. Ideally, examples will share the same basic diversity of characteristics that are present in the subjects in the claim. It is difficult, for example, to pass federal laws targeting education in all of the United States. The needs of states like California are very different than those of states like Massachusetts. You need to carefully scrutinize the characteristics of the population described in the claim and check to see if the examples provided share the same essential characteristics.

3) *Are negative examples accounted for?* If one side of an argument provides three examples to support their side and the other provides one to show that the argument is not true, which side should prevail? If the claim is universal in nature (all X are Y), any counter example that is representative of the population described in the claim must be answered. Where the arguer is making a more limited generalization, negative examples must still be accounted for, but could theoretically be overwhelmed by superior numbers. Suppose you make the claim that most illegal drugs are life threatening and cite as grounds the examples of heroin, cocaine, and methamphetamine. If your opponent points out that no one has overdosed on marijuana, you would be able to respond that one example does not overcome the number of examples that you have provided. You could also note that simply because no one has overdosed on marijuana, it does not mean that it is not life threatening. It comes down to your definition of life threatening. Definitions will be addressed in a later chapter.

4) *Which examples best represent the true characteristics of the population?* This standard is applied when evaluating two competing examples. Imagine a debate on the proposition that the First Amendment should be viewed as absolute. The side supporting the proposition argues that the First Amendment must be protected because newspapers should have the right to freely discuss political issues, citizens should have the right to protest in public, and government should not tell people that they cannot practice their religion. In response, the other side argued that the First Amendment should not be viewed as absolute and Walmart should have the right to restrict the sale of music containing offensive lyrics in their store. Which side has provided more representative examples? Because the First Amendment only protects the citizen from government violations of the right to free expression, the Walmart example would not be representative of a First Amendment issue.

IDENTIFYING THE ARGUMENT FROM ANALOGY

Justices and judges are servants of the law, not the other way around. Judges are like umpires. Umpires don't make the rules; they apply them. Nobody ever went to a ballgame to see the umpire (Roberts, 2005).

In arguing from analogy, an arguer attempts to prove that two events are either literally or figuratively similar enough to warrant their comparison. Literal analogies involve comparing subjects that are objectively fairly similar. This type of argument can be very useful, because it allows an arguer to project that events and circumstances present in one event may well occur in another. Policy makers regularly argue this way when basing a new policy on the results of a similar, already existing policy:

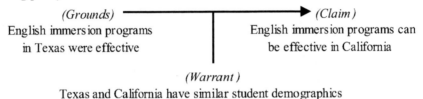

(Grounds)
English immersion programs
in Texas were effective

(Claim)
English immersion programs can
be effective in California

(Warrant)
Texas and California have similar student demographics

The grounds in the argument from analogy establish that a compared subject has certain qualities. The claim projects those properties to a different subject. The warrant either implicitly or explicitly indicates that the compared events are substantially similar.

Figurative analogies involve the same grounds, warrant, and claim relationships as their literal counterparts, but compare dissimilar subjects. Because figurative analogies involve comparisons of subjects that are intrinsically dissimilar, they are not strong arguments from a logical perspective. Compared to other argument forms, figurative analogies are the weakest form of reasoning (Rybacki and Rybacki, 2000). They can, however, have a strong persuasive impact. Arguers will use figurative analogies to attempt to explain an unfamiliar subject by comparing it to something the audience is familiar with (and may have strong feelings about). When feminists argue that women should avoid marriage because it is a form of slavery, the image of slavery may raise emotional imagery in the minds of audience members. The critical question, however, is whether the non-voluntary practice of the institution of slavery is substantially similar to the voluntary (and easily terminated) institution of marriage.

TESTING THE ARGUMENT FROM ANALOGY

1) *In what essential respects are the compared subjects similar?* The key when examining analogies is to look to the essential characteristics of the compared subjects, not just the tangential similarities. When comparing countries, for example, the arguer should be able to demonstrate that they share similar forms of government, that they share key values. Obviously all countries have citizens, but it is not sufficient to justify the comparison of nations on the broadest possible similarity. Analogies that compare the United States to Canada, for example, would be stronger than those that compared the U.S. to Iran.

2) *In what essential respects are the compared subjects dissimilar?* When looking at the essential qualities of the compared subjects, if it is determined that the dissimilarities outnumber the similarities, the analogy should be dismissed. When debating handgun restrictions, advocates of restrictions frequently compare Japan's handgun homicide rate to that in the United States. Such comparisons ignore, however, both the histories and the constitutions of the compared countries.

SUMMARY

The Toulmin model provides a useful method to analyze the grounds, warrant, claim, backing, rebuttal, and qualifier that may be found in an inductive argument. When testing arguments from authority, it is important to analyze the expertise of the source and potential bias, as well as the recency of the evidence. When examining arguments from sign, examine the frequency with which the two events in contention accompany each other and look for circumstances that may have confused their professed relationship. With causal arguments, ask if there is a probability that the relationship between grounds and claim is coincidental, if the effect is present whenever a sufficient cause is present, and if a necessary cause is ever absent when the effect is present. When analyzing arguments from example, look to the number and quality of examples, as well as the extent to which any negative examples have been accounted for. Finally, when arguing analogies, examine the similarities and differences of the essential characteristics of the subjects being compared.

REFERENCES

Adler, Ron and Neil Towne. *Looking Out Looking In.* Harcourt Brace, 1996.

Ingraham, Laura. *Shut Up & Sing.* Massachusetts: Regnery, 2003.

Lichter, Robert, Stanley Rothman, and Linda Lichter. *The Media Elite.* Hastings House, 1990.

Roberts, John G. Quoted in Savage, David. "Roberts Sees Role as Judicial Umpire" Los Angeles Times. September 13, 2005.

Rybacki, Karyn, and Donald Rybacki. *Advocacy and Opposition: an Introduction to Argument.* 4th Ed. Boston: Ally and Bacon, 2000.

Stewart, Jill. "How the Los Angeles Times Really Decided to Publish its Accounts of Women Who Said They Were Groped." *Capitol Punishment.* October 14, 2003

Toulmin, Steven. *The Uses of Argument.* Cambridge: Macmillan, 1958.

Toulmin, Stephen, Richard Rieke, and Allan Janik. *An Introduction to Reasoning.* New York: Macmillan, 1984.

WWW.CNSNews.com. "Bush Wins High Marks for Speech." September 21, 2001.

Winebrenner, T.C. *Exercises in Critical Thinking.* El Corral. 2004

EXERCISES

Chapter 2: Identifying and Testing Inductive Arguments

1. Read an editorial from a newspaper. Identify an argument from cause, sign, example, analogy, or authority. Using the appropriate test, analyze the argument.

2. Using InfoTrac, research two articles that support the same side of an argument. Create two arguments from authority that utilize your research.

3. Using either a live or televised speech, identify and analyze the speaker's use of argument from sign, cause, analogy, example, or authority.

4. Using InfoTrac, research the word "analogy." Describe a recent use of argument from analogy by a speaker or writer. Test the analogy.

5. Read the Letter to the Editor section of a newspaper. Using the Toulmin model, diagram one of the arguments that you find.

CHAPTER 2

Chapter

3

Fallacies

In Chapter 2, we examined the structure of argument and began our examination of methods for analyzing arguments. In addition to understanding the various tests of arguments, it is important that you also have a good grasp of the most common fallacies of reasoning. A *fallacy* is any argument that violates accepted standards of sound reasoning. While fallacies are not grounded in logic, they may be persuasive and are, therefore, tempting to use. Calling your opponent a name to harm his credibility can be effective, but it is fallacious. Further, fallacious arguments can backfire if the audience becomes aware that the arguer is attempting to mislead them.

As you examine the various fallacies, you will notice that many of them correspond to the types of argument discussed in Chapter 2. Additionally, it is more important that you understand the errors of reasoning associated with each fallacy than it is to focus on the labels attached to the fallacies. While it is useful to be able to name the fallacies (being able to recite Latin names will undoubtedly make you sound more educated), audiences are not as likely to be persuaded by your charge that your opponent committed an "ad populum" fallacy as they would be if you explained the reasoning error behind the fallacy. Finally, what follows is not an exhaustive listing of all fallacies, but what is covered are the most commonly used and discussed errors in reasoning.

HASTY GENERALIZATION (JUMPING TO CONCLUSIONS)

Hasty generalization is a fallacy that is associated with argument from example. A hasty generalization occurs when we draw a conclusion based on insufficient examples. Those examples may be insufficient if they are too few in number or if they are not representative of the population in question. This is an amazingly common fallacy. Recall that one test of *arguments from example* looked to the number of examples provided by the arguer. When an opponent argues from example, pay attention to the population that they are discussing in the claim. If the population includes a large number of people, for example, the sample should be relatively large. The qualifier (or absence thereof) should provide some clue as to the size of the population being addressed. Secondly, in addition to the possibility of providing too few examples, an arguer can commit the fallacy of hasty generalization if they ground their argument in examples that are not representative of the population. In an interview on Fox News, the director of an organization which seeks the total separation of religion from politics argued that President Bush should not have asked the nation to pray following the attacks on the World Trade Centers and that religion has motivated virtually all acts of evil. She based this argument on the grounds that religious people were involved in the attacks on the Trade Centers. Clearly this argument is fallacious, both in terms of the number of examples provided (consider the total number of religious people in the world versus those who committed the atrocities), as well as the fact that fanatics do not represent the perspective of the mainstream. (By definition, fanatics would not share the same perspectives as the average person of faith.)

Like many fallacies, hasty generalizations may be based partly in fact. It is true, for example, that fanatics attacked the World Trade Centers. The argument becomes fallacious, however, when the arguer attempts to make more of the claim than the evidence allows. It is a natural human tendency to want to make generalizations to explain our world, but without adequate evidence, we should resist the temptation.

BEGGING THE QUESTION (CIRCULAR REASONING)

When begging the question, an arguer uses as proof to support a conclusion some part of that conclusion. To beg the question is to assume as fact something that you are trying to prove. Arguers will beg the question when at a loss for real proof. Be alert for evidence that seems to simply be a rephrasing of the claim: "Any restrictions on freedom are evil because it is wrong to limit liberty."

As you will read later, in debates, it is often important to provide clear definitions of terms. When creating definitions or when examining your opponent's definitions, be on the lookout for circular definitions. For example, if a topic included the word "justice," it is not sufficient to merely define the term as "the act of being just." This definition begs the question and fails to provide a clear definition of the term.

FALSE DILEMMA (EITHER/OR FALLACY)

Generally speaking, whenever arguers indicate that there are only two possible alternatives in a situation, they have committed the fallacy of faulty dilemma. There are times when only two alternatives exist (when one is in a lake with no help in sight, you must stay afloat or drown), but in most circumstances there are multiple options available. Those who would argue, for example, that we must subsidize the arts or they will perish ignore that many artists actually make it on their own, producing work that people want to buy.

When debating, you need to be especially wary of the false dilemma when it occurs in questioning. On the topic of the role of feminism in American society, your opponent might ask, "Do you support or are you opposed to the agenda of the American feminist movement?" This is clearly a false dilemma because there is a lot of ground that exists between blanket support and opposition.

POST HOC

As was mentioned in Chapter 2, *post hoc, ergo propter hoc* means "after this, therefore because of this." It is more widely known as the *post hoc* fallacy. This fallacy is associated with argument from cause. It is easy to commit this fallacy because it is difficult to establish that a particular event actually caused a second event. Consequently, it is tempting to reason that, because one event preceded another event, it must have caused that event. Even when one event precedes a second event many times, an arguer confuses correlation with causation if he assumes that the first event caused the second event. In recent years, many Americans have turned to herbs and other homeopathic cures for illnesses. Under FDA testing, a few of these "natural medicines" have been found to be effective. Some users, however, reason that because they feel better after taking a particular herb, the herb must have caused them to feel better. Perhaps there was a relationship. Or, maybe, the user was simply experiencing the placebo effect in which the belief in the efficacy of a drug caused results. Perhaps the malady simply went away on its own. The bottom line is it is very difficult to establish causal relationships. Researchers use very specific guidelines to control for extraneous causes when determining the true causes for effects.

In the aftermath of Hurricane Katrina, which ravaged Louisiana in the Fall of 2005, many commentators jumped to the conclusion that the hurricane was caused by global warming.

> The hurricane that struck Louisiana yesterday was nicknamed Katrina by the National Weather Service. Its real name is global warming...Unfortunately, very few people in America know the real name of Hurricane Katrina because the coal and oil industries have spent millions of dollars to keep the public in doubt about the issue. In 2000, big oil and big coal scored their

biggest electoral victory yet when President George W. Bush was elected president-and subsequently took suggestions from the industry for his climate and energy policies (Gelbspan, 2005).

In addition to asserting a causal connection between hurricanes and global warming, the author quoted above asserts a connection between the Bush administration's environmental and energy policies and the hurricane. Yet the author fails to establish even a simple correlation between President Bush's tenure in office and increase in global temperatures. One cannot conclusively argue that no connections between the various factors which have been asserted exist but the arguer has the burden of proving those causal relationships.

SLIPPERY SLOPE

Another fallacy related to argument from cause is the slippery slope argument. When an arguer asserts that one action will lead to a series of less desirable actions, he/she may be committing the slippery slope fallacy. The thing to look for is that the arguer will simply assert each causal link in the chain leading to the catastrophic end. Keep in mind that one policy frequently does lead to a sequence of both negative and positive effects. A Zen comparison would be the image of a rock dropped into a pool of calm water, causing a series of ripples. Arguers, however, have a burden to prove the links between those various effects. Those that argue, for example, that moments of silence in public schools will lead to student-led universal prayer, followed by teacher-led prayer, followed by sectarian prayer, followed by the isolation of all non believers, have committed the slippery slope fallacy. To legitimately make those claims, the evidence supporting each link in the chain must be provided.

Debaters need to be on the lookout for the slippery slope fallacy. Part of the game of debate can involve painting the worst possible picture of your opponent's case. (It is generally better advice to be more reasonable because you risk losing credibility with your audience if your reasoning seems too catastrophic.) Debaters will argue that a policy will cause a series of events that will lead to the most catastrophic ends. If the linkages to those ends are not challenged, it becomes difficult to deny the pathos that will be generated by the seriousness of the final effect in the chain. One great way to challenge the slippery slope is to look to *empirical* (observable) examples that demonstrate that similar policies have not lead to catastrophic consequences. When arguing against bans on assault rifles, some have concluded that any restrictions will lead to confiscation of all guns. The fact that machine guns were banned in the 1930s and confiscation has not yet occurred would seem to disprove the slippery slope.

AD HOMINEM (NAME CALLING)

Ad hominem is Latin for "to the man." *Ad hominem* occurs when a speaker attacks or speakers attack some aspect of their opponent or their opponent's sources, such as their appearance or intelligence. The focus of debate should be on the worth of ideas. Part of the reason that many novice arguers get very angry and defensive when arguing is that they view any argument as a personal attack. Arguers must understand that their personalities, while interesting, are irrelevant to the argument. What matters are the ideas. Consider the abysmal example of argument set by former President Clinton's advisor, James Carville, who went on a smear campaign against Paula Jones (one of several women who accused then President Clinton of sexual misconduct).

> Carville is famous for saying of Jones, "Drag a hundred dollars through a trailer park and there's no telling what you'll find." Carville's attacks were followed by a barrage of similar character assassinations from members of the media who referred to her variously as a "bimbo," the "Dogpatch Madonna," and a "Trailer Park Tramp" (Human Events, 7).

The attacks on Paula Jones, while disturbing, point to the fact that skilled arguers may defer to fallacies because they know they can be effective in forwarding their case. Think, however, of the ethical ramifications of dismissing the word of a woman, who has accused a man of sexual misconduct, on the grounds that she is poor.

While it is true that personal issues related to a source should not be relevant in a debate, there are times when issues such as character could play a role in a legitimate argument. A person who has been convicted of perjury, for example, might not be viewed as a credible witness. It is perfectly legitimate to question the qualifications of a source, or to examine their potential bias on an issue. It is not acceptable, however, to simply call them names and dismiss their opinion without explaining the grounds for the dismissal.

Questions to Ponder

What is character? To what extent does a source's character impact their believability?

In competitive debate, it is never permissible to make personal attacks on an opponent. To dismiss, for example, the arguments of a male opponent on the issue of abortion because he is not a woman is to commit an *ad hominem* attack. In parliamentary debate, such attacks will be subject to an objection on the grounds of "personal privilege." We will discuss this point later in the text.

TU QUOQUE

Tu quoque is a special case of the *ad hominem* fallacy. It means, "you also." This fallacy occurs when we dismiss an opponent's argument or source because they failed to follow their own advice. When a person who has advocated moral standards, for example, violates those standards, it does not weaken the importance of the standards; it simply points to the weakness of the person who committed the transgression. Again, the attack is on the behavior of the person, not on the wisdom of their argument. A teenager who tells their parents that they cannot consistently argue that taking drugs is wrong when they drink is correct if they mean that their parents' behavior is inconsistent with their philosophy. They cannot, however, indict the wisdom of the admonition against taking drugs—it stands regardless of their parents' behavior. It would be silly and counterproductive to suggest that because someone has violated a principle, the principle cannot be sound. Everyone makes mistakes; the alternative is to live a life without standards so that you never risk violating them.

AD VERECUNDIAM (FALLACIOUS APPEAL TO AUTHORITY)

In Chapter 2, we examined the argument from authority and the standards required to legitimize the use of expert opinion to support a claim. A deferral to authority is fallacious if it violates those standards, particularly if the source is not an expert in the field or if we have no need to defer to authority because the judge is able to adjudicate the disputed claim without the aid of an outside expert. Such an unwarranted use of authority occurs when someone defers to a newspaper editorial to determine who to vote for in an election, or when they buy a product on the advice of a celebrity.

Additionally, if an arguer attempts to deter challenges by citing an authority, he/she has committed a fallacious deferral to authority. When competing claims are presented in an area in which the judge is not expert, citing an authority may well give a debater an advantage in the eyes of the audience. It is not logical, however, to argue that because your opponent has no evidence, they cannot credibly argue a point. At times, simple reason can demonstrate that a point is either not relevant or not valid, irrespective of support from an expert.

AD POPULUM (BAND WAGON)

The *argumentum ad populum*, or appeal to the popular, is a fallacy that occurs when an arguer claims that something is good, justified, or desirable because it is popular. The *ad populum* fallacy is an incorrect appeal to authority in which we defer to the wisdom of the masses. Remember that slavery once had popular support. Arguing that something must be good because lots of people like it, however, assumes that the masses are always correct. This fallacy is common and is the motivating force behind advertising. Advertisers feed upon the human desire to be accepted as part of the group, the "in crowd," and base advertisements on the grounds that because everyone is buying something, you should too. Political campaigns similarly promote any poll data that supports their candidate to show that he/she is the one that everyone seems to be voting for.

What is and isn't an acceptable deferral to the popular gets a bit tricky in a democracy. For example, subsequent to the conflict in Vietnam, a common doctrine that has guided the use of the U.S. military recommends the establishment of popular support for any potential intervention. Following the attacks on the World Trade Centers and the Pentagon, the President rallied to get both the support of the American public and the world behind (potential) U.S. military intervention. It is, however, the obligation of the President to uphold the Constitution and defend the country, regardless of public opinion. In many states, laws can be passed by popular vote in the form of propositions that appear on the ballot. With some regularity, voters have passed propositions that the Supreme Court has found unconstitutional. In a democracy, the voice of the people is critical. It must, however, be balanced by the rule of law.

APPEAL TO IGNORANCE (*ARGUMENTUM AD IGNORATIUM*)

If we argue that our opponents cannot disprove a claim and, therefore, the claim must be true, we have committed the fallacy of appeal to ignorance. The use of proof to support a claim simply increases the probability that a claim is true; it does not guarantee it. Similarly, the absence of proof to support a proposition may weaken its argumentative value, but it does not guarantee that the claim is either true or false. There are two varieties of this fallacy. The first occurs when we reason that something must be true because no proof to the contrary exists: "Aliens must exist because they have been clever enough to avoid our ability to detect them for generations." The second form of the fallacy contends that something cannot be true because no proof for its truth exists: "We cannot have souls, because there is no scientific method for identifying them." Realize that virtually all advancements in the sciences were faced with skepticism on the grounds of lack of empirical (observable) evidence. The notion that germs were the cause of disease was dismissed because

CHAPTER 3

germs could not be seen. It was not until the microscope was developed that the theory that germs caused illness became widely accepted. It is important to remember that the lack of proof may be a sign that a claim is false; it may also simply be a sign that we have not yet developed a means of discovering the proof.

That is not to suggest that we should accept asserted positions without proof. Certain fields of argument actually require that, absent proof, we conclude that the opposite is true. In law, for example, if the prosecution does not prove its case, we presume in favor of the defendant. In this arena, a *presumption* has been intentionally assigned to the defense. This is done so that, where a discrepancy in proof exists, the outcome will favor the accused. The justice system utilizes this standard for proof because it adheres to the philosophy that it is better that the guilty be freed than the innocent imprisoned.

Similarly, in academic debate, we hold that the person who brings a claim has the burden to prove it. As a matter of philosophy, however, we recognize that a claim supported by proof is more probably true. We cannot categorically and conclusively claim that the absence of proof means that a claim is false. The distinction being drawn here is really between belief and truth. Claims with evidence are more believable. The existence or absence of evidence, however, does not guarantee truth.

STRAW MAN

The straw man argument occurs when we misrepresent an opponent's argument to make it easier to attack. The name is derived from the image of establishing a straw figure and then easily knocking it over. Opponents of California's Proposition 187 labeled it the anti-immigration initiative and argued that it discriminated against immigrants. Factually, the proposition limited aid to undocumented or illegal immigrants only (Mailman, 3). Obviously, the fear that all immigrants would be impacted by the proposition generated a great deal of concern.

Straw man arguments are very common in academic debate, because much of debate involves first stating your opponent's position and then responding to it. As we will discuss in a subsequent chapter, it is important to listen carefully to an opponent's argument and invent counter arguments that actually address their central point. It may seem easier to misrepresent their position, but it will be easier for them to defeat your argument if it is based on the straw man fallacy. They need only point out to the audience that you have misrepresented their argument and, therefore, addressed the wrong issue. Having argued the misrepresented position will mean that you have neglected their actual argument.

NON SEQUITUR (IRRELEVANT REASON)

This fallacy occurs whenever an arguer provides support for a claim that has little relevance to the claim. Subsequent to the attacks on the World Trade Centers and the Pentagon, opponents of spaced based anti-ballistic missile systems argued that the attacks proved that we do not need ABM systems. Of course, the fact that enemies of the United States did not use a ballistic missile (this time), does not indicate that there is no need for ABM systems (Weinberger, 41). This fallacy can result from simply neglecting to explain the relationship between the grounds and the claim. It is not enough, for example, to argue that there is racism in society and to conclude that we need affirmative action. Absent an explanation that demonstrates that affirmative action would provide a satisfactory response to the problems caused by racism, there would be no reason to accept the grounds as support for the claim.

Keep in mind that the audience will determine relevance. An argument that we should not eat meat because Hindus believe in Kharma is likely to be viewed as a *non sequitur* to most non-Hindus. Arguers, therefore, must endeavor to explain the relevance of their arguments and adapt their arguments to the beliefs and values of their audience.

INCONSISTENCY

We argue inconsistently when we argue from contradictory premises or argue for contradictory conclusions. It is difficult, for example, to argue that we should not eat animals because all animal life is sacred and concurrently conclude that abortion is morally acceptable. Where an advocate argues that all life must be protected, he/she takes on the burden of defending all life. It seems inconsistent to oppose abortion on the grounds that life is important and concurrently support the death penalty. Arguers must think about the logical extensions of their premises and modify them as necessary to avoid conclusions that they do not want to defend. The advocate that is pro-life and pro-death penalty could argue, for example, that they support the protection of innocent life.

It is important to keep on the lookout for inconsistencies in debate because there are plenty of opportunities for advocates to create contradictions. In addition to having to worry about not contradicting yourself, you must also worry that you and your partner do not contradict each other. Being able to point out to the audience that opponents have contradicted themselves can be an effective way to gain the upper hand in a debate.

FAULTY ANALOGY

The fallacy of faulty analogy results from comparing two groups that are more dissimilar than similar or similar groups that have one important dissimilarity. Grossly erroneous comparisons are those that are similar in unimportant ways and dissimilar in important ones. The faulty analogy will appear solid, however, as the advocate attempts to highlight similarities. The key to defeating them is to point out that those similarities are not as relevant as the ways in which the compared groups are dissimilar. In an argument against high-density urban development, Steven Hayward (1999) argued,

> High-density development doesn't reduce congestion. The superficially appealing idea is that if we all live closer to where we work and shop, shorter car trips and mass transit will replace all those long car rides. But the real world doesn't work that way. What happens at a cocktail party when a new wave of people shows up and the population doubles? Is it harder or easier to get to the bar and cheese tray? Is it harder or easier to carry on a conversation and move around the room?

There may be valid reasons to reject high-density growth in cities. Clearly, however, cities are not cocktail parties, and the transportation options available in a city are much more substantial than those available in your apartment. The compared groups then (high density city growth and crowded cocktail parties) are alike in that they are both potentially crowded. They are, however, different in virtually all other aspects.

Derrick Jackson (2003), a columnist for the Boston Globe, provides us with another excellent example of the misuse of analogy:

> For the world's greatest weapon of mass destruction, Bush would leave the world alone. In a couple of months, the tobacco treaty will be presented to the World Health Assembly. If it is adopted, it will go out for ratification. Only 40 nations need to ratify it for it to go into effect in the countries that approve it. If the United States does not get behind the treaty, it will be every bit as cynical on cigarettes as it accuses Hussein of being with weapons inspections…That is another way of telling the world to get lost as we give aid and comfort, if you go by the actual carnage, to the globe's most dangerous terrorists.

It is undeniable that cigarettes contribute to more than their fair share of premature deaths and illnesses world-wide. There are, however, a few obvious differences between weapons of mass destruction and cigarettes. The individual smoker, for example, must claim some responsibility for the practice of smoking. Even if you assume a scenario in which underage smokers are lured into the habit through the use of sinister subliminal advertising, people can and do quit. By comparison, when you are the victim of a nuclear or biological attack, you typically do not have much control over your fate. Even if you assume that the author meant that non-smokers are victimized by second hand smoke, there have been a number of laws passed to protect the rights of non-smokers against second hand smoke. It is illegal, for example, to smoke in bars and restaurants in California. Unfortunately, no similar legislative remedy exists for biological or nuclear attacks.

EQUIVOCATION

An arguer commits the fallacy of equivocation when he/she implies that two words have the same meaning when, in fact, they do not. Julia Roberts, star of Pretty Woman and sometimes political commentator observed:

> Republican comes in the dictionary just after reptile and just above repugnant...I looked up Democrat. It's of the people, by the people, for the people (Drudge, 2001).

Ms. Roberts equivocates between the word Democrat (a member of the political party) and democracy (government by the people). You might also notice the ad hominem nature of the argument. While the above example demonstrates an equivocation in comparison with a known meaning of a term, sometimes an arguer will commit the fallacy of equivocation by using the word in two different ways within his/her argument. Many puns are based on this form of equivocation:

> The scholarship office said that it was the place for poor students to sign up for financial aid. I have never done too well at school so I guess I qualify as a poor student. Sign me up!

Arguers must be careful to use a term consistently throughout their argument. You should be especially vigilant when examining arguments involving ambiguous words such as "big, large, small, short, old, etc." If I say that Texas is one of the biggest states in the union, do I mean in terms of geographical size or do I mean total population? Making sure that ambiguous terms are clarified is one way of making sure that your opponent does not "shift" his/her arguments in the debate.

SUMMARY

Understanding fallacies is an important part of developing your critical thinking and argumentation skills. Fallacies are persuasive because they pose as valid arguments. Explaining why an argument is fallacious is substantially more effective than simply identifying the fallacy being committed. While not an exhaustive list, the following fallacies are very common:

- **Hasty generalization**: occurs when we draw a conclusion based on insufficient examples.

- **Begging the question**: an argument that uses as proof to support a conclusion, some part of that conclusion.

- **Faulty dilemma**: whenever arguers indicate that there are only two possible alternatives in a situation.

- **Post hoc**: because one event preceded another event, it must have caused that event.

- **Slippery slope**: an arguer asserts that one action will lead to a series of less desirable actions.

Ad hominem: a speaker attacks—or speakers attack—some aspect of their opponent or their opponent's sources, such as their appearance, intelligence, or their character.

- *Tu Quoque*: when we dismiss an opponent's argument or source because they failed to follow their own advice.

- **Fallacious appeal to authority**: deferral to authority is fallacious if the source is not an expert in the field or if we have no need to defer to authority.

- *Ad populum*: when an arguer claims that something is good, justified, or desirable because it is popular.

Appeal to ignorance: when we argue that our opponents cannot disprove a claim and, therefore, the claim must be true.

Straw man: when we misrepresent an opponent's argument to make it easier to attack.

Non sequitur: whenever an arguer provides support for a claim that has little relevance to the claim.

Inconsistency: when we argue from contradictory premises or argue for contradictory conclusions.

Faulty analogy: an argument that compares two groups that are more dissimilar than similar.

Equivocation: an arguer uses a term inconsistently or implies that two terms have the same meaning when they do not.

REFERENCES

Barry, Vincent, and Douglas Soccio. *Practical Logic.* New York: Hold, Rinehart, Winston, 1988.

Coulter, Ann. "Tabloid Trash With a Presidential Seal." *Human Events.* October 2, 1998.

Drudge, Matt . "Julia Roberts unloads on Bush." *The Drudge Report.* http://www.drudgereport.com/julia2.thm." March 16, 2001.

Gelbspan, Ross. "Katrina's Real Name." *Boston Globe.com.* August 30, 2005.

Hayward, Steven. "Suburban Legends." *National Review.* March 22, 1999.

Jackson, Derrick. "Real Weapons of Mass Destruction Planted in the U.S." *Daily Breeze.* March 7, 2003. A 13

Mailman, Stanley. "California's Proposition 187 and Its Lessons." *New York Law Journal.* January 3, 1995.

Rieke, Richard D. and Malcolm O. Sillars. *Argumentation and Critical Decision Making.* New York, Longman, 2001.

Weinberger, Casper. "After the Terror." *Forbes.* October 15, 2001.

EXERCISES

Chapter Three: Fallacies

1. Using editorials and Letters to the Editor, identify five fallacies. Label the fallacies, include complete source citations, and provide enough of the text of the quotations that the fallacies are clearly evident.

2. Using print advertisements, identify five fallacies. Include a copy of the advertisement and discuss the fallacy in each advertisement.

3. Using InfoTrac, research the term "fallacy." Discuss an article that analyzes fallacies.

4. Examine the text of a recent political speech. Identify and discuss any fallacies that you find.

An Overview of
Parliamentary Debate

A BRIEF HISTORY

As we examined in Chapter One, the study of debate, at least in terms of its rhetorical origins, is quite old. While Aristotle is regularly credited for his contribution to the general study of rhetoric, Protagoras (481-411 B.C.) is known as the father of debate. His students in Athens regularly engaged in debates on a variety of issues. As long as there have been academies and universities, debating (at least on an intramural level) has been an important part of their curricula. The first English-speaking intercollegiate debate probably pitted Cambridge University against Oxford in the early 1400s (Freeley, 19). The last two hundred years have seen a real proliferation in the development of intercollegiate debate (the bulk of that happening in the last 100 years). In recent history, intercollegiate debate has come to be practiced throughout much of the free world and, over the last few years intercollegiate debate has even become popular in China. Much of the spread of debate throughout the world can be attributed to healthy exchange programs and debate exhibitions among foreign universities interested in debate.

The Birth of NDT, CEDA, and Parli

In 1947, the National Debate Tournament (NDT) was established. The NDT was not only a tournament, but also came to be the title given to a specific style of debate that would dominate competitive academic debate until the early 1970s. NDT debate utilizes one topic for the entire year. The topic is always phrased as a call for a change in public policy. This was, and to some extent still is, an excellent form of debate. The emphasis of NDT is on the arguments and evidence associated with the variety of policies which are possible under the year's topic. Unfortunately, however, the NDT emphasis on evidence and argument mutated the activity so that high rates of delivery (some over 300 words per minute) and extremely narrow cases (to try to trick the other team) have become pervasive. Faced with what they saw as an event that was not promoting effective speech communication behaviors, many directors of forensics programs sought an alternative. It came in the form of the Cross Examination Debate Association or CEDA.

Established in the early 1970s, CEDA's intended focus was for students to debate value-oriented claims, in a style that would emphasize humor and persuasive delivery. CEDA's popularity grew throughout the 1970s and 80s, until it all but supplanted NDT. It has been said that those who ignore history are destined to repeat it and, sadly, CEDA gradually evolved to so closely resemble NDT that in the mid-1990s they began debating the same resolution and have all but merged. Just as the problems with NDT debate inspired the success of CEDA, the problems associated with the over utilization of evidence and high rates of delivery in CEDA created the need for a new style of debate. Consequently, parliamentary debate, which had been practiced in England, Canada, and in many other countries, has grown to dwarf NDT/CEDA debate in the United States.

In the United States, parliamentary debate is governed by two organizations: the American Parliamentary Debate Association (APDA) and the National Parliamentary Debate Association (NPDA). In 1994, the first National Parliamentary Debate Association Tournament was held (Trapp, 2). Parliamentary debate has grown dramatically since that first national tournament. Today, the NPDA rankings list more than 300 colleges and universities as parli participants. Particularly on the West Coast, parliamentary debate, or parli, is the dominant form of debate practiced at forensic tournaments. Every weekend, NPDA-sanctioned tournaments occur throughout the United States. At the conclusion of the year, a number of different organizations (the NPDA being the most prominent) sponsor national championship tournaments. In addition to domestic competition, teams from around the world (including the United States) take part in the World Universities Debating Championships. The "Worlds" tournament utilizes a parliamentary debate framework. It is interesting to observe how a common debate framework can bring together students from around the world, each from different educational backgrounds.

THE EXTEMPORANEOUS NATURE OF PARLI

Contrasted with its predecessors CEDA and NDT rather than focusing on one topic for the entire academic year, parliamentary debate is extemporaneous in nature. *An extemporaneous speech is one in which the speaker may be familiar with the subject matter, but is not certain of the exact nature of the topic.* Students competing in parliamentary debate are obliged to argue a different topic each time they debate, with a limited amount of advanced preparation time. A typical debate tournament will involve at least six preliminary rounds and four to five elimination rounds of debate. Parli debaters may, therefore, debate eleven different topics at any given debate tournament. The extemporaneous nature of parliamentary debate makes it a nearly ideal environment in which to practice and develop both analytical and communication skills. When time allows, it is always best to prepare a speech thoroughly before delivering it. Working professionals understand, however, that they rarely have much advanced notice before speaking. They must be able to prepare a speech on short notice and think on their feet while delivering it. Not knowing the topic weeks in advance compels parli debaters to have a broad base of knowledge and the skill to speak articulately without much preparation time. In fact, parli debaters get only fifteen minutes to prepare for each debate!

NO WRITTEN EVIDENCE ALLOWED

The rules and nature of evidence in parli are intentionally different from those in CEDA/NDT. There are pros and cons associated with those differences. Recall that one of the factors that led to dissatisfaction with CEDA/NDT was the over utilization of evidence at the expense of analysis and delivery. In an effort to limit the amount of evidence actually read in the debate and to encourage the development of analysis, the rules of parliamentary debate ban the reading of quotations in the debate. Debaters can cite sources and quotations from memory, but they may not bring prepared materials into the debate. Critics of parliamentary debate argue that the ban on written evidence leads to incorrect paraphrasing and all but eliminates the other team's ability to challenge the veracity of sources quoted in the debate. One of the great advantages to CEDA/NDT is that debaters learn to research and challenge their opponent's arguments from authority. This is substantially easier to do when the complete written text from which a quotation is drawn is available for analysis during the debate.

On the other hand, the difference between the uses of authority in parli versus CEDA/NDT can be viewed simply as a difference in emphasis. In CEDA/NDT, quotations and argument from authority represent the primary/front line grounds for the claims being presented. In parli, debaters are expected to provide analysis and information that would be available to a well-read audience, and any sources that are cited and paraphrased represent backing to that analysis and information. Parli is much more interested, therefore, in the inferences or analysis that can be drawn from the opinions of experts than it is in simply deferring to the authority of experts as the final word in the debate.

PARLI EMPHASIZES A RENAISSANCE EDUCATION

Because parliamentary debaters do not know the topics that they will be debating in advance of the debates, they must be prepared to speak on a wide range of issues. Parliamentary topics range from philosophical maxims such as "This house believes that the ends justify the means" to more specific questions of policy (similar to those debated in NDT/CEDA), such as "This house believes that the United States Federal Government should implement a ban on assault weapons." Consequently, parli debaters must be exceptionally well-read.

It is interesting to observe that parli debate draws upon the exact types of knowledge that you should be gathering in your undergraduate general education requirements. To be a truly educated person is not to simply have a great deal of depth of knowledge in one area. Truly educated people have both a breadth of knowledge and a desire to continue to deepen and expand that knowledge. The breadth of the general education requirements, like the range of topics debated in parliamentary debate, has the potential to make us deeper, clearer thinkers. One fun aspect of parliamentary debate is that it gives students the opportunity to argue issues that they have learned about in their college courses.

Many of the topics debated involve issues of philosophy, theology, and values. A well-prepared parli debater will have read the works of philosophers such as John Locke, Plato, and Descartes. Philosophers deal in timeless questions, which are issues that are as relevant today as they were in antiquity. Locke's theory of the social contract, for example, forms the basis for much of American democracy. It is also useful to explore philosophy and theology from multiple perspectives. Consider the importance today of knowing not only the Judeo-Christian perspective on human rights, but also those values held by Muslims in the Middle East.

In addition to issues overtly associated with values and philosophy, parli debaters must be prepared to debate current events and public policy. Many college students feel that they don't need to study current event issues because they don't see the direct connections between national and international affairs and their lives. One hopes that the events of September 11, 2001 will forever dispel that notion. Good debaters, and frankly good citizens, need to be reading a major newspaper, watching good-quality national news, and reading one or more news magazines (such as *Time*, *US News and World Report*, or *Newsweek*) regularly. Becoming expert on current event issues will help you to articulate sharper positions on events that educated people talk about, not only in debates, but also in social conversation. Being unaware of current events greatly limits your conversational range and, therefore, limits your ability to expand your network of personal and professional contacts.

Like current event issues, it is also important that parli debaters have strong backgrounds in classic public policy issues. You are probably already familiar with a number of these issues: the death penalty, animal rights, euthanasia, capital punishment, gun control, the legalization of marijuana, abortion rights, and censorship. These issues slip in and out of the headlines during elections and at other times. They exist almost perpetually as the basis for public debates, and many of these issues are the centerpieces defining the political agendas of the major political parties in the United States and elsewhere. While it is convenient to separate matters of philosophy from issues of current events and public policy, you may have already observed that values and philosophy form essential premises in many of the current event/public policy questions. How, for example, can one debate the death penalty without some understanding of the meaning of life and of the social contract?

PARLI PROPOSITIONS ARE FACT, VALUE, AND POLICY

The focus of any debate is the proposition or resolution. Note that in academic debate, the terms topic, resolution, and proposition are used interchangeably. While CEDA/NDT debate focuses only on propositions of policy, parliamentary debate utilizes as its propositions the three types of declarative claims: claims of fact, claims of value, and claims of policy. We will be discussing the necessary elements of establishing a case (the stock issues) for each type of claim in subsequent chapters. At this point, it is important that you merely be able to identify the three types of claims. You will also note that propositions may be prefaced with "this house believes." This phrasing is simply intended to reflect that parliamentary debate is very loosely modeled after the British Parliament. Unless otherwise defined, the "house" is assumed to be the three participants in the debate chambers: the Government team, the Opposition team, and the judge (the Speaker of the House).

Claims of Fact

Claims of fact are provable through empirical grounds (evidence from things which have been observed) and involve a past, present, or future controversy. Factual proposition will generally attempt to identify the characteristics of something or describe a relationship between two or more things. Consider the following propositions of fact:

Resolved: rap music causes violence.

Resolved: that social security has failed us.

The melting pot metaphor is a historical myth.

The war on drugs has failed.

Nice guys finish last.

All's well that ends well.

You probably noticed that the last two topics differ from the others in that they are substantially more metaphorical. Metaphorical topics are very common in parliamentary debate and test the debater's ability to analyze the topic and debate its merits using concrete examples that illustrate the metaphorical relationships implied by the topic. While more open to interpretation, metaphorical topics may have language which skews them more towards fact, value, or policy or may be so vaguely worded that any classification would be acceptable.

Claims of Value

Claims of value make judgments about persons, places, things, or ideas. Value propositions will typically include an evaluative term or phrase. Expressions such as "more important than," "desirable," and "better than" all indicate that that a proposition is calling for a judgment about something. The following are claims of values:

Resolved: the right of privacy is more important than any other Constitutional right.

Freedom is detrimental to equality.

Dogs are better than cats.

The United States Supreme Court has overemphasized the separation of church and state.

Shrek is the best children's movie to be released in the last five years.

Restrictions on the possession of handguns would be desirable.

The distinction between claims of fact and value may seem somewhat academic but factual claims are comparatively more objective and the burdens established by factual claims are usually more readily apparent than those associated with value claims. If you were debating a proposition of fact such as "Resolved: that pornography causes violence against women," you would probably have a fairly clear idea of what you would need to prove to win the debate. Suppose, however, the topic was, "Freedom of expression is more important than public safety." The later topic, a claim of value, is clearly more ambiguous, requiring a value judgment comparing two fairly broad subjects. As we will examine in subsequent chapters, providing clear definitions of terms and criteria for clarifying the evaluative term are critical components of debating values.

It is also important to remember that the boundaries of fact and value sometimes blur. The resolution "This House values standards over compassion" appears to be a value topic, comparing two apparently opposing values. If the "House" is interpreted to mean the Speaker and the other participants in the debate, the Speaker will decide whether standards are more desirable than compassion, based upon the advantages and disadvantages of the application of each. If, however, "House" was defined as "American Society," the proposition could be defended as a claim of fact. The Government's burden would be to show that today, American Society values standards over compassion. The judge would simply look at examples presented by both sides that support or refute the idea that society values one over the other.

Claims of Policy

A claim of policy calls for a change in public action. Policy claims typically include the word should. Claims of fact and value will form the support for policy propositions. Claims of fact will be used to describe the way things are, to provide the factual grounds in the form of statistics and objective observations about a controversial condition. Claims of value will be used to make judgments about those facts and to describe the values that will motivate our policy choices. Policy propositions, however, go further than the descriptive and evaluative functions of fact and value claims to attempt to persuade the audience that some change in the way we conduct our lives is warranted. The following represent claims of policy:

The United States should significantly change its foreign policy towards the Middle East.

The death penalty should be banned.

The United States should hold companies responsible for the products that they sell.

This House should change its foreign policy towards the United States.

This House would rage against the machine.

You'll note that the last proposition is a metaphor. Debaters constructing a case on this topic would have wide latitude to construct a case that simply represented a "rage against the machine." Many policy claims are much clearer, indicating an agent of action (who will do the policy), an action (the thing to be done), and a desired effect: "Resolved, that the United States Federal Government should decrease fuel emissions to increase air quality."

You might have also noticed that the last proposition uses the word would rather than should. There is some controversy in academic debate as to whether would is indicative of a fact or a policy. If interpreted as a fact, would implies that the

Government must show that something is likely to happen. If interpreted as a policy, the debate shifts from what is likely to happen to what should happen. In academic debate, debaters will frequently argue that the language of the topic supports their interpretation of whether the topic is a fact, value, or a policy. These arguments are important because of the different burdens associated with the proposition types.

Policy debate topics are very common in parliamentary debate, perhaps because the burdens associated with these topics are clearer. It is interesting to note that parli debate began with a commitment to debate claims of fact, value, and policy, and the current trend is clearly a preference for debating policies. The same type of evolution occurred in CEDA debate, which began debating value claims and is now exclusively debating policies. Values are arguably harder to debate, but they are the necessary precursors to policy discussions. If we enact public policy without first knowing what we value/hope to achieve, our policies will probably fail.

BASIC BURDENS IN PARLIAMENTARY DEBATE

It is important to understand that the responsibilities of the various speakers in the debate and the structure of the debate are influenced by three interrelated concepts: presumption, burden of proof, and burden of rejoinder. While, as you will later learn, other burdens are associated with the Government and Opposition roles, these three concepts provide the foundation for the argumentative environment in which the debate occurs. These concepts are important to understand, not only because they are critical to academic debate, but also because they help to shape the environment of any forum in which argumentation is present.

Presumption

Presumption is the notion that one side's position in the debate is initially favored. Debates occur over figurative ground. The ground in a debate is made up of the existing beliefs, values, and policies that are held by the current system or *status quo*. The side in the debate that has presumption (is favored) represents the *status quo*. Presumption does not mean that one side will necessarily win; it just means that they have a strong hold over the ground until "some sufficient reason is adduced against it" (Whatley, 112). Presumptions can be divided into two kinds, artificial and natural.

Artificial presumptions are those that have been assigned for some purpose. Certain fields of argument have intentionally established presumptive ground. The field of law, for example, has assigned a presumption for the defendant (in a criminal matter) and the respondent (in a civil matter). To some degree, the scales of justice do not begin at a balance; they actually begin tipped in favor of the defense. This artificially assigned, field dependent form of presumption stems from the belief that the defendant is innocent until proven guilty. Assigning presumption to the defense has the structural effect of giving the plaintiff (in a civil matter) or the prosecutor (in a criminal matter) the first and last word in the courtroom. The thought here is that speaking first and last helps compensate for the burden of having to overcome the presumption of innocence assigned to the defense.

Natural presumptions arise from the inherent nature of challenged persons, practices, beliefs, and values. When debating policies, the old adage, "if it ain't broke, don't fix it," applies. We have a natural presumption against change, and that is a good thing. With change comes risk. Every change we make has effects that we cannot predict. Buy a new car and you would be able to predict that your auto insurance, payment, and registration fees will increase. You might not be able to predict that you needed that extra money for an unforeseen expense. Decision makers whose decisions impact people's rights, money, and well-being have to be particularly hesitant about being too quick to act.

Natural presumptions also occur in the form of the people, beliefs, and values we favor. Arguers who do a good job of analyzing their audiences will choose arguments and authorities that their audience favors. You might have noticed that politicians will attempt to claim that they have presumption on their side by asserting that public opinion is on their side. Ultimately, it is important to remember that the only presumption that really matters is that which exists in the mind of the judge because he or she will be the one making the final decision (Rieke and Sillars, 77).

Questions to Ponder

In the context of a criminal trial, do you think natural presumption lies with the prosecution or with the defense? In a civil trial, does it rest with the plaintiff or the respondent?

Academic debate propositions may reflect both natural and artificial presumption. Policy propositions carry clear natural presumptions against change. The Opposition's team is generally (there is an exception that we will discuss in a subsequent chapter) the defender of the *status quo* (current system) and, therefore, enjoys presumption. The natural presumption is not always clear on propositions of fact and value. Where, for example, does the natural presumption rest on the topic: This House believes that up is better than down? Indeed, particularly on metaphorical propositions, identifying where the natural presumption rests can be very difficult. As a consequence, academic debate assigns presumption artificially to the Opposition's without regard to whether or not presumption seems to naturally flow their way based upon the language of the proposition.

Presumption in academic debate has both structural and substantive effects. In terms of the structure of debate, the Government that has the burden of overcoming presumption speaks first and last. With regard to the substantive issues in the debate, if there is any doubt as to whom to vote for in a debate, presumption would require that the judge vote for the Opposition. Further, the assignment of presumption to the Opposition means that the flip side of presumption, the burden of proof, is assigned to the Government.

Burden of Proof

The burden of proof is the requirement that the advocate not enjoying presumption present sufficient reasons to overcome that presumption. Once presumption is located, the burden of proof is assigned. What constitutes "sufficient reasons" is, like presumption, sometimes artificially assigned. In a criminal procedure, one artificially assigned burden of proof is "beyond a reasonable doubt." This may seem like an extremely high burden of proof to meet, but the burden is based upon the principle that it is better that the guilty be freed than the innocent be imprisoned. In a civil trial, the plaintiff is arguing that they have been harmed in some way. Typically, the restitution for that injury is money. The burden assigned in a civil trial is a preponderance of the evidence. It is obviously easier to present a preponderance of the evidence in a trial than it is to have that evidence eradicate reasonable doubt. The lighter standard of proof is based upon the principle of justice that holds that it is less offensive to err when taking your money than taking your freedom. Recall the infamous O.J. Simpson case in which Mr. Simpson was acquitted by the criminal jury, but lost the civil case.

In academic debate, the Government has burden of proof. This burden results both from the artificial assignment of presumption to the Opposition's and from the basic rule of burden of proof. *The basic rule of burden of proof is that whoever asserts must prove* (Patterson and Zarefsky, 27). Remember that the Government has the task of proving the proposition (the central claim being debated) true. Because the Government brings forth the claim, they have the burden to prove it.

Another ramification of the basic rule of burden of proof is that every claim in the debate implies both presumptions and burdens of proof. The fact that the overall presumption in the debate is assigned to the Opposition does not mean that they can simply assert the truth of any claim and demand that the Government prove the opposite. It is true that the Government carries the burden to prove the topic true, but the Opposition must adequately defend itself.

Burden of Rejoinder

Burdens in a debate are traded, much like a ball in a tennis match. The Government must begin with a *prima facie* case. *A prima facie case is one that "on its face," or "at first glance," is sufficiently constructed to temporarily suspend the presumption for the Opposition.* While we will be discussing the necessary elements of a prima facie case in subsequent chapters, understand now that the prima facie case simply gets the Government's foot in the door. Once presented, however, it mandates that the Opposition now meet its burden of rejoinder. The burden of rejoinder requires that each side in the debate respond to the other or lose the arguments that they are silent on. The burden of rejoinder, then, alternates back and forth, subsequent to each speech in the debate—like a tennis ball being hit back and forth over the net. Neither side can simply argue that, because they have presumption or because they presented a prima facie case, they have won.

A critical element in debates, implied by the burden of rejoinder, is the need for clash. Clash is the lifeblood of debate. *Clash refers to the act of engaging your opponent's arguments in as direct a manner as possible.* In debate, it is tempting to avoid your opponent's arguments in deference to your own. While it is wise not to let your opponent's argument become the focus of the debate, once introduced, you must provide some form of a response to those arguments. In Chapter 7, we will discuss point-by-point, or direct refutation, as a method for maximizing clash in the debate. Keep in mind that the goal of a debate is to test the probable truth of the proposition. If you have watched political debates, you have probably been frustrated by the lack of clash exhibited. The typical political debate may seem more like two ships passing in the night than a sincere attempt at engaging ideas through argument. Each politician provides a prepared speech on a subject that they feel comfortable discussing (regardless of the announced topic of the debate). Rarely does real clash occur and, as a consequence, the topic of the debate is not truly tested.

When clash occurs throughout a debate, a much clearer picture of the probable truth of the proposition, as interpreted by the Government's case, emerges. As the individual issues are raised, clashed with, rebuilt, and clashed with again, they are shaped and refined. By the last speeches in the debate, what emerges, at least in theory, are the strongest issues for and against the proposition. Clash, within the context of the structure of the debate, provides the engine by which the probable truth of the proposition is tested.

THE STRUCTURE OF PARLIAMENTARY DEBATE

Parliamentary debate is modeled loosely after the British Parliament. While parliamentary debate is practiced in a number of ways both here and abroad, we will be focusing on the structure practiced by the National Parliamentary Debate Association (NPDA). The debate occurs within the context of the "House." The House is made up of the Government team, the Opposition team, and the Speaker of the House (the judge). The Government team is charged with supporting the proposition or resolution. The Opposition team attempts to persuade the Speaker of the House that the proposition should not be adopted. The Speaker serves as both an evaluator of the arguments in the debate and as a referee of sorts (keeping time, ruling on procedural issues, etc.).

Constructive Speeches

The debate is divided into two types of speeches: constructive and rebuttal. During the four constructive speeches (two from the Government and two from the Opposition), the Government and Opposition introduce any arguments new to the debate that they wish to elaborate on through the two rebuttal speeches. In addition to introducing arguments, each constructive speech subsequent to the Prime Minister's constructive should include refutation of the preceding speech. Think of the constructive period then as the time allotted in the debate for staking out the Government and Opposition's ground and for the formulation of positions that may be used throughout the debate. As the constructives proceed, those arguments are refined until we reach the rebuttal period.

Rebuttal Period

The rebuttal period of the debate consists of two rebuttals: the first from the Opposition, the last from the Government. The rebuttals are a time for summary and final refutation. A commonly recognized rule in debate is that no new arguments are allowed during the rebuttal period. This rule largely protects the team speaking second to last (the Opposition), as they would have no opportunity to address new arguments if they were brought up in the last Government speech. New examples supporting old lines of argument are typically allowed where the example is not introducing a new theme in the debate. If, for example, the Government were debating the merits of the death penalty and had been arguing that people sentenced to life in prison may actually kill while in prison, adding the name of another inmate who had taken a life while incarcerated would not be a new argument, just a new example. If the Government used that new example as a reason to modify the proposal they had offered in the first speech, they would be guilty of making a new argument.

The following represents the structure of parliamentary debate as practiced by the NPDA. You should familiarize yourself with the abbreviations that are frequently used to describe the speeches. The Prime Minister is the PM. The Leader of the Opposition is the LO. The Member of Government is the MG. The Member of the Opposition is the MO. You will note that the Government has the first and last speech. You will also observe that that both teams have the same amount of total speaking time. Controlled and equal speaking time is an important defining characteristic of debate.

STRUCTURE OF PARLIAMENTARY DEBATE

Constructive Speeches	Purpose	Time
Prime Minister (PM)	Define Keywords Establish Criteria Meet Criteria Burdens	7 min.
Leader of Opposition (LO)	Examine/Counter Define Examine/Counter Criteria Direct Refutation of PM Case Present Opposition's Case	8 min.
Member of Government (MG)	Defend Definitions and Criteria Defend Government Case Extend Case with New Analysis Argue Opposition's Case	8 min.
Member of Opposition (MO)	Defend Leader of Opp's Case Argue Member of Govs. Responses Extend Opposition's Case	8 min.

Rebuttal Speeches	Purpose	Time
Leader of Opposition	Review Key Opp. Arguments	4 min.
Prime Minister	Answer Key Opp. Arguments Rebuild and Retell Gov. Case	5 min.

SPEAKER RESPONSIBILITIES

Prime Minister Constructive

The Prime Minister's constructive speech introduces the proposition to the audience and establishes the key elements necessary to developing a prima facie case for the proposition. The speech will begin with a statement recognizing the Speaker of the House (the judge), the Opposition team, and the Member of Government. The PM will then introduce the proposition, define the terms in the proposition, provide criteria, and then provide a case that meets the remaining stock issues relevant to the type of proposition being debated.

Leader of the Opposition Constructive

The Leader of the Opposition's constructive speech begins with the same recognition statement made by the PM. The LO must then examine any definitions provided by the PM and either accept those definitions or provide reasons to reject those definitions and then counter define. The LO will then begin to argue the PM's case using direct point-by-point refutation (clash), keeping in mind the stock issues relevant to the type of proposition being debated. Once the PM's case has been properly attacked, the LO is free to present arguments which refute the resolution, but might not be directly associated with the arguments presented by the PM. Arguments not directly associated with the Government's case are referred to as *off case* arguments.

Member of Government Constructive

The primary job of the Member of Government is to retell and rebuild the Government's case that was presented by the Prime Minister. The process of rebuilding the case involves retelling the story of the case, responding to any arguments made by the Leader of the Opposition, adding new examples and analysis to support the case, and pointing out any areas of the case that the Opposition neglected to argue.

Member of Opposition Constructive

Where the Member of Government is charged with the task of defending the Prime Minister, the Member of the Opposition must defend the positions advanced by the Leader of the Opposition. The MO's job is to review the key arguments voiced by the Leader of the Opposition, argue the responses made by the Member of Government, point out any Opposition arguments that have not been responded to, and provide new arguments and analysis supporting the Opposition's case.

Leader of Opposition Rebuttal

It may seem odd that the Leader of Opposition Rebuttal follows immediately after the Member of Opposition Constructive, but this order allows the Government to have the last rebuttal (in keeping with the assignment of burden of proof to the Government). The task of the Leader of the Opposition rebuttal is to extend any arguments that they made during the LO constructive that they feel the Member of the Opposition didn't adequately address. Additionally, the Leader of the Opposition must summarize the key reasons why he/she believes that the Opposition has won the debate. Part of that summary will involve continuing to clash with Government perspectives.

Prime Minister Rebuttal

As the last speech in debate, the Prime Minister has the ability to look back upon each of the speeches in the debate and decide which arguments are truly important. The primary job of the Prime Minister is to, once again, retell the story that he presented in the Prime Minister constructive. In rebutting the main points of the Opposition, the Prime Minister must pay particular attention to those highlighted by the Leader of the Opposition's rebuttal. In addition to extending those points of the Government's case that have been clashed with, the Prime Minister should point out which of the Government's key points had been ignored throughout the debate.

QUESTIONS AND OBJECTIONS

Points of Information

Virtually all argumentative forums include some structure that allows for a question and answer period. Learning how to handle questions is an important skill to develop. In parliamentary debate, questions come in the form of Points of Information. The question period is limited to the time following the first minute and before the last minute of each of the four constructive speeches. There are no questions allowed during the rebuttal period. To ask a question, you simply rise, wait to be recognized, and ask one well-worded question. Keeping in mind that questions are charged against the speaker's time, the speaker has the right to control the number of questions asked. Questions serve to clarify issues and establish ground for future argument. In addition to asking questions, Points of Information may be used to make very short statements.

Points of Order

Where Points of Information are questions or statements posed to the other team, Points of Order are essentially objections to a potential violation of the rules of parliamentary debate. If you feel a rule has been violated, you simply stand, say Point of Order, and explain the rule violation to the Speaker of the House (judge). Probably the most common rule violation is that a new argument has been made in rebuttals. Once the Point of Order is made, the judge stops the time and renders a decision.

Points of Personal Privilege

Points of Personal Privilege are essentially objections that a personal foul has been committed. Such fouls take two forms: personal attacks (*ad hominems*) and gross misstatements of argument. Debaters who feel they have been personally insulted or who feel that their arguments have been grossly misrepresented may rise, say Point of Personal Privilege, and explain the charge. The judge will stop the time and make a ruling on the issue.

SUMMARY

Parliamentary debate, with its emphasis on extemporaneous analysis, philosophical reasoning, and persuasive delivery, emerged to fill a void created by perceived deficiencies in NDT and CEDA debate. Parliamentary debate encourages its participants to be broadly educated. Topics debated in parliamentary debate are either metaphorical or literal in nature and are phrased in the form of fact, value, and policy propositions.

Presumption, burden of proof, and burden of rejoinder act to shape the structure of debate and the environment in which the key issues in the debate are argued. A parliamentary debate is divided into four constructives and two rebuttals. In addition to the major speeches in the debate, Points of Information, Points of Order, and Points of Personal Privilege help to clarify issues and enforce adherence to the rules of parliamentary debate.

REFERENCES

Freeley, Austin. *Argumentation and Debate*. 8th Ed. California: Wadsworth, 1993.

Patterson J.W. and David Zarefsky. *Contemporary Debate*. Boston: Houghton Mifflin, 1983.

Rieke, Richard D. and Malcolm O. Sillars. *Argumentation and Critical Decision Making*. New York, Longman, 2001.

Trapp, Robert. *Parliamentary Debate* in *Intercollegiate Forensics*. Ed. T.C. Winebrenner. Kendall/Hunt.

Whately, Richard. *Elements of Rhetoric*. Ed. Douglas Ehninger. Carbondale: Southern Illinois UP, 1963.

EXERCISES

Chapter Four: An Overview of Parliamentary Debate

1. Create fifteen propositions (five of fact, five of value, and five of policy).

2. Think of a new policy that is being advocated. Identify the new policy and the change that it will create. Discuss which side has the burden of proof and which side has presumption. Is the natural presumption (factors such a public sentiment) for or against the change?

3. Using InfoTrac, research the term "burden of proof." Find an article that discusses the role that the burden of proof played within the context of a recent controversy. Cite and discuss the article.

4. Using InfoTrac, research the term "presumption." Find an article that discusses the role that presumption played within the context of a recent controversy. Cite and discuss the article.

5. Attend a forensics tournament and watch a Parliamentary Debate. Discuss the roles that the burden of proof and presumption played in the debate.

CHAPTER 4

Research: Discovering and Supporting the Issues

Whether you are researching a topic that has been assigned in your argumentation class or you are on a debate team and researching a case that has become popular at tournaments, you will find that you are extremely lucky to be debating in the era of the Internet. Prior to the advent of the electronic information age, debaters would spend hours in the library only to find that the books they needed had been checked out or were not yet available. Clearly, there are still many advantages to researching the "old fashioned way," but contemporary researchers find that on-line research offers both convenience and speed. Indeed, the primary challenge for the contemporary debater is how to best weed-through and manage the plethora of information that is now so readily accessible. This chapter provides some useful tips that should help you to research more efficiently. We begin by discussing where to start if you have been given a topic to debate in an argumentation course. We will address some strategies for preparing for tournament debating later in this chapter.

Brainstorming the Proposition

Begin your analysis of the proposition you have been assigned by exploring the meaning of each of the key terms. You will eventually need to have definitions for these words (see Chapter 6) when constructing your case, so it may be a good time to examine the possible meanings of the words from a variety of different contexts. Check the reference section of your library to determine if they carry dictionaries related to specific fields of endeavor. For example, if the topic involves a legal issue, you should track down a copy of *Black's Law Dictionary*. Black's is a respected source and will help you to understand the meaning of the terms from a legal perspective. Where no field-specific dictionary is available, you can find definitions of field dependant terms within the pages of records, journals, and books. For example, if you are looking for a legislative definition of "war on drugs," you may wish to review the records of a specific congressional hearing. If the language in the proposition does not require clarification from an expert in the field, you may refer to common usage dictionaries, such as *Websters*, to define the key terms.

Once you have done a preliminary analysis of the meaning of the terms in the proposition, you should consider the variety of issues that are likely to emerge as the proposition is debated. *Issues are questions generated by the various claims and sub-topics associated with a central claim or proposition.* If the proposition were "the legalization of the recreational use of marijuana is desirable," you would need to think about all the potential issues associated with that claim. Does smoking marijuana pose a health hazard? What cognitive risks does it create? A useful way to brainstorm the issues is to draw a line down the center of a piece of paper and create a column for the potential claims that would support the proposition and a column for potential claims that would serve as Opposition ammunition.

Proposition: This house would legalize euthanasia

Definitions from *Websters New World Dictionary*

Legalize: to make legal or lawful

Euthanasia: act of causing death painlessly to end suffering

Arguments in Favor	Arguments Opposing
The terminally ill suffer.	Doctors can control pain through medication.
If death is certain, why prolong suffering?	Doctors may misdiagnose.
Increases the freedom of patient.	Will encourage patients to die rather than burden their families.
Gives doctors options.	Violates the medical oath to "do no harm."
Is legal in other countries.	The United States should set an example.

While not exhaustive, this analysis provides a starting point for the research of the proposition. As you look through subject headings and when you are entering keywords, you can refer back to your brainstorming sheet for ideas. As your research progresses, you will add issues to your brainstorming brief. Eventually, you will have developed a good visual representation of the potential arguments in the debate.

FACTS AND OPINIONS

When it is time to gather support for the claims that will be the building blocks of your case, you will need to find two broad categories of evidence: fact and opinion. Each form of evidence provides unique qualities that fulfill different requirements in your case.

Evidence of Facts

Evidence of facts provides reports on observable conditions. Factual evidence has the potential to be verified as objectively true or false. Like other forms of argument from authority (see Chapter 2), factual evidence requires that the source have the ability to accurately report on the observed conditions. Having the ability to objectively witness an event increases the likelihood that the reported data will be an accurate account of the events. For example, a reporter who is at a political convention is better equipped to report information than a colleague back at the television station who must rely on second-hand information. While it is often necessary to rely on the accounts of others to determine what has or hasn't happened, the more people that are involved between the actual witness and the printed account, the greater the likelihood that distortion of the event will occur.

Evidence of facts may be found in a number of different forms. Clearly, news accounts of an event constitute evidence of facts. *Examples and illustrations* reported in newspapers and magazines provide excellent sources of evidence of facts that you could incorporate into your case. Examples and illustrations can provide pathos for your argument when they involve real people involved in the issues surrounding the proposition.

Statistics are another type of evidence of facts that can greatly enhance your case. Statistics provide the big picture where examples and illustrations can reflect the more personal level of issues. Consider again the euthanasia topic that we brainstormed earlier. An example of an individual who suffered from a terminal disease gives the judge a sense of how the issue impacts lives. A statistic that reports the number of people who suffer from terminal diseases provides the judge with perspective concerning the extent of the problem. *Descriptive statistics* report the results of polling of an entire population of subjects. If all critical care doctors in a state were polled concerning their opinion on euthanasia, the results would be a descriptive statistic. *Inferential statistics* poll a subset or sample of the population and draw inferences about the population based on that sample. If a researcher randomly polled a portion of the state's critical care physicians and then concluded that the results were representative of the state's critical care physicians in general, the statistic would be inferential. Because of the complexity associated with gathering accurate statistics, it is important that you carefully test statistics using the standards described under test of authority in Chapter Two.

Experiments comprise the last category of evidence of facts. Researchers at colleges and universities, as well as private institutions, publish reports that attempt to explain the relationships that exist between variables. Virtually every profession and academic discipline publishes journals that report the results of studies and experiments conducted by respected members of their communities. Typically, experiments involve the manipulation of an independent variable or variables to study the effect on a dependant variable or variables. Researchers with critical care patients might study the impact of family support (the independent variable) on patient comfort (the dependant variable). Extraneous variables are factors that enter into the relationship between the independent and dependent variables and potentially skew the results of the study. Was it really family support that impacted patient comfort or was it differences in the communication skills of critical care nurses? To guard against the effects of extraneous variables, the researchers must carefully design their studies to increase the likelihood that their conclusions are valid. Arguers should be aware of the methodology of any experiments that they quote. Because research methodologies can be very complicated, arguers may ultimately have to defer to the expertise of their sources. Consequently, you should be able to describe the credentials of the researchers you quote.

Evidence from Opinion

Unlike evidence of facts, evidence from opinion is inherently subjective. Where factual testimony reports on events and conditions that are verifiable, opinion-based testimony provides an interpretation of the facts. It is common for an author to utilize both evidence of facts and evidence from opinion to develop his/her argument. Consider this quotation by *New York Times* editorialist Thomas Friedman:

> A few Palestinian leaders and commentators have been speaking about what a mistake it was for Arafat to have turned down the Clinton plan for a Palestinian state; Palestinian legislators have voted no confidence in Arafat's Cabinet and pushed forward more responsible alternative; and secular Palestinians have begun openly questioning suicide bombing. These trends are bad news for Hamas, Islamic Jihad, Iraq and Iran. So, they have been pushing out even more suicide bombers to trigger a Sharon reaction that would rally Palestinians around Arafat's failed leadership (Friedman, 2002).

The first section of the quotation (up to the words "These trends") is factual testimony. The author is simply reporting on the behavior of Palestinian leaders and commentators. When the author writes of the implications of the behavior and the motives behind the bombings, he is providing an opinion.

Opinion evidence relies heavily upon the credentials of the source. While testifying about facts requires a level of expertise (the ability to accurately report the events), the credentials of the author are especially important when the author is making subjective evaluations of the facts. As was noted in Chapter Two, we want to be as certain as possible that the author is an expert in the field being discussed and that the author is reasonably free of bias. In debates, it is common to hear two experts who provide differing opinions concerning the same set of facts. Audiences will defer to the expert whose opinion is the most consistent with their presumptions on the issue and who has the greatest perceived level of expertise in the field.

SOURCES OF EVIDENCE

In this section, we will examine the various sources of information that you may turn to when researching for debate. While it is clear that on-line database research services, such as InfoTrac, have made research easy, fun, and time-efficient, your college library remains an excellent place to start your research. Because it is difficult to keep up with all the possible sources of information, it is always a great idea to talk to a reference librarian. Reference librarians are constantly updating their knowledge of potential resources, and they are invaluable guides to understanding the wealth of information available in the library. A short chat with a reference librarian can save you a lot of time and lead you to sources that you might otherwise not have found. Let's examine some of the advantages and disadvantages to a few of the resources available to you.

Books

Books remain one of the best resources that you can turn to when starting your research. Books can provide a comprehensive review of the topics associated with the proposition that you are debating. Because books may not be as current as periodicals, they serve different research purposes. Even dated books can provide valuable context on a topic. Once you have read the key books on a topic, you can turn to periodicals to research more current information. Most libraries have electronic databases that list their holdings. The electronic database will be searchable by subject and author. While your initial research will probably rely on a keyword subject search, you may eventually use the author index as your research reveals the names of key authors on your topic. As you are reviewing the results of the electronic index search, be sure to look for any related subjects that are listed. These subjects can provide additional lines of research that you may want to follow.

Periodicals

While books offer the advantages of context and depth, periodicals can provide very specific, recent information. There are a variety of different periodical indexes that you should familiarize yourself with. If you are interested primarily in researching popular magazines, the *Reader's Guide to Periodical Research* is a great place to start. Many libraries have both a hard copy (bound) and an electronic version of the *Reader's Guide*. It is researchable by subject and very easy to use. It is, however, limited to "popular" periodicals. Specialized periodicals, such as Government publications and scholarly journals, are generally not included in the *Reader's Guide*. A useful index on topics related to the Social Sciences (most debate topics are) is the *Social Sciences Index*. This index is organized like the *Reader's Guide*, but includes many specialized journals. Like the *Reader's Guide,* the *Social Sciences Index* can usually be found in both hard copy and computer searchable versions. For legal periodicals, look for the *Index to Legal Periodicals*. It is a surprisingly easy index to use (organized like the *Reader's Guide* and *Social Sciences Index*), and it indexes the law reviews and law journals that are published by major law schools. Law journals can provide excellent analysis on debate topics associated with legal issues (most policy topics will have legal ramifications). In addition to helping you understand the issues surrounding a legal question, law journals provide citations to key court cases and laws.

Government Documents

If you are debating an issue of public policy, you should consider researching Government documents. The Federal Government publishes a wide variety of documents, ranging from the records of Congressional meetings to books on highly specialized topics. Not all libraries will carry Government documents. The Federal Government designates a large number of libraries (approximately 1300) as Federal Depositories. Many of these Depositories can be found at large universities. After you have narrowed your Government documents search down to a specific title and call number, phone ahead to the nearest university to determine whether they carry the title.

There are a number of different Government document references you may wish to utilize. The *Monthly Catalog of United States Government Publications* can be used to index a wide variety of Government Documents. Government Depositories may use the *Catalog* as an index to their holdings. It is searchable by subject, keywords, and title. The *Congressional Record* is a compilation of the daily hearings that take place on the floor of the House and Senate. This is an excellent source because, in addition to the remarks of lawmakers, the *Record* includes supplementary reference materials that may be included in the Congressional hearings. The *Congressional Information Service (CIS) Index* is a gateway to virtually all Congressional publications. The index is updated monthly and is fairly simple to use. Begin your search using keywords in the index section. After you have found an interesting document, use its call number to look it up in the abstract section of the index.

Newspapers

If you are looking for evidence of facts, newspapers are a good place to start. Not all newspapers are created equal, and the larger papers typically make is easier for you to access their back issues. Major newspapers, such as the *New York Times* and the *Christian Science Monitor*, provide on-line access to many of their most important stories. In addition, most libraries will carry indexes for and back issues (usually not in hard copy) of the major newspapers. In addition to evidence of facts, newspapers will provide opinion evidence in the form of editorials. Editorials provide a potentially valuable source of analysis on issues. However, depending on the author of the editorial and their area of expertise, a well-researched book or journal article will provide more expert opinion than the editorial pages of a newspaper.

Scholarly Journals

Virtually every academic discipline produces a journal of the writings of its best thinkers. Scholarly journals provide an excellent source of expert testimony because they are generally peer reviewed. Before an article is published in a peer-reviewed journal, it must pass the scrutiny of a group of experts in the field. Compare that process to the World Wide Web, where anyone with an opinion may have a web page. Examples of scholarly journals include the *Journal of the American Medical Association (JAMA)*, the *Quarterly Journal of Speech, Argument and Advocacy, The American Bar Association Journal*, and *Psychological Abstracts*. Scholarly journals provide their own indexes, and many may also be indexed through the larger indexes (such as the Social Sciences Index).

The World Wide Web

The "Web" can provide excellent background information on an issue. You need to be extremely selective, however, in the material that you take from the Web. Think of the Web as a library without a librarian. While libraries have criteria they follow regarding what is and is not admitted into their holdings, the Web has no gatekeeper. In fact, anyone with the proper software and on-line service can "publish" a web page. There are a few things you should remember when researching the Web.

Keep in mind that the Web is not primarily intended to be a student research facility. Web sites are produced for a variety of reasons, many of which have little or no value to you as quotable material. Many sites are simply advertising. If you were researching the efficacy of a drug, the manufacturer's web page is going to give you a one-sided (biased) perspective. Additionally, there are a lot of "soap box" web pages out there. These sites provide a one-sided venue that allows their authors to express their viewpoints. There are, however, some valuable sites, such as those that report the results of research projects at Universities. Unfortunately, there are also far too many sites dedicated to pets.

When citing web pages, you should indicate the title of the web page; the author (if identifiable); and be able, if asked, to present the address of the cite (URL). Like quotations derived from published materials, you must be able to demonstrate a sign of authority when quoting web pages. If the site is produced by an institution (a university, think-tank, the Federal Government, etc.), cite the name of the institution. If the site is not primarily associated with an institution, cite the name of the individual or group that produced the site. If you cannot identify the source of the site, it is not going to be of any value to you as a source of quotations. Anonymous quotations taken from web sites should generate no credibility. Where the site is primarily attributed to a single author, you should be able to indicate that the author is an authority in the field, and you should also be able to cite published materials that the author has produced. The titles and subjects of those publications will reflect the author's expertise and bias. Finally, because web pages are regularly updated, make sure that you cite the last date the page was updated.

InfoTrac

The InfoTrac service that you have access to as a result of buying this textbook provides an invaluable method of researching for your debate. InfoTrac is a full text database that you can search by subject, author, title, keywords, and a variety of other index strategies. As of this writing, InfoTrac is providing its users with access to over 12,600,000 articles. The database is updated each business day. Holdings range from popular magazines to specialized journals (Thomson, 2002).

To utilize InfoTrac, you will need to have access to the Internet. Simply enter the site's address (as of this writing: http://www.Infotrac-college.com). You will be prompted to enter your password and asked a few registration questions. Once you are registered, you will be able to access InfoTrac by simply typing in your password.

ORGANIZING YOUR MATERIALS

Preparing for a Classroom Debate

So you have done a lot of research and it is sitting in piles surrounding you on the floor of your room. Now what do you do with it? In subsequent chapters, we will be discussing the stock issues that you will be using to build your case. You will eventually need to support these stock issues with the evidence that you have found. Because there is very little time during a debate to search for a quotation in a stack of magazines or books, now is the time to begin to organize your evidence into usable *briefs*. A brief consists of a main argument and a series of supporting claims, each supported by evidence. Recall the brainstorming exercise that we examined on the euthanasia issue. On the side supporting euthanasia, we identified five arguments: 1) the terminally ill suffer, 2) suffering should not be prolonged, 3) patient freedom is increased, 4) doctors have more options, and 5) it is legal in other countries. Assuming you were debating euthanasia, you would read your research and find quotations that would support those arguments. Additionally, you would find quotations that support other lines of argument on your topic that you may not have considered during the brainstorming phase. You should add those arguments to your brainstorming brief and consider how your opponent might respond.

As you read the material that you have gathered, you should highlight quotations that support key arguments on your side of the topic. Next to each highlighted paragraph, write a sentence that summarizes the main claim that the paragraph supports. Keep quotations short enough that they do not bore your audience and do not use up too much of your speaking time, but long enough to provide evidence of the author's analysis. You may edit information that is not useful to the point being made, so long as you do not violate the author's intended meaning.

Each argument from authority should follow this basic format:

(Claim)   Biosolids not proven to create health risks
(Citation)   Staff Writer, Solid Waste Report, Sept. 20, 2002 v33 i32 p1
(Quotation)   "The panel found no evidence of an urgent public health risk from exposure to land-applied biosolids. But the finding was tempered by the lack of studies available on human exposure."

After you have collected the quotations that you may use in the debate, you are ready to organize your materials in brief form. At the top of the page, type or write your main argument. For example, one page/brief might be dedicated to the argument that patients should have the right to choose to end their suffering. Next, include all the evidence and claims that fit under that general heading. Perhaps you gathered evidence from legal, medical, and theological perspectives. Your brief could follow this structure:

Patients should have the right to end their suffering.

1. Theology supports a patient's right to choose
   (supporting material: source citation and quotation)

2. The medical industry supports the right to die
   (supporting material: source citation and quotation)

3. It is consistent with other legal freedoms
   (supporting material: source citation and quotation)

Once you have gathered and briefed the main arguments supporting your side of the debate, you should place the briefs in folders with labels that clearly indicate the subject of the brief(s) that are inside. This may sound like excessive organization, but it will pay off. If you are on the Government team, you will find it useful to have your evidence easily accessible when the time comes to prepare the Prime Minister's Speech (the first speech in the debate). If you are on the Opposition team, you may also wish to prepare certain arguments in advance. We will be discussing the structure and stock issues for your case in subsequent chapters. Additionally, when you are responding to arguments during the debate, you will not have the time to go hunting through stacks of magazines and books to find an appropriate quotation. If you are nervous during the debate (it is natural to feel somewhat frazzled), the last thing you want is confusion over where your research is. Taking the time to organize your arguments will help to make the debate easier and a lot more fun.

Preparing to Debate at Tournaments

As mentioned in Chapter 4, debaters competing at Parliamentary Debate tournaments are not allowed to bring evidence into the debate. The goal of this prohibition on written evidence is to encourage the debaters to focus more on analysis and delivery and less on prepared briefs. While debaters cannot bring prepared briefs into the debate, many tournaments allow contestants to refer to materials prior to debating. Keep in mind that tournament debaters only have fifteen minutes to prepare for each debate, so it is important to be somewhat familiar with potential issues prior to referring to briefs. But because Parli has evolved to a place where it is common for debaters to argue very specific issues, having a well-researched file of arguments and evidence on a wide variety of issues may mean the difference between winning and losing. There are three sources of issues that you should brief: current events, great thinkers and historical documents, and "canned" cases.

Researching Current Events

Topics associated with current events are extremely popular in Parli. There are really two categories of current events topics. The first involves issues that come in and out of the public spotlight. Issues such as affirmative action, the death penalty, and euthanasia have been debated for generations, but are made timely by court cases and recent examples in the media. Tournament debaters should develop briefs that outline the key arguments on both sides of these issues, but you will obviously want to brief the most recent information on the issue. However, in addition to understanding the current state of the topic, be sure that you brief relevant historical information. For example, how have related laws evolved? Which groups have supported or opposed the issues? How have comparable countries treated the issues?

The second category of current events topics includes issues that have only recently come to the public forum. Many of these issues will attract the media's attention for only a limited time, either because they reach a natural closure point or because something more important pushes them out of the limelight (at least temporarily). Successful Parliamentary debaters will read a variety of newspapers and watch national news broadcasts and commentaries. Newspapers, such as *The New York Times*, *The Washington Post*, *The Wall Street Journal*, and *The Christian Science Monitor*, are examples of quality newspapers that will give you a sense of the important issues of the day. News commentaries, such as the *O'Reilly Factor*, *The Beltway Boys*, the *McLaughlin Group*, and *This Week*, provide interesting analysis and are good indicators of the types of topics you may be debating at tournaments.

Ideally, then, tournament debaters will prepare a variety of briefs on current events issues. These briefs can be placed in folders, indexed alphabetically, and kept in some form of portable file holder. In addition to continuing to research new issues, you will need to continually update your older briefs. A good tournament debater never stops researching. Just as you think you have researched all there is to know, you will discover a new issue to investigate. Consider this list of current events issues that were briefed by debaters at the 2002 Willamette Debate Institute. While no list can be exhaustive of all possible current events issues, the debaters at this institute did a great job of covering a lot of key issues. Because of space limitations, I have included files indexed through letter H.

Sampling of Topics Researched at the Willamette Debate Institute

Affirmative Action
Air Traffic: Air Traffic Control Privatization
Air Traffic: Guns in Cockpits

79

Amtrak: Privatization
Animal Research
Argentina: Economic Crisis
Caspian Sea Oil Development
Children: Child Soldiers
Children: Mandatory Child Abuse Reporting
Children: WTO & Child Labor
Colombia: Plan Colombia
Corporate Accounting: Bush Reform Proposal
Corporate Accounting: Senate Reform Bill
Cyprus: Internal Conflict
Death Penalty: Mentally Retarded
Death Penalty: Moratorium
Drugs: Anti-Drug/Anti-Terrorism Advertisements
Drugs: Drug Courts
Drugs: Drug Testing
Drugs: Legalizing Marijuana
Drugs: Peyote vs. First Amendment
Drugs: Plan Colombia
Education: Bush Education Reform Plan
Education: Charter Schools
Education: ESL Reform
Education: School Prayer
Education: School Violence
Education: Sexual Education
Education: Standardized Testing
Elections: Instant Runoff Voting
Elections: Native Americans Clause in CFR Act
Environment: Endangered Species Act
Environment: Kyoto Protocol
Environment: Mixed Oxide Fuel
Environment: Solar Energy
Environment: Sustainable Farming Grants
Environment: SUV Emissions Standards
Environment: Yellowstone Snowmobiles
European Union: Dollar vs. Euro
Gay Adoption
Genetically Modified Organisms
Health Care: Drug Patents
Health Care: Mental Health Parity
Health Care: Prescription Drug Coverage
Health: AIDS Epidemic & Solutions

Health: Vaccination of Children
Health: West Nile Virus

Because tournament debaters must be prepared to debate both sides of an issue, each of your briefs should include some background history, arguments for and against the proposition, potential plans to meet policy implications, disadvantages to those plans, and solvency arguments (reasons why proposed policies will not solve the problem). Your briefs should also include supporting authorities for each of the main arguments developed. When you prepare your arguments at the tournament, you will have the ability to quickly refer to your briefed arguments, recall the key positions, and paraphrase authorities to support your arguments.

Researching Great Thinkers and Historical Documents

In addition to current events based topics, many of the topics that you will encounter at debate tournaments will require you to be familiar with the theories and documents that have been generated by the great thinkers of history. Political scientists, philosophers, economists, theologians, and experts in other areas have developed theories that are regularly used in debates. For example, the theory of maximizing the greatest good, attributed primarily to John Stuart Mill, can be easily adapted for use as a criterion in a debate. Because it is difficult, perhaps impossible, to retain such a broad range of knowledge, it is useful to brief the key theories of these thinkers and to include the briefs in your files. Here is a sample of thinkers and historical documents that you should be familiar with.

A Sampling of Great Thinkers and Historical Documents

Saint Thomas Aquinas
Aristotle
Jeremy Bentham
The Bill of Rights
Noam Chomsky
Jesus Christ
The Constitution of the United States
Rene Descartes
Declaration of Independence
Ralph Waldo Emerson
Federalist Papers
Michel Foucault
Ghandi
David Hume
William James
Thomas Jefferson

Immanuel Kant
John Locke
James Madison
The Magna Carta
Karl Marx
John Stuart Mill
Muhammad
Friedrich Nietzsche
Plato
Ayn Rand
Jean Jacques Rousseau
Adam Smith
Socrates
The Universal Declaration of Human Rights
Voltaire

Researching "Canned" Cases

Many debate teams are researching and preparing detailed cases that can be used to support appropriately worded broad or metaphorical topics. The practice is controversial. Some argue that canned cases should be encouraged because they are simply well-prepared Government positions. Supporters of canned cases contend that debaters should not be penalized for working hard. On the other hand, opponents argue that canned case tend to focus on very narrow case areas and represent an unfair burden for the Opposition. A canned case, for example, may focus on one particular bill that is being considered in Congress.

From a purely strategic perspective, there are advantages and disadvantages to utilizing canned cases. It is difficult for the Government to develop a brilliant case in the fifteen minutes that they are allocated for preparation. Canned cases can provide the Government with the strategic advantage of being able to present a well-researched, thoroughly thought-out position on an issue that it is unlikely the Opposition will be prepared for. The down-side to this strategy is that it can become tempting to use a canned case to support virtually any proposition, without regard to whether or not it is consistent with the meaning of the proposition. Many judges are aware of this practice and will give a loss to the Government if the Opposition effectively argues that the case does not support the proposition (i.e., is not topical). Because it requires experience to determine when the canned case will fit the proposition, novice debaters should avoid running canned cases.

Even if you don't choose to run canned cases to support the proposition, you will need to research the canned cases that other teams are running. When possible, it is best to approach the research of canned cases from a team perspective. Following a tournament, debate squads should meet and discuss both theoretical issues that they may have found interesting and/or confusing, as well as any cases that seemed to be exceptionally well-researched, polished, and recurring. (These qualities may not be limited to canned cases, but they tend to correlate with them.) Teams can then be assigned to brief the cases. Finally, because there is frequently overlap between current events issues and canned cases, briefing current events may help to prepare you for some of the canned cases that will be lurking out there.

SUMMARY

Thoroughly understanding the proposition you are debating is the first step to developing and defending your arguments. By brainstorming, defining, researching, and briefing the key issues in the debate, you will develop both an understanding of the topic and an arsenal of evidence that you can refer to in the debate. Sources of evidence include books, periodicals, scholarly journals, Government documents, the World Wide Web, and databases such as InfoTrac. Tournament debaters should develop briefs on current events issues, the theories of great thinkers and important historical documents, and canned cases.

REFERENCES

Allen, E.L. *From Plato to Nietzsche.* New York: Fawcett, 1957.

Friedman, Thomas. Editorial. *New York Times* published in *The Daily Breeze.* Sept. 25, 2002.

Maran Graphics. *Internet and World Wide Web Simplified.* 3rd Ed. Chicago: IDG Books, 1999.

Staff Writer. "Biosolid policy under review." *Solid Waste Report*, 33. Sept. 20, 2002.

Thomas, H. *Living biographies of Great Philosophers.* New York: Garden City Books, 1959.

Thomson Learning. *InfoTrac: User Guide for Instructors.* Ohio: Thomson, 2002.

EXERCISES

Chapter Five: Research

1. Find a newspaper editorial that utilizes both evidence of facts and opinion. Identify the fact and opinion evidence in the editorial.

2. Brainstorm ten arguments supporting and ten arguments opposing a proposition. List those arguments using the format described in this chapter.

3. Using InfoTrac, research "academic debate." List three articles that appear in the journal *Argument and Advocacy*. Summarize one of those articles.

4. Using InfoTrac, research "media bias." List three article citations on the subject. Read an article that interests you and summarize its content.

5. Research one of the Great Thinkers listed in this chapter. Discuss his or her primary theoretical contributions.

Chapter

6

Arguing Propositions of Fact and Value

CONSTRUCTING THE GOVERNMENT'S CASE

As we observed in Chapter 4, the Government team must present a *prima facie* case in support of the proposition if they hope to temporarily suspend the presumption that is enjoyed by the Opposition. As you will soon learn, the burdens associated with defending the different types of proposition are sometimes shared, but are sometimes unique. Because they do not call for a change in public action, claims of fact and value have more in common with each other than they do with claims of policy. And, while the content of debates may vary (may be field-specific), the basic burdens associated with proving propositions of fact and value true are basically the same (field invariant). To be able to effectively build a prima facie case for a proposition, you must first be able to identify the stock issues relevant to the proposition type. *Stock issues are those burdens that apply to a specific type of proposition, regardless of the subject of the proposition.* It is important to note at the outset that there has always been some disagreement within the debate community as to what constitutes the stock issues, particularly regarding propositions of fact and value (Bartanen and Frank, 49). What follows, however, are issues commonly utilized as stock issues on propositions of fact and value. We begin our discussion of case construction with a stock issue common to each of the three types of propositions: the Government's burden to be topical.

Stock Issue One: The Case Must Be Topical

Once you have correctly identified the type of claim you are debating, you must choose a case area that supports each of the keywords in the topic. When debaters argue for a proposition, they are not simply arguing for the subject suggested by that proposition. *Topicality is the requirement that the Government team present a case that both supports each of the keywords of the topic and does not stray from the boundaries established by those words.* The issue of topicality is said to be *a priori*, in that it is the issue that the judge will evaluate before any other. Furthermore, topicality is said to be an absolute voting issue in the debate. Unlike less important issues in the debate, if the Government loses topicality, they lose the debate.

Topicality is an important burden in debate because it forces the Government to identify the ground that they will defend and simultaneously indicates the ground that they cannot occupy. This requirement prevents the Government from shifting their advocacy as the debate progresses. Suppose you were attempting to support the topic "This House believes that rap music causes violence." You define rap music by using testimony from a musician who described the key characteristics of rap music. Your case goes on to argue that many notorious rappers have been involved in, and have perpetrated, violent acts. Your case would not be topical because, at best, it demonstrated that many rappers caused violence, not that rap music caused violence. In this example, you would have violated topicality because you did not stay within the boundaries of the topic.

It is also possible to present a case that meets your definitions, yet loses on topicality, because the Opposition is able to persuade the judge that your definition does not reasonably represent the true meaning of the topic. Returning to our rap music topic, if you had defined rap music by citing examples of notorious violent rappers, and then run your case enumerating the violent acts that they had been involved in, the Opposition could argue that your definition of music was too broad and inaccurate and that the "music" should be the focus of the debate. If they were able to persuade the judge to accept a more limited definition that excluded rappers, your case would no longer be topical.

In addition to staying within the topic, remember that the burden of topicality requires that you support each of the keywords of the topic. Suppose you were supporting the topic: "This House believes that *Shrek* is the best children's movie to be released in the last five years." In support of the proposition, you presented the reasons that you believed that *Shrek* was a great children's movie. Nothing about this case construction puts you outside of the topic; you fail, however, to sufficiently support each of the keywords of the topic. The language of the topic implies both a comparison and a timeframe for that comparison. Supporting the claim that *Shrek* is a great children's movie is not the same as supporting the claim that it is the "best" children's movie to be released in "the last five years." To be topical you would need to compare *Shrek* to other children's movies that came out in that five-year timeframe.

Topicality issues in parliamentary debate can get tricky because of parli's use of metaphorical topics. Topics such as "This House believes that all's well that ends well" give the Government some latitude in their interpretation of what is and isn't their ground. When debating metaphors, the crucial thing to look for is that all characteristics described by the metaphor are represented by the Government's case. The intention of the "all's well" metaphor is not to describe events that start well and that end well. The metaphor has always been taken to mean that even negative means can lead to positive ends. The Government interpretation should represent the metaphor as it is commonly understood, and it should carefully support all of the characteristics of the metaphor, or it risks being challenged as non-topical.

Stock Issue Two: The Case Must Be Significant

Where the burden of topicality requires that the Government remain in the topic, the burden of significance requires that the Government present a case that adequately represents the topic. *An insignificant case is one that, while potentially topical, is too small in either quantity or quality to represent the characteristics of the primary subjects in the proposition.* The burden of significance is the requirement that the Government not make a hasty generalization.

In the illustration below, the large circles represent the resolution and the set of possible case areas. The smaller circles represent the case that the Government has established to support the resolution. You'll note that the case area in non-topical illustration is relatively large, but outside of the parameters of the resolution. By contrast, the case area in the hasty generalization illustration is within the parameters of the resolution, but relatively small. A case that is a hasty generalization may well be topical; it is simply too insignificant to support the topic. A case that is not topical may be quite significant; it simply supports a different resolution.

HASTY GENERALIZATION VERSUS TOPICALITY

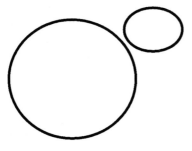
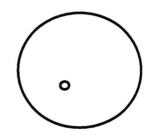

NON-TOPICAL   HASTY GENERALIZATION

Suppose the proposition being debated was that "might makes right." If the Government team argued that using the United States military in Afghanistan was necessary, they would be reasonably topical. The Opposition could argue, however, that they only represented one example (Afghanistan) in which the topic was true. The Opposition would be contending that the Government was guilty of a hasty generalization. If, however, the Government constructed a case that argued that diplomatic solutions to conflict are justified, the Opposition would contend (hopefully) that they are not topical because "might" implies the use of force. The definition of "might" would obviously play a role in that discussion.

When supporting propositions of fact and value, you must be mindful of the significance of the case you are presenting. Begin by considering the size and implications of the proposition you are supporting. Where propositions include qualifying language (words such as "some," "more often than not," and "generally speaking"), the language of the qualifier will provide clues about the number and size of examples that you must provide. If you were assigned to the Government side of the topic "This House believes that, more often than not, might makes right," your burden would be to persuade the judge that force was the correct strategy at least 51 percent of the times it was used. Part of that burden will be met throughout the debate as you refute Opposition examples of when might did not make right. While it is clearly impossible for the PM to present all possible cases of when might made right, his/her burden would be to demonstrate examples that represented the range of experiences in which might made right. Perhaps the PM might demonstrate the truth of the topic historically, in the present, and by advocating future use of might. When debating propositions of fact and value, the Government will generally better represent the topic by presenting one or two examples from a range of possible contexts than to focus only on one.

At times, however, you will be debating proposition of fact and value that do not have qualifying language. When no qualifying language exists, you can generally assume that the Government's burden is to show that the proposition is more often than not true. Because debate propositions probe the probable truth of generalizations, we do not assume (absent a qualifier that indicates a stricter burden) that the Government must prove the topic to be universally true. If you were debating the topic "Sexual education in the public schools has failed," your burden would not be to prove that all sexual education programs have failed all students. Your burden would simply be to show that sexual education has generally failed.

Because it is tempting to confuse correlation with causation, propositions that assert causal relationships mandate relatively rigorous tests. If the proposition was "Pornography causes crime," the Government, in their criteria, would need to establish whether they intend to prove a sufficient, necessary, or contributory causal relationship (see Chapter 2). Keep in mind, as we observed in Chapter 3, the Government will have to explain exceptions to the cause/effect relationship.

In sum, the Government must provide a case that is a significant representation of the topic. At times, qualifiers that provide a threshold for the ratio of examples that the Government must win are present in the proposition. As a rule of thumb, when propositions of fact and value do not include qualifying language, assume that the Government burden is to prove the topic true, more often than not, or true "on balance." Some topics, such as those that include a narrow casual relationship, may require fewer cases to prove the truth of the topic. Ultimately, the Government should be able to explain why they have focused on a certain set of examples as sufficient to support the resolution.

Stock Issue Three: The Government Must Define Terms

One of the greatest powers of the Government rests in its presumptive right to define terms. As you have read, the burden of proof rests with the Government, and presumption is enjoyed by the Opposition. In the area of assigning definitions and picking the case area, however, a stipulated presumption is assigned to the Government. This simply means that the Prime Minister, as the first speaker in the debate, has the right to offer definitions and assign the case area. The Opposition, in turn, must show good reasons for rejecting those choices. Because the Government enjoys presumption with regard to definitions, the Opposition has the burden to demonstrate that the Government has abused its discretion. Argument over the meaning of the topic may progress throughout the speeches in the debate and generally form the basis of any topicality argument.

Definitions Establish Ground

Proposition of fact and value, particularly metaphorical propositions, are often quite vague and broadly worded. When the Government defines terms, they are saying that, for the purposes of this debate, these words will have a specific meaning. In reality, there might be multiple possible interpretations of the words in the proposition, but the Government will want to narrow the meaning of the topic to provide *debatable ground.*

Debatable ground implies that the proposition has been interpreted to provide sufficient argumentative choices for both the Government and the Opposition. Clearly, it is in the best interest of the Government to define terms in such as way as to limit the amount of ground that they have to defend. On the other hand, a case that is based upon definitions that are too narrow will be susceptible to challenge by the Opposition. Suppose you were the Government on the topic "This House believes that the war on drugs has failed." Further suppose that you know a lot about drug testing in the

NFL, so you define drugs as steroids. Based upon that definition, you construct a case around steroid abuse in the NFL and the failure of the League to prevent it. You have constructed a case that clearly meets its definition; the problem is that the definition is vulnerable to challenge because it is so narrow. In all probability, a smart Opposition team would attempt to counter define to expand the definition of "drugs" and would also argue that your case is a hasty generalization. (There are lots of drugs that are being warred against; your case is only one example of a drug that is not widely used in the general population.) If, however, the Opposition chooses not to argue your definition, your case area will be the focus of the debate. The Opposition will not be able to argue that any other form of drug enforcement has been successful. (Technically, they can still point out the merits of other forms of drug enforcement. You will just be able to say that they are irrelevant given the definition of "drugs" that they failed to argue.)

The "war on drugs" example raises another issue that is important when constructing your case and assigning meaning through definitions. When you are examining the topic for the first time, ask yourself what you think is the intended meaning of the proposition. What is the "spirit of the resolution?" *The spirit of the resolution refers to the notion that there is a recognizable social controversy surrounding the topic.* With regard to the topic "This House believes that the war on drugs has failed," most people you ask would tell you that the "war on drugs" refers to the Federal Government's anti-drug efforts. Those efforts might include strategies such as border interdiction, education, and rehabilitation. The NFL drug testing case would not be consistent with what most people would understand as the "spirit of the resolution." That is not to say that you must always adhere to the intent of the topic. Sometimes, that intent is not at all clear, particularly on metaphorical topics. Even where it is clearly discernable, there is no rule that says that the Government must adhere to the spirit of the resolution. Be aware, however, that *artificial presumption* already rests against the Government (see Chapter 4). If you construct a case that is diametrically opposed to what your audience thought about when they first heard the topic, you may also be opposing the *natural presumption* that audience will hold against the case. In trying to be clever by strategically defining the topic, be aware of how your audience may receive your interpretation. If you think the advantage of constructing a case based upon a "clever" interpretation of the proposition will hurt you more than help you, you might consider a more middle of the road interpretation.

A final word on division of ground involves the notion of defining/interpreting the proposition as a truism. *A truism is a case that, on its face, cannot be argued.* A form of the fallacy of begging the question, a truism usually occurs when the Government has interpreted the topic in such a way as to remove virtually all Opposition ground. If the topic were "This House believes that contemporary feminism benefits

American women," and the Government defined "This House" as contemporary feminists, the topic would have been defined as a truism. *An easy way to check the effect of definitions on the meaning of the proposition is to substitute the definition for the term it is defining.* Substituting "contemporary feminists" for "This House" creates the proposition "Contemporary feminists believe that contemporary feminism benefits American women." If the Opposition does not counter define, they are stuck with trying to argue that contemporary feminists do not believe that their philosophy is advantageous to women. Most judges of parliamentary debate would quickly side with the Opposition if they were to argue that the ground in the debate had been unfairly divided because the topic had been defined to create a truism. Once again, the Government is almost always better off strategically when it chooses definitions and case interpretations that provide fair ground for both sides. When you begin with an interpretation that the judge will find objectionable, you have to defeat both the arguments voiced by your opponents and the presumption against the legitimacy of your case that you have created in the mind of your judge.

When to Define

It is typically not necessary for you to define every word in the proposition. The critical issues are whether or not the meaning of the term is controversial and will have a substantial impact upon the ground division in the debate. "This House" generally does not need to be defined. When the topic is phrased "This House believes," the assumption is that the debaters are attempting to persuade the judge, as the Speaker of the House, to believe the proposition. However, when debating policy proposition, the "house" may need to be defined to determine the specific agent that will implement the policy (see Chapter 7).

When terms are *equivocal* (have more than one accepted meaning) or vague and may impact both the clarity of the issues discussed and the ground in the debate, the Government should define them. If the Government fails to define, the right to define shifts from the Government to the Opposition. Metaphorical topics are particularly prone to problems with vagueness and equivocation. Consider the proposition, "This House believes that all's well that ends well." What does "well" mean? Even more literal topics present challenges. In the proposition "This House believes that freedom of expression is more important than national security," the Government would, at a minimum, need to define "freedom of expression," "more important," and "national security."

How to Define

Common Usage

After you have decided which terms seem controversial, decide whether the key terms in the proposition lend themselves to definition through popular usage or may require more field-specific definitions. When you turn to a dictionary such as *Websters*, you will find words defined in terms of their common usage. The numbered definitions in standard dictionaries generally reflect how commonly used the definition is. The natural presumption of the audience is likely to lean towards the more commonly used definitions of terms. The proposition "This House believes that liberty is more important than equality" requires clarification of the terms "liberty," "more important," and "equality." When we turn to *Websters New World Dictionary* (277) for clarification of the meaning of "liberty," we find:

> **liberty** 1. freedom, etc. 2. a particular right 3. an impertinent attitude 4. U.S. Navy permission for an enlisted person to be absent from duty for 72 hours or less.

The best definition for the purposes of the debate would probably be either the first or second definitions listed. The Government could develop a case using definition number 4 and argue that the Navy should issue leave based upon a criterion other than equality, but that wouldn't be consistent with the common usage of the term "liberty" and would, therefore, be more vulnerable to challenge.

Synonym

You'll note that the first definition of "liberty" was its synonym, "freedom." Synonyms are words that have similar denotative and connotative meanings as the words they define. An advantage of using a synonym to define is that often, you can think of a synonym that may be more familiar to the audience than the word you are trying to define. Defining the "right to be let alone" as "privacy" may help clarify the meaning of the word for the audience. The drawback to synonyms is that their usage risk defining in an equally unclear, perhaps circular fashion. When, for example, we define "liberty" as "freedom," we don't really clarify the term much. If, however, we were to define "liberty" within the context of the various Bill of Rights freedoms that protect it, we would be providing a clearer perspective on what we mean by the word.

Examples

Sometimes examples can help to clarify the meaning of a word. Because the case that will ultimately be constructed to support the proposition will be based on examples, it makes sense to use examples when defining the key terms in the proposition, as well. When debating the proposition "This House believes that the war on drugs has failed" and the Government wishes to focus its case on marijuana and cocaine, then it might choose to define drugs by using marijuana and cocaine as examples of the types of drugs that the war on drugs has failed to control.

Negation

To define by negation is to clarify the meaning of a term by indicating what the term does not mean. For example, eligibility to compete in intercollegiate forensics is generally limited to students who have not completed an undergraduate degree and who have not competed for more than four years. Negation can also be combined with other forms of definitions to show both what is included and excluded within the meaning of a term. A proposed definition of driver eligibility might provide inclusive qualities such as being at least 17, having past extensive driver training, and having maintained a good academic record, as well as excluded qualities (negation) such as not having been convicted of drug or alcohol-related offenses.

Qualities

Particularly when debating metaphorical propositions, it may be important to define key terms by isolating the characteristics and qualities they represent. A debate on the proposition "This house believes that cats are better than dogs," in which the topic is taken literally, will not be particularly deep. A better debate would require that the Government isolate the qualities and characteristics of dogs and cats in its definition of terms, and then proceed with a case that makes comparisons of analogous subjects that share those characteristics. Perhaps "dogs" could be defined as representing the quality of loyalty, and "cats" could represent independence. The Government case could then look at the value of having allies that are loyal to the United States in voting patterns in the United Nation versus those allies that tend to vote independently.

Context

The context in which the words in the topic appear, as well as the social controversies that provide the basis for the propositions, are important to recognize when formulating the definitions. At times, it is better to define the proposition in terms of its key phrases rather than focusing on individual words. Using the proposition "Resolved: The Right of Privacy is more important than any other Constitutional right," it makes more sense to define the expression, "right of privacy," than to individually define, "right," "of," and "privacy."

Field Dependent Terms

Where commonly used words and phrases lend themselves to definitions taken from standard dictionaries, words and expressions used in specific contexts may be more appropriately defined through the use of specialized sources. Dictionaries such as *Black's Law* provide definitions based upon their usage within a particular field. If you needed to define the First Amendment, it might be better to use a source expert in the field of law than to defer to the "common usage" of the term. In addition to specialized dictionaries, field dependent terms can be defined by deferring to the opinions of experts found on web pages, in books, magazines, journal articles, and newspapers. If, for example, you were debating the merits of "United States foreign policy in the Middle East," you might want to turn to sources from the State Department to provide the definition of "foreign policy."

Finally, when debating issues related to philosophy (metaphorical topics are frequently based in philosophy), grounding your definitions in the theories of relevant philosophers can be very effective. For example, if you were debating the proposition "This House believes that the ends justify the means," you might turn to John Stuart Mill's theory of utilitarianism to define the proposition. Once again, it would make more sense to define the phrase "ends justify means" rather than the individual words of the proposition.

Stock Issue Four: The Government Must Provide Criteria

Where definitions explain the meaning of the topic, criteria provide the standards by which we will determine whether or not the topic is true. So fundamental is the development of criteria to evaluating non-policy propositions that Ronald Matlon has argued that two stock issues, providing criteria (what he calls the "definitive stock issue") and meeting the criteria (the "designative stock issue"), should be the central focus of analysis in non-policy debate. Criteria use is really not complicated; in fact, we regularly use criteria outside of academic debate. Let's say you want to buy a new car and you are trying to decide on what is the "best" car for you. You are on a limited budget (if you aren't, good for you), you like to camp (so you need room), and you want something reliable (not too old or run-down). You have decided then on the criteria for the "best" car for you: 1) cost, 2) cargo sizes, and 3) dependability. The trick now is to find a car that meets your criteria.

Another way of thinking about criteria in academic debate is that it serves as a statement of what the Government must prove in the debate and, therefore, provides the mechanism or yardstick by which the judge can decide if the Government has met its burden. Like definitions, criteria serve to establish ground and burdens in the debate. Therefore, when they create the criteria, the Government must be careful not to overly limit the Opposition ground. Ideally, the criteria provide an objective mechanism by which the truth of the topic is discerned. As is true of definitions, if the Opposition can provide reasons to reject the criteria, the judge may allow them to supplant the Government criteria with their own.

In addition to indicating what is to be included when determining the truth of the topic, the criteria also act as a filter to determine what is excluded. Continuing with the example of buying a car, if our criteria require that we look to cost, cargo room, and dependability first, it implicitly excludes supplanting that criteria for something like appearance or audio system. This exclusionary function of criteria acts to further limit the ground that the Government must defend. When the Government claims that it need only prove that X is true to win the debate, any Opposition discussion of Y becomes irrelevant.

Criteria on Propositions of Fact

Criteria on factual propositions generally function to provide a threshold for determining when the relationships described in the proposition are probably true. A *threshold is a point at which we can agree that enough proof has been established to meet the burden implied by the proposition.* When developing a criteria for the factual proposition "Social Security has failed us," the Government must decide what the key measures for failure of that system are and at what point of poor performance we would indicate that they have failed (threshold). Perhaps failure could be measured by 1) the ability of the system to provide a competitive return on the worker's investment, 2) the ability of the system to endure, and 3) the ability of the system to maintain its recipients beyond the poverty level. The Government could establish a threshold for the first criterion based upon the percentage of increased return they believe that an alternate system, such as investment in the stock market, might provide. The threshold for the second criterion could be a requirement that the system be able to survive to provide for any generations that contributed to it. For the third criterion, the Government could establish a threshold for when the percentage of recipients who have fallen below the poverty level is unacceptable.

Criteria may be *independent* or *dependent*. When criteria are *independent*, winning any single criterion is sufficient to prove the probable truth of the proposition. When criteria are *dependent*, each criterion must be won for the proposition to be deemed probably true. The Government should indicate whether their criteria are independent or dependent and should explain why. The question is simply whether or not each criterion is significant enough to serve as a test of the probable truth of the topic. Some criterion may be more significant than others. When looking to the Social Security topic, the third criterion, "The ability of the system to maintain its recipients beyond the poverty level," might be viewed as a significantly sufficient test of the proposition to be deemed independent. Meeting the first criterion, the question of whether or not the system provides a competitive rate of return would probably not be enough to justify the conclusion that the system had "failed."

Propositions that establish causal relationships may appear simple on their face, but what type of causal relationship does the Government need to establish? With regard to the proposition "Rap music causes violence," the Government could establish criteria based upon either a sufficient, necessary, or contributory relationship between rap and violence. Clearly it would be more difficult for the Government to establish a sufficient or necessary causal relationship than it would be to prove that rap merely contributed to violence. It is important, however, that the Government make clear what its burden is in the criteria.

Other factual topics will require more imagination when divining criteria. Metaphorical topics can be particularly challenging. Consider the topic, "This House believes that nice guys finish last." The criteria you establish for this topic will be relative to the qualities you assign to "nice guys" and to "finishing last." You may interpret "nice guys" to be those countries that use non-protective trade measures. "Finish last" might be interpreted as suffering from large trade deficits. In addition to criteria related to those qualities, an important element to include when debating this type of generalization is the percentage of "nice guys" who must finish last before the topic is true. When a generalization does not include a qualifier, you should assume the threshold is "more often than not." Debaters frequently refer to this as "on balance" criteria. As name implies, "on balance" means that the judge will simply weigh the number of examples supporting the topic against those opposing it. If the topic proves to be truer than not, the Government wins.

After having indicated what the criteria should be, the Government must indicate why the criteria provided represent the best measure for assessing the probable truth of the topic. Essentially, the Government must justify and support its decision to utilize the criteria that they have advanced. The reasons for choosing the criteria may vary, but minimally, the Government should be able to base its justification on the basis that the criteria represents a fair division of ground and that the criteria is consistent with the language and subject matter of the proposition. With claims that are clearly drawn from a particular field of expertise, the Government might be able to argue that their criteria are similar to the types of standards that would be applied by that field. Propositions involving guilt, innocence, or product liability might utilize criteria drawn from the legal field.

In sum, when constructing criteria on propositions of fact, remember that the criteria is attempting to establish a mechanism that will help the judge decide whether or not the topic is probably true. Your goal when establishing criteria on factual topics should be to indicate what is to be proved and how you will go about proving it. Finally, you must provide analysis that supports your choice of criteria.

Questions to Ponder

Develop criteria for proving the claim: The War on Drugs has failed.

Criteria on Propositions of Value

Sometimes it is difficult to determine whether a proposition is a claim of fact or a claim of value. Both types of propositions may involve inferences about facts. While the similarities between the two types of claims can be confusing, more often than not, you should be able to recognize the difference. Claims of fact tend to be provable by more objective means, using evidence that is readily observable. Value claims, however, tend to be more subjective and require that we make judgments about persons, places, things, or ideas. Sometimes value claims make clear comparisons between two or more values. Because of their highly subjective nature, providing clear criteria is particularly important when debating value claims.

What Are Values?

A highly respected theorist in the area of values, Milton Rokeach, contends that values are "core conceptions of the desirable within every individual and society" (16). Values exist at a much deeper level than our beliefs and, as a result, are much less prone to change. Values may exist at both individual and group levels (Rokeach). Some theorists speculate that our values are established very early in childhood. As core conceptions, values can sometimes be expressed in fairly simple terms. Among those things that are considered values are: life, liberty, equality, justice, security, quality of life, peace, wisdom, and happiness (Rokeach). Additionally, in academic debate, broader concepts are discussed as values. For example, debaters may compare the value of Freedom of Speech to the value of National Security. These broader concepts may actually represent a conglomerate of values. When we say we value Freedom of Speech, we are expressing our support for values such as liberty, self-respect, expression, etc.

Values can be found throughout arguments. We may talk about them within the context of a value proposition, but they play important roles in other types of claims, as well. In claims of fact, the choices we make to support an inference reflect values. In policy claims, the problems we choose to focus on, as well as the solutions we construct to solve those problems, are necessarily associated with values.

Criteria Weigh Values

Value criteria serve to weigh competing values. Each value that is being compared can be extremely important. Values such as justice, freedom, peace, life, quality of life, and happiness are valued by American society. Many propositions, however, require that you make a case for why one should be valued over another. *Value hierarchies* prioritize values. Recall Patrick Henry's famous statement, "Give me liberty or give me death." This statement reflects a hierarchy in which liberty is valued over life. The American system of capitalism reflects a hierarchy that favors freedom over equality. (Within the context of the philosophy of capitalism, these are competing values because a society in which everyone shares the same social status must limit the individual's freedom to make choices that might jeopardize their social position.) In other contexts, however, equality is valued over freedom. Despite the fact that wealthier neighborhoods pay more in property taxes, these school districts cannot receive more tax revenues than are allotted to school districts in poorer neighborhoods. Hierarchies, then, are context-specific.

Sometimes the proposition establishes the hierarchy that is to be debated. The proposition, "This House believes that the right of privacy is more important than any other right" clearly establishes the hierarchy the Government must support. The criteria for the proposition must then determine why it is that privacy should enjoy a place at the top of the hierarchy. A key part of establishing a value hierarchy is demonstrating why one value should be favored over another. When arguing the privacy topic, one way the Government might support its hierarchy involves the question of whether privacy should be viewed as an *instrumental* or as a *terminal* value. *Instrumental values are the means to achieving a desired outcome. Terminal values are the ends we hope to achieve.*

In debates, criteria frequently reflect that values are instrumental to achieving goals. With regard to the privacy topic, the Government would begin its criteria by discussing the goals that privacy helps us to achieve. The Government might argue that privacy is the most important right because it protects our ability to enjoy other rights. To make clear to the judge how this concept should be used to evaluate the debate, the Government should include a statement, sometimes referred to as a *decision rule*. A decision rule is simply a statement that expresses exactly what the Government's burden in the debate is. On this topic, the Government could contend that privacy allows us to successfully pursue freedoms, such as the ability to associate with whomever we please or the ability to research and read material that others might find offensive. If the Opposition accepted this criterion, the Government burden for the debate would be to demonstrate that privacy is the instrument that allows us to enjoy other rights. The Government's criteria could resemble the following:

> The Government's burden today is to demonstrate that privacy is more important than any other right. To meet this burden, we will argue that privacy is utilized more than any other right to pursue our freedoms. We are contending that the worth of a value lies in its utility. Our decision rule, therefore, is if the Government can prove that privacy is more instrumental than other rights in achieving desired ends, a ballot for the Government is warranted.

Another option for the Government is to create criteria in which the value of privacy is viewed as a goal to be achieved (terminal value). When utilizing this strategy, the Government would begin by demonstrating why privacy should be viewed as the most important right to be achieved. They might argue, for example, that privacy is the most important right because it is the right most needed. The Government's case would then attempt to prove that privacy was threatened and that it is needed. Utilizing the terminal value strategy, the Government's criteria could be as follows:

> To support the proposition that privacy is the most important value, we begin by arguing that privacy, or the "right to be let alone," is particularly needed in the modern world. Perhaps more than any other right, we will contend that privacy is uniquely threatened. Further, we will argue that other rights enjoy much more protection than is extended to privacy. We will be contending, therefore, that a measure of a value's importance can be found in the extent to which it is needed. Our decision rule, therefore, is that if the Government can prove that privacy is the most needed right, a Government ballot is warranted.

Rather than establishing values to be compared, many propositions simply ask the Government to make a judgment about something. The same basic criteria options apply, but the Government must infer the relevant value from the context of the proposition. On the topic "This House believes that the method of conducting Presidential elections is detrimental to Democracy," the Government might begin to establish its criteria by determining the value or valued outcome that is harmed by the current method of conducting elections. Teams might argue that the Right to Vote is fundamental to Democracy, and if the Government can show that the method of conducting elections infringes on the Right to Vote, then the Government will have proven the proposition true. As the Government develops its case, it may uncover a value hierarchy. One criticism of the method of conducting Presidential elections is that the projection of elections results based upon East Coast polling data discourages some voters on the West Coast from voting. A case utilizing this example would be establishing a hierarchy that holds the Right to Vote above the right of the press to project those results.

In sum, when establishing criteria on value topics: 1) The Government should indicate which value should occupy the top of the hierarchy. 2) The Government should indicate why that value is the most important value. 3) The Government should provide a decision rule that indicates what its burdens are relative to the value.

Develop criteria for the claim:
This House values standards over compassion.

Stock Issue Five: The Government Must Meet Its Criteria

Thus far, we have been concerned with arguments associated with how the debate will proceed. The definitions established the meaning of the topic and divided Government and Opposition ground. The criteria further defined ground in the debate by articulating what the Government must prove to win the debate. The remainder of the Government's case is dedicated to meeting the burden that they have established for themselves in their criteria. This is done through a combination of storytelling and identifying and supporting claims.

Storytelling

Storytelling is an important part of debate. In virtually all argumentative contexts, stories are being told and evaluated by an audience. In the courtroom, attorneys tell competing stories. In a murder trial, the prosecution will tell the story of how the defendant committed the crime. Their story will involve the defendant's motive, means, and opportunity to murder the victim. The defense has two options, and these are not mutually exclusive. They can attempt to weaken parts of the prosecution's story. Perhaps they will present a witness that will indicate that the defendant could not have been at the crime scene when the murder was committed. They can also offer a counter story. The defense could present witnesses that implicate a second suspect. The jury would then evaluate the competing stories.

Like a trial, a debate involves storytelling. The evaluation of argument as storytelling is sometimes referred to as the *narrative paradigm* (Fisher, 1987). The Government team will tell a story that supports the proposition; the Opposition will attempt to shoot holes in that story and/or tell competing stories. Two criteria are used to evaluate the competing narratives. The first criterion looks to whether the story is organized in such a way that the pieces make sense together (coherence). The second criterion questions the extent to which the story is consistent with what the audience considers to be true (fidelity).

You should keep the storytelling model in mind when constructing your case. When brainstorming arguments to support your criteria, ask yourself if the arguments are consistent with what the audience believes to be true. When structuring your arguments, check to see if the structure of the case presents a coherent argument for the proposition. Let us turn now to a discussion of structure.

Structuring the Government's Case

Claim, support, explanation is the basic model for structuring the arguments in your case. As we observed in Chapter 2, a well-constructed claim should be relatively simple and to the point. Support your claim using one of the types of grounds we discussed in Chapter 2 (example, analogy, authority, sign, or cause). Next, it may be useful to explain the relevance of the argument to the burdens established by the criteria. Some arguments simply establish the early stages of a story that eventually leads to proving the criteria true. Many arguments, however, are more directly related to the criteria, and their relevance should be explained. Essentially, the explanation is telling the judge why he or she should care about this argument. Forcing yourself to make explanations about the relevance of arguments to the criteria will help you stay on target. The many arguments that will make up your case can begin to resemble a forest in which all that you (and the judge) can see are the individual trees. The criteria represent the big picture. They provide the standards by which the resolution will be interpreted. If the main arguments in your case become incoherent, you risk creating the impression that you have not met the burdens established by the criteria.

Sub Points, Observations, and Contentions

The main arguments that the Government will advance to support its criteria are referred to as contentions. Typically, the Government will offer 2 or 3 contentions. Each contention is made up of sub points. A sub point is simply an argument (claim, support, explanation). Contentions that are sufficiently developed to meet the criteria are referred to as *independent*. It is possible to develop a case with many independent contentions. The advantage of independent contentions is that the Government will meet its criteria and, therefore, win the debate if it successfully carries even one. Finally, the Government may use *observations* to highlight arguments in the debate that do not make sense as contentions. Procedural issues, such as definitions and criteria, are often placed within the framework of observations. The following is an example of one possible case structure that utilizes observations, contentions, and sub points. There are many possible permutations of this structure, but it provides a good basic framework from which to begin.

Introductory Remarks
   Ingratiation
   Statement of Support of Resolution

Observation One: Definitions
   Definition of key term #1
   Definition of key term #2
   Definition of key term #3
   Definition of key term #4

Observation Two: Criteria
    A. *The value, goal, or standard*
    B. *The support for the value, goal, or standard*
    C. *Decision rule: how the judge will use the value, goal, or standard as criteria*

Contention One: The first main argument that meets the criteria

    A. *The first claim necessary to develop the story of Contention One*
        1. *Supporting material (example, analogy, cause, sign, authority)*
        2. *Possible explanation of the relevance of the sub point to the criteria (if appropriate)*
    B. *The second claim necessary to develop the story of Contention One*
        1. *Supporting material (example, analogy, cause, sign, authority)*
        2. *Possible explanation of the relevance of the sub point to the criteria (if appropriate)*
    C. *The third claim necessary to develop the story of Contention One*
        1. *Supporting material (example, analogy, cause, sign, authority)*
        2. *Possible explanation of the relevance of the sub point to the criteria (if appropriate)*

Additional Contentions

OPPOSITION STRATEGIES

The Opposition's burdens when debating propositions of fact and value are fairly simple. You've learned that the Government must meet five stock issues: it must be topical, it must be significant, it must define terms, it must provide criteria, and it must meet its criteria. If the Government fails to adequately meet these burdens, it may lose the debate. The Opposition's strategy, therefore, is to attempt to show that the Government has failed to meet one or more stock issues.

The Opposition has two broad argumentative strategies that it can utilize. The first strategy is *direct refutation*, which is the process of first identifying your opponent's argument, then providing a counter response to that argument. After identifying the Government's argument, the basic structure of the Opposition's counter response should follow the *claim, support, and explanation* model. The Leader of the Opposition, then, will spend a large portion of his or her time directly refuting the various elements of the Government case, trying to show that they have failed to meet one or more of the stock issues. Arguments that are applied through direct refutation to the Government's case structure are referred to as *on case arguments*. *Off case arguments* are Opposition arguments that do not directly apply to the main arguments of the Government's case. Like the Government, the Opposition may structure arguments in the form of *observations*. The first observation the Opposition may make concerning the Government's case is that the case is not topical.

Arguing That the Government Is Not Topical

After hearing the Government's case, the Opposition must decide whether or not they are going to accept the case as topical. The Opposition should ponder what the proposition means and compare their interpretation of the meaning of the topic to the Government's. Topicality is an all or nothing issue for the Government. If the Opposition can prove that the Government is not topical, the Government loses. Because topicality is an all or nothing issue for the Government, judges will frown on Opposition teams who argue topicality when, in fact, the case is reasonably topical. Given the metaphorical nature of many of the topics in parliamentary debate, it is important that both teams have familiarized themselves with famous metaphors so that they can clearly represent the intended meaning of metaphorical topics.

Problems with topicality tend to stem from one of three sources. The first source of topicality violations occurs when the Government ignores important terms in the proposition when developing their case. If the topic were "This House believes that intercollegiate athletics is a form of academic fraud" and the Government's case focused on violations of NCAA regulations, they would have ignored the word "academic" in the proposition. The topic calls for an indictment of athletics as it relates to academia, not as it relates to organizations that govern intercollegiate athletics.

The second source of topicality violations occurs when a Government team provides a definition for a term that they fail to meet. Referring once more to the "intercollegiate athletics is a form of academic fraud" proposition, the Government team might have defined academic fraud, but failed to meet their definition by showing that something about athletics perpetrates a fraud in terms of its relationship with academia.

These two sources of topicality problems (ignoring a term or the Government's failure to meet its own definition) lend themselves to topicality attacks that are easy to develop and structure. The Leader of the Opposition would simply begin his or her speech by saying that they have an observation concerning topicality. The first part of the topicality argument is referred to as the *topicality standard*. A topicality standard is simply a rule that establishes the burden that the Government must meet to be topical. If the problem stems from a mismatch between the Government's own definition and their case, the standard is simply the Government's definition. If the problem stems from a term that the Government has ignored or failed to properly define, another standard must be used. A commonly used topicality standard is that "all words of the resolution have meaning." This rule is based upon the theory that removing any single word from the topic substantially changes the meaning of the topic. After presenting this standard, the Leader of the Opposition would go on to the second part of the topicality observation that involves showing how the Government has violated the standard. The final part of the topicality observation simply reminds the judge that if the Opposition can demonstrate that the Government is not topical, the Government loses. The following represents a basic structure for a topicality argument, utilizing the "academic fraud" example.

> *Observation: The Government Is Not Topical*
>   *A. Standard: All words of the resolution have meaning.*
>   *1. The resolution requires that fraud be perpetrated against academia.*
>   *B. Violations*
>   *1. The Government ignores the word "academic" in the proposition.*
>   *2. The Government's case argues that athletics has cheated the NCAA—not that athletics defrauded academia.*
>   *C. Topicality is a voting issue*
>   *1. Topicality divides ground in the debate.*
>   *2. Topicality promotes testing of the proposition.*

The third source of Government topicality violations occurs when Government has provided a definition to justify their case, their case meets that definition, but the Opposition believes that the definition is inconsistent with the true meaning of the word given the context of the resolution. Remember, that if the Government defines "day" as "night" and the Opposition fails to counter define, "day" will mean "night" for the purposes of the debate. At times, therefore, it is necessary that the Opposition provide counter definitions as the basis for the topicality argument, and to expand the ground that they will be allowed to argue on during the debate. The subsequent section addresses the steps you should follow when arguing the Government's definitions. The standards discussed for evaluating definitions can be used within the context of a topicality argument or simply for challenging a definition so that the Opposition can expand their ground in the debate. When used within the context of a topicality observation, you would simply adhere to the same model discussed above and utilize one of the definitional standards to justify a counter definition. You would then go on to show how the Government fails to meet the new definition and is, therefore, not topical. Let us turn now to a discussion of methods used to challenge a Government definition.

Arguing the Government's Definitions

The Leader of the Opposition should analyze each of the Government's definitions to determine if the Government has "reasonably" defined terms. A *reasonable definition* of terms: 1) is consistent with expert or lay definitions of a term, and 2) provides fair division of ground in the debate. If one or more of the Government's definitions are not reasonable, the Leader of the Opposition may choose to provide counter definitions. The Opposition should remember, however, that not all definitions matter. If the Government is not gaining a strategic advantage from a definition, there may be no need to argue it. If, however, the Government's definitions have allowed them to run a case that is not on its face topical or if their definitions have overly limited negative ground, the Opposition should counter define.

To offer a counter definition, the Opposition must first demonstrate what is wrong with the Government's definition. To do this, the Opposition should offer a *definitional standard*. Definitional standards are criteria that help the judge to assess who has provided the best definition for the debate. The following standards are commonly used in debates:

Common Usage: The best definition is one taken from the way a term is used by the masses.

Field Expert: The best definition is one taken from experts in the field.

Specificity: The best definition is one that narrowly defines what is included within the meaning of a term.

Inclusion/Exclusion: The best definition includes both what is included within the meaning of a term and what is excluded from its meaning.

Framer's Intent: The best definition interprets words consistently with the commonly recognized controversy surrounding the proposition. This can be a difficult standard to establish, as many topics do not have a clearly definable intent.

After the Opposition has established a standard by which to evaluate definitions, they must apply the Government's definition to the standard and argue why it doesn't meet it. Once this has been done, the Opposition must offer a counter definition. If the Opposition simply indicts that Government's definition as inadequate but fails to provide an alternative, the judge will be forced to use the Government's definition. Recall that the Government enjoys presumption on its choice of definitions, so the Opposition must meet the burden of demonstrating why the Government's choice of definitions should be overturned. After providing a counter definition, the Opposition should explain why their definition better meets the standard that they have provided. This step is important because it is inconsistent to indict the Government's definitions as vague and then to provide equally vague counter definitions.

In summary, these are the steps the Opposition should follow when arguing a definition:

1. Provide a definitional standard
2. Apply the standard to the Government's definition
3. Provide a counter definition
4. Apply the standard to the counter definition

Arguing Hasty Generalization

One of the Government's burdens is to present a case that is a significant representation of the proposition. During preparation time, before the Prime Minister presents the case, the Opposition should think about how potentially large the proposition is. The Opposition should look to both the language and type of topic to help it make a determination of whether the Government's case is a hasty generalization. To adequately test philosophical topics, the Government should draw on examples from a variety of areas. Where the topic is limited to a single subject, it may still be important for the Government to cover more than one example of that subject. If the topic was that "gun control measures have, on balance, been effective," the Opposition should consider the variety of gun control measures that could be involved in the debate. If the Government attempted to limit the discussion to one gun control measure, the Opposition might question whether that limitation provides an adequate test of a proposition on the general question of gun control.

Like topicality, hasty generalization can be presented as an observation. The first argument in the observation should indicate what would fulfill the burden of proving the generalization true. The second argument in the observation should explain to the judge why the Government's case falls short of meeting that standard. Finally, the impact of the argument should be explained. The Opposition could claim that if they win the hasty generalization argument, they should win the debate, or they can claim that, because the topic is broader than the Government's interpretation recognizes, they should be able to examine the proposition in its totality. This second argument allows the Opposition to run arguments that oppose the proposition in general, greatly expanding their ground.

Arguing Criteria

It is particularly important for the Opposition to carefully evaluate the Government's criteria. Whether arguing propositions of fact or of value, the Opposition should determine if the Government's criteria fairly and clearly divides the ground in the debate. The most obvious ground allocation problem occurs when the Government's criteria establishes a *truism*. The criterion is a truism if it assumes the very question that the proposition poses and, therefore, provides no ground for the Opposition team. Suppose the topic was that "Freedom of Speech is more important than National Security" and the Government offered a value and a decision rule as their criteria. In the value section, they argued that expression is the most important value. Their decision rule was that if they show that Freedom of Speech protects expression better than National Security, they should win. Because "expression" is virtually synonymous with "Freedom of Speech," the Government's criterion is a truism. Of course, Freedom of Speech upholds expression better than National Security. If the Opposition accepts the criteria, they would be granting the supremacy of Freedom of Speech. Even if the Government has not created a truism, their criteria may still unfairly skew the ground their way, or it may be unclear. In either case, the Opposition should offer counter criteria.

A useful strategy to follow when arguing propositions that require the Government to prove that one thing is more important than another is to argue that the Opposition's burden is to demonstrate either that the opposite is true or that the two things are equal. If the proposition were "This House believes that equality is more important than freedom," it would be easier for the Opposition to demonstrate that freedom is of equal importance to equality than it would be to prove that freedom is more important than equality.

When arguing the Government's criteria, the first step is to show what is wrong with their criteria. If they have not presented criteria, the judge may accept that as a reason to reject the Government's case altogether. Minimally, failure to present criteria is grounds for the acceptance of the Opposition's counter criteria. Additionally, lack of clarity or creating a truism can be grounds for rejecting the Government's criteria. If those criteria are based upon a primary value or goal, the Opposition can present reasons why they believe their value or goal is superior to the Government's. Finally, the Opposition must present counter criteria. As when arguing definitions, it is pointless to criticize the Government's criteria if you are not going to offer an alternative.

Arguing the Government's Contentions

When arguing the Government's contentions, focus on the burden that has been established by the criteria. It is easy to get caught up in each of the arguments that the Government has presented, but the criteria represent the "big picture." Your primary question regarding each of the Government's arguments should be: how does the argument fulfill the burden established by the criteria? You don't need to argue every point. Some arguments are not particularly consequential. Such arguments may be used to establish part of the Government's story, but may not directly impact their criteria. If you run into arguments that are simply facts or non consequential to the criteria, you may choose to ignore them. Remember, however, that any arguments you choose not to argue are conceded to your opponents.

In addition to challenging the relationship between the Government's claims and the criteria, the Opposition will need to analyze each of the Government's main points. You can begin by identifying the type of argument that is being made (cause, sign, example, analogy, authority—see Chapter 2), and then applying the relevant tests to their argument. If, for example, they present an authority to support a point, you should analyze the credibility of that authority. If appropriate, make arguments indicting their source's qualifications or potential bias. If possible, present information from authorities that support your perspective and argue that they are superior sources.

As you are arguing the Government's main points, look for opportunities to point out any informal fallacies (see Chapter 3) that might have occurred. Be especially vigilant with regard to contradictory arguments made by the Government. You may notice contradictions within a speech or between speeches. As the debate progresses, you will want to look for contradictions between the Prime Minister and Member of Government.

In addition to looking for contradictions, look for opportunities to *turn* your opponent's argument. You turn an argument when you prove that the claim is not only false, but the opposite of the claim is true. Imagine that the Government's case is supporting the proposition "This House believes that the death penalty is undesirable." Their criterion is that life is the most important value and if they can demonstrate that the death penalty devalues life, they should win. Their case argues the death penalty sends the message that killing is alright. You could easily turn these arguments by contending that not using the death penalty undermines the value of life for two reasons. First, when innocent people are killed and their murderers allowed to live, it sends the message that murderers can kill and the State will support them for the remainder of their days. Second, convicted murderers might well kill again while in prison. This also violates the value of life.

Developing the Off Case Story

Recall that direct refutation of the Government's case serves the function of poking holes in their story. After you have argued the major points of the Government's case, you may have time to present your story. The Opposition's story on propositions of fact and value comes largely in the form of counter examples. These counter examples may be structured in much the same way as the Government's contentions. These arguments are referred to as *off case* because they do not directly relate to the Government's case structure; rather, they attack the resolution in general. Be aware, however, that all arguments in the debate must relate to either the

Government's criteria or the Opposition's criteria. (As a matter of strategy, it is ideal if they relate to both.)

Recall the example introduced earlier in this Chapter: "This house believes that the Right of Privacy is more important than any other right." Depending on the criteria, the Opposition might offer examples of other rights that it feels are at least equally important. Like the Government's contentions, the Opposition's off case will usually consist of sub points made up of claims and grounds. The following represents a potential structure for an off case argument on the privacy topic:

Off Case Argument One: The Right to Life Is More Important than Privacy

    A. *Life Is a Right Protected by Government*
       (Supporting Material)

    B. *Life Is Threatened by Terrorism*
       (Supporting Material)

    C. *Privacy Laws Assist Terrorist*
       (Supporting Material)

    D. *Without Life, Privacy Is Irrelevant*
       (Supporting Material)

SUMMARY

Propositions of fact and value share similar qualities. To meet their prima facie burdens, the Government must be topical, be significant, define terms, provide criteria, and meet the burdens established in the criteria. The Opposition's case consists primarily of focusing on weaknesses in the Government's case through the use of direct refutation and off case arguments. Both the Government and the Opposition should utilize the claim, support, and explanation model when making individual arguments. Individual arguments should fit within the framework of the narratives that each team is attempting to create.

REFERENCES

Bartanen, Michael, and David Frank. *Nonpolicy Debate.* Scottsdale: Gorsuch, 1994.

Brownlee, Don. "Approaches to Support and Refutation of Criteria." *CEDA Yearbook,* 1990, 9-25.

Matlon, Ronald J. "Debating Propositions of Value." *Journal of the American Forensic Association 14,* 1978, 194-204.

Rokeach, Milton. *Beliefs, Attitudes and Values.* San Francisco: Jossey-Bass, 1968.

Rokeach, Milton. *Understanding Human Values.* New York: Free Press.

Websters New World Dictionary. New York: Simon and Schuster, 1979.

EXERCISES

Chapter 6: Arguing Propositions of Fact and Value

1. Construct criteria for the topic: "Freedom is more important than equality."

2. List the ten most important values in your life.

3. Pick two of the types of definitions described in this chapter. Make an argument that describes why one is better than the other.

4. Structure a contention that supports the proposition: "Cats are better than dogs."

5. Using InfoTrac, cite and describe the findings of one article that examines the connection between violent media and violent behavior.

6. Choose a fact or value proposition from the Appendix. Develop an argument for that proposition.

Arguing Propositions of Policy

CONSTRUCTING THE GOVERNMENT'S CASE

As you learned in Chapter 4, policy propositions call for a change in public action. Of all of the types of propositions, policy claims are probably the most popular in academic debate. Part of the reason for their popularity stems from the greater ambiguity associated with arguing non-policy propositions. It is important to remember, however, that facts and values form the basis for arguments for change. Unless we know the facts associated with a problem and are clear on values that influence our potential choices, we are likely to construct policies that don't address the real problem, don't solve the problem they are supposed to address, or create bigger problems than they are attempting to solve. Some have referred to propositions of fact and value as "pre-policy" in their orientation. There is some truth to this characterization, but in addition to preceding policy disputes, claims of fact and value are used to construct policy cases. We begin our analysis of policy propositions by examining the stock issues associated with the Government's burdens when supporting claims that call for a change. You will observe that a few of the stock issues are shared with non-policy propositions.

Stock Issue One: The Case Must be Topical

As was discussed in Chapter 6, the Government team must present a case that reflects the keywords of the proposition. Policy propositions ask the Government to create a proposal to solve a problem. It is, therefore, the policy that the Government advocates that must be topical. Some policy propositions will clearly indicate the type of policy that the Government must construct. The proposition "This House would lift the embargo on Cuba" would obviously require that the Government support the policy of lifting the embargo on Cuba. Any deviation from the policy explicitly indicated in the proposition would be readily apparent to the Opposition and would be easily challenged as non-topical.

A second type of policy proposition indicates the general area the policy must be drawn from, but leaves the specific elements of the policy to the Government to determine. The proposition "This House would substantially alter its foreign policy towards one or more Middle Eastern nations" allows the Government to choose both the type of policy that will be altered and the specific nation or nations that will be the focus of the debate. To be topical on this type of proposition, the Government must be careful to meet each of the keywords of the topic. Part of their burden would be determined by the meaning of "foreign policy" and "Middle Eastern."

A third type of policy proposition in parliamentary debate is the policy metaphor. Far from specifying the type of action the Government must take, policy metaphors simply suggest that some type of action should occur. The topic "This House would let the hammer fall" gives the Government a lot of room to be creative in generating a topic that will fit the metaphor. To be topical on metaphorical propositions, the Government should identify the characteristics that are present in the proposition. (This will be done through definitions.) For example, letting "the hammer fall" seems to imply some type of violent action. (Within this context, a "hammer" could be argued to be the mechanism that strikes the firing pin of a bullet or shell in a handgun or rifle.) The plan that the Government constructs, therefore, would probably involve some type of violent action (perhaps military intervention).

Definitions may play an important role in establishing a topical case on policy propositions. Within the Parliamentary debate community, there are two perspectives on the issue of Government definitions on policy propositions. The first, and the dominant, perspective is that Government teams should define terms just as if they were debating a non-policy proposition. (For a more thorough examination of definitions, see Chapter 6.) Definitions in this context would provide the judge with a general idea of the meaning of the language of the topic, and the Government's proposal would then have to fall within the boundaries created by that language. Topicality would, therefore, be partially evaluated by comparing the Government's definitions to the policy that they had created.

The second perspective is that the Government's proposal acts as an *operational definition* of the proposition. An operational definition explains the meaning of the proposition by describing the operation implied by the proposition. If the topic were "This House would significantly alter its foreign policy towards Iraq" and the Government's plan was to invade the country, the operational definition of "significantly alter its foreign policy" would be the invasion detailed in the plan. When the Government operationally defines, it is not saying that its plan is the proposition. Instead, the Government is arguing that their plan is one example of the proposition.

The problem with operational definitions is that, because they allow the Government to supplant the language of the proposition with their plan, they may tempt the Government to virtually ignore the true meaning of the terms of the topic. The Opposition could then provide a counter definition of the terms of the proposition and challenge the plan as non-topical.

On metaphorical topics, it is particularly important to provide definitions that describe the characteristics implied by the metaphor. Definitions on metaphorical topics help to provide justification for your interpretation of the metaphor. On the topic "This House would still the fires within," the Government team should define "still the fires within." Rather than defining the words individually, they might simply explain what they believe the metaphor means. They might define "still the fires within" as attempting to achieve domestic calm, as opposed to dealing with international strife. They could then develop a plan that was aimed at reducing domestic terrorism. As they developed their plan, they would want to be mindful of the need to keep it consistent with the characteristics that they had ascribed to the proposition in the definitions.

Stock Issue Two: The Government Should Articulate Criteria

There is some controversy in the debate community with regard to the role of criteria in policy debate. Some believe that the Government need not articulate criteria when debating policy propositions. As we discussed in Chapter 6, criteria play an important role in debating propositions of fact and value. When debating policy propositions, the implicit criterion is that the Government must show that, "on balance," the advantages of adopting the proposal or plan outweigh the disadvantages associated with its adoption. While it is true that an "on balance" criterion is implied by all policy propositions, the Government should indicate whether or not this is the criterion it wishes the critic to utilize when evaluating the debate.

Beyond the implied criteria of "on balance," the Government has other options when formulating criteria. One commonly utilized criterion is *cost benefit analysis*. Cost benefit analysis is commonly confused with "on balance," but requires that the advantages and disadvantages of the Government's plan be reduced to their monetary worth (Brownlee & Crossman, 1989). If the topic were "This House would drill for oil in the Arctic Reserve," the Government could utilize cost benefit analysis to prove that the monetary gain exceeded the monetary cost of the Alaskan drilling project. The primary argument against cost benefit analysis is that it is impossible to quantify in dollars the cost of all things that will be impacted by a policy. In Alaska, for example, there may be significant environmental impacts associated with new drilling.

Another criteria option for the Government is to create a value or valued objective as a primary goal for the policy to achieve (Lewinski, Mezler, and Settle, 1973). This type of criteria is part of a policy-making strategy known as the *goals criteria case*. By focusing on a particular goal, the Government can argue that anything not related to its criteria is irrelevant to the debate. Utilizing a goals criteria strategy on the Arctic drilling propositions, the Government might argue that reducing reliance on foreign sources of oil should be the primary focus of the U.S. energy policy. The criteria would go on to offer the decision rule that if the Government can demonstrate that its plan will reduce reliance on foreign oil, the Government should win the debate. Obviously being able to choose a single goal by which to measure the success of its policy provides the Government with a huge strategic advantage. Not only can it limit what its policy will be expected to achieve, it can limit the Opposition's discussion of the negative outcomes of its policy. We will discuss the structure for the goals criteria case later in this chapter.

Stock Issue Three: The Government Must Show a Significant Problem Exists

Recall that presumption rests with the Opposition. One of the reasons presumption is placed with the Opposition on policy propositions is because of the risk involved with change. The first step in establishing that the risk is worth assuming is in developing the need for change. To develop the need for change, you must show that something valued is being threatened or actually harmed.

Demonstrating that something valued is being threatened is an obvious point at which values meet policy argument. Begin by establishing why the threatened subject is valued. Perhaps lives are being threatened. You should make an argument that expresses why we have a moral obligation to protect life. Perhaps the environment is being threatened. You should explain why valuing the environment is important.

Once you have established what is being threatened, you should describe the nature of the threat. Where possible, both qualitative and quantitative forms of support should be used. Qualitative support comes in the form of illustrations and examples that add pathos to your argument. If you are addressing a humanitarian crisis, use examples of real people, whose stories you may have read in magazines, newspapers, or books. Quantitative support comes in the form of the statistics you may use to describe the breadth of the problem. Quantitative support alone may lack the pathos necessary to motivate your audience to sympathize with your problem. Additionally, some problems do not lend themselves to easy quantification. How, for example, would you quantify the harm caused by restricting First Amendment rights? In some circumstances, however, qualitative support alone may be inadequate. Unfortunately, one or two examples of lives impacted by a problem are rarely the basis upon which policy makers will enact major change. Whether using quantitative support, qualitative support, or a combination of both, you must argue that the consequences of ignoring the problem will be dire.

Stock Issue Four: The Government Must Show an Inherent Barrier to Solving the Problem

Inherency is the requirement that the Government articulate the reasons for the status quo's inability to solve the problem. If the status quo can or will solve the problem on its own, there is no need to adopt the proposition. The inherency burden looks to the cause of the problem discussed in the significance section of the case. Inherency is an important element of policy construction because without acknowledging the fundamental cause of a problem, it is difficult to determine if the plan will solve it.

The root causes of problems act as barriers to solving them. These barriers can be found in either structures or attitudes. *Structural inherency refers to barriers created by laws and regulations.* Voting laws that discriminated against women and minorities were structural barriers to equality in voting. Tax laws that put excessive burdens on Americans are structural barriers to fair taxation. *Attitudinal inherency refers to barriers created by beliefs, attitudes, or values.* The belief that taxation is excessive may lead some to provide smaller contributions to charities. The belief that what is inexpensive must lack value may cause some community college students to take course work less seriously. Sometimes barriers to solving problems are both attitudinal and structural. Statistics tend to show that teen drivers are more prone to accidents than drivers with more experience. Increasing the age at which teens may get licenses would address the structural barrier (the law) to reducing the number of teen auto accidents. Attitudinal barriers, such as the belief in immortality that seems to be prevalent among teenagers, will be more difficult to address (Cox, 1975).

Stock Issue Five: The Government Must Provide a Plan That Solves the Problem

After having presented a problem and indicating what is causing it to continue, the Government must present a plan that solves it. It is not necessary for the Government to completely solve the problem. No laws are able to achieve 100% solvency. The extent to which the Government must solve is somewhat subjective.

The costs associated with the plan and any possible negative side effects (disadvantages) have to be weighed against the positive effects (advantages) that the plan is able to solve for. If the plan, relative to its costs, appears to solve for too little, the Government will lose the debate on the basis of lack of solvency.

The plan should contain all the major elements necessary to address the problem and the inherent barrier(s) described earlier in the case. The plan is usually organized into major components known as "planks." The following outline describes commonly utilized plan planks and their responsibilities:

Plank One: Agency. In the Agency plank, the Government will describe who will be responsible for oversight and implementation of their plan. Typically, this will be either an existing or new United States Government agency. Good policy debaters are familiar with existing Government agencies, such as the Environmental Protection Agency (EPA), and will match their area of expertise to the problem area and assign them to oversee their plan. Propositions in Parliamentary Debate may also call for the use of international agencies, such as the United Nations, or foreign governments. Regardless of the specific agency used, the Government Team should be able to justify their choice of agency. Why, for example, would the EPA make a good oversight agency? When choosing an agency, it is important to consider the kinds of things that they will be required to do and determine whether or not your choice has the authority to and is capable of fulfilling those duties. Additionally, the Government should be careful to avoid using agencies that they have identified as part of the problem in the significance/inherency sections of the case. If the inherency section of the case identified specific attitudes as barriers to solving the problem, the Government needs to indicate why those attitudes will not impact the membership of its agency.

Plank Two: Mandates. Simply put, the mandates plank explains what the agency will do. Will laws be made or repealed? The Government has the right to make the mandates as specific or general as they would like. Specific mandates have the advantage of being easier to enforce, because they provide clear measures of what the agency is required to do. If the plan required that the Attorney General ban the use of military tribunals and he failed to do so, he would be subject to whatever punishment the Government had outlined in the enforcement section of its plan. General mandates have the advantage of allowing the agency some flexibility to adapt to change. If the topic involved the implementation of a tax reduction, a specific mandate that ignored the possibility of a decrease in surplus revenues would leave the Government open to Opposition arguments that the plan will lead to deficits. General mandates that simply indicated that the decrease would be implemented but allowed for the flexibility of changing the amount or the timing of the decrease, depending on the economic climate, might avoid some Opposition arguments.

A final element that the Government may wish to add to the mandates plank is the timeframe for the implementation of the plan. Without a specified timeframe, the assumption is that the Government accepts that the plan will be implemented immediately. Immediate implementation of the plan may be desirable if the problem requires immediate attention and the chances of solving the problem will not be adversely impacted by a sudden change in the current system. Sometimes, however, the status quo is not quite ready for immediate plan implementation. Suppose that the plan required the reduction of fossil fuel-based transportation. The Government could argue that alternative fuel sources could supplant fossil fuels, but the technology necessary to allow that to happen may not be immediately available. If the Government had evidence indicating that a specific alternative fuel source could be ready within a specified timeframe, they could use that evidence to support a delayed implementation date for the plan. The drawback to delaying the timeframe is that it leaves the Government open to Opposition counter proposals that might solve the problem faster than the Government's plan. (See arguing the counter-plan in this chapter.)

Plank Three: Funding. In the funding plank, the Government will describe how they intend to pay for their plan. Ideally, they should be able to give some indication of how much the proposal will cost, as well as where the funding will come from. Because parliamentary debate propositions deal with a wide variety of agents, the Government team must make sure that it utilizes a funding mechanism that is consistent with the authority vested in its agent. Where the agent is part of the United States Government, Federal funding is assumed. To avoid adding to already strained Federal budgets, the Government Team may want to specify a method for raising revenue. Suppose that one of the advantages of the plan is that it saves money. The money saved could be diverted to paying for the plan. The Government might also wish to raise taxes. Remember, however, that the Opposition can argue that the Government's fundraising efforts will have negative side effects (disadvantages).

Plank Four: Enforcement. In this plank, the Government team can specify how it will attempt to insure that the agency entrusted to implement the mandates will actually do their job. Enforcement is particularly important if the inherency section of the case indicated that attitudes might influence the desire of agency members to cooperate. Examples of possible enforcement measures include fines and imprisonment. The Government team can utilize any measure that it thinks would deter circumvention of its plan. As is true of any aspect of the Government's plan, the Opposition will be able to argue that disadvantages may result from the methods that the Government has chosen for enforcement.

Develop a plan that restricts the possession of handguns.

Stock Issue Six: The Government's Plan Must Be Advantageous

The final stock issue that the Government must meet involves the outcome of its plan. As you recall, the Government argued that problems exist in the status quo. To meet the need created by these problems, the Government presented a plan. *The beneficial results of the plan are referred to as advantages.* The advantages should primarily demonstrate that they meet the need created by the problem.

In addition to advantages associated with the problem, the plan may produce advantages not directly related to the problem, but still significant. For example, a plan that seeks to address the problem of dwindling supplies of fossil fuels by using alternative energy sources may produce advantages related to cleaner air. The cleaner air advantage can be related to decreases in asthma and other health-related issues.

When crafting the story that is the Government's case, the advantages produced by the plan must apply to the criteria in the debate. Recall that, if no criteria are articulated, the implicit criterion in a policy debate is "on balance." If the criterion is "on balance" the Government's burden will be to show that its advantages outweigh the disadvantages created by the policy. (The Opposition will be presenting the disadvantages.) If the criteria involve a value or goal, the Government must be able to demonstrate that its advantages meet the value or goal.

BASIC STRUCTURE FOR THE GOVERNMENT'S CASE

While there are a variety of options available for structuring a case on a policy proposition, the following outline reflects the policy stock issues discussed in this chapter. The example supports the proposition "This House would significantly alter the method of conducting Presidential elections." Note that the outline includes only the claims associated with the arguments; the advocate would be required to add the necessary supporting materials.

Introduction
Ingratiation
Statement of Support of Proposition

Observation One: Definitions
Significantly: From *Websters*, "important"
Alter: From *Websters*, "to change"
Method of Conducting Presidential Elections: "the process by which the
President of the United States is selected"

Observation Two: Criteria
A. Goal: Defense of the Right to Vote
(Support for and explanation of the Right to Vote)
B. Decision rule: If the plan increases protection of the Right to Vote, a
Government ballot is warranted

Contention: Media Coverage of Presidential Elections Harms the Right to Vote
A. Media coverage is part of the method of conducting elections
(Supporting evidence/analysis)
B. Early projection of election results discourages voting
(Supporting evidence/analysis)
C. Discouraged voters are effectively disenfranchised
(Supporting evidence/analysis)
D. The problem is inherent because media sources race to project the results
(Will not self-censor)
(Supporting evidence/analysis)

The Plan

Plank One: Agency—Necessary legislation shall be implemented through
Congress. The Federal Communication Commission will provide oversight of
election coverage.

Plank Two: Mandates—Broadcast of Presidential election results prior to the
close of the polls in all States shall be prohibited. Nothing in the plan shall be
construed to prevent the announcement of local and State elections after all of
the polls in impacted areas are closed.

Plank Three: Funding—Funding requirements should be minimal and allocated
through general Federal revenues.

Plank Four: Enforcement—Violations of the ban shall be punishable by fines and revocations of FCC licenses.

Advantage One: The ban on projections will encourage voting.
A. No winner will be declared until all polls are in.
   (Supporting evidence/analysis)
B. West Coast voters will not feel that their vote doesn't count.
   (Supporting evidence/analysis)
C. The Right to Vote will be made more meaningful.
   (Supporting evidence/analysis)

Advantage Two: The ban will help to reduce the media's influence on elections
A. Media have too much influence on elections.
   (Supporting evidence/analysis)
B. Media influence is contrary to Constitutional protections.
   (Supporting evidence/analysis)
C. Banning early projections defends the Right to Vote.
   (Supporting evidence/analysis)

Strategic Issues

Questions to Ponder

If you were the Government team on the Presidential elections topic, what case area would you run? If you were the Opposition team, what would you argue against the early projections case?

The outline supporting the Presidential elections topic reflects at least two key strategic considerations that you should be familiar with. First is the strategy of *preemption*. Opposition arguments are preempted when answers to those arguments are built into the case structure. This strategy is useful because it allows the judge to hear your answer to potential Opposition arguments before the Opposition has a chance to initiate them. Additionally, preempting arguments in the constructive speeches saves valuable rebuttal time by not forcing you to answer an Opposition argument for the first time in rebuttals. To preempt an argument, first determine what you think the other team is likely to argue. The early projections case seems to invite at least two arguments. First, it is vulnerable to a topicality attack because media coverage may not be viewed as part of the "method of conducting Presidential elections." You will note that this argument is preempted in two places. First, the definition of "method of conducting Presidential elections" defines the method as "the process" by which Presidents are selected. This definition is sufficiently broad to include virtually anything involved in the Presidential election (including debates, fundraising, primaries, etc.). Second, the A sub point of the Contention argues that media coverage is part of the method of conducting the election. Thus, the topicality argument is preempted in two areas.

A second preemption occurs in the plan. Advanced debaters sometimes refer to portions of the plan that preempt Opposition arguments as *plan spikes*. One possible Opposition argument would be that the plan would create the disadvantage of discouraging coverage of the outcomes of local and State races that might be on the Presidential election ballot. The mandates section of the plan makes it clear, however, that the media would be free to cover the results as soon as all polling in the affected State had concluded.

A third preemption involves the second advantage of the case. An obvious disadvantage to this case is that it limits the Freedom of the Press by not allowing them to cover the results of the election until all of the polls are closed. While there are exceptions to the First Amendment (yelling fire in a crowded movie theater, libel, etc.), the plan does infringe upon the press. The second advantage, however, can be weighed against the First Amendment argument that the Opposition will likely make. The Government could contend that, while it is true that the plan may restrict the First Amendment, the advantage to the constitutionally protected right to vote outweighs the harm to the First Amendment.

A second strategic issue reflected in the outline involves the use of the Government's criteria. This particular case outline represents what is sometimes referred to as a *goals criteria* format. The goals criteria format limits the arguments in the debate by focusing only on those that impact the stated criteria. You will note that both of the advantages meet the Government's criteria goal of defending the Right to Vote. If the Opposition does not provide a counter criteria/goal, they will have to limit their discussion to how the Government's case impacts the Right to Vote. One consequence of accepting the Right to Vote criteria would be that any impact to the First Amendment would be irrelevant because it is not the focus of the criteria. As was discussed in earlier sections involving criteria, the ability to initiate criteria provides the Government with great strategic opportunities.

CONSTRUCTING THE OPPOSITION'S CASE

Topicality and Definition Considerations for Policy Arguments

Many of the topicality issues discussed in the preceding chapter apply when arguing policy propositions. Definitions remain a potential source of topicality problems and, therefore, the strategies discussed in Chapter 6 regarding contesting definitions may still be useful to you. The Government's plan is their example of the proposition and, as a consequence, will be the focus of your topicality analysis.

When evaluating if the Government is topical, think about the meaning of the key terms in the proposition and the burdens that they represent. Look next at the Government's plan and ask yourself if the plan and the Government's definitions represent reasonable interpretations of the topic. This determination is particularly difficult on metaphorical topics, but don't be too quick to allow the Government to run any case it chooses simply because the topic is a metaphor. Their definitions should explain the characteristics of the metaphor, and there should be a clear relationship between those characteristics and the plan. If, however, you think that the Government is reasonably within the topic and has upheld the burdens created by the key terms in the topic, then you should not argue topicality.

If the Government's definitions are skewed, present and support a definitional standard and a counter definition (see Chapter 6). If the Government's definitions seem reasonable, but their plan does not meet their definitions, utilize their definition as the standard for the particular topicality issue and show how the plan violates it. For example, suppose that the proposition requires that the Federal Government implement a comprehensive medical policy. Further suppose that the Government's definition of Federal Government is adequate, but their plan utilizes the various states to implement the medical policy. You would argue that, based upon the Government's own definition of Federal Government, the plan's utilization of State Governments is not topical. You should frame the topicality argument using the standards, violations, and impact structure described in Chapter 6.

Extra Topicality

Extra topicality is a topicality consideration unique to arguing policies. As you have read, the Government must present a plan that represents each of the keywords of the topic. In addition, it cannot exceed the authority granted it by the proposition. If the Government goes outside the proposition to find solutions to its problem, it is said to be *extra topical*. For example, if the proposition requires a decrease in the civilian possession of handguns, a plan mandate that requires training as a prerequisite for ownership might be viewed as extra topical. After all, if you receive a gun after having been trained to use it, no restriction on handguns is actually occurring. The Government's only authority on the handgun proposition is to provide a plan that restricts possession; it cannot aid possession. You can utilize the same standards, violations, and impact structure previously described to present an extra topicality argument. Unlike standard topicality, extra topicality is typically not an all or nothing issue for the Government. If the Opposition demonstrates that one of the Government's plan planks is extra topical, any advantage stemming from that plank will not be allowed. This may not result in an automatic Government loss, but it will certainly reduce the number of advantages that their plan is able to produce. In our example, the Government could not claim safety advantages from gun training. If the extra topical plank was associated with the Government's only or primary advantage, the Government will probably not be able to claim that the plan is sufficiently advantageous to warrant implementation.

Effects Topicality

A final topicality consideration unique to arguing policies is the requirement that the Government not rely on the effect of its plan to meet its topicality burden. In other words, if the Government's plan is not topical, it is irrelevant if the advantages derived from the plan seem to be. The only burdens associated with the advantages are solvency and the extent to which they outweigh the disadvantages. Topicality can only be evaluated by looking to the plan language. Continuing our handgun restrictions example, if training is not a restriction on handguns, the Government's topicality burden cannot be met by claiming that some people will not pass the training and will, therefore, be restricted. To be topical, the plan or training would have to be a restriction. The effects topicality defense premises the Government's topicality on the Government's solvency. If everyone passes the training, no "significant restrictions" will result.

Arguing That the Government's Plan Is Insignificant

Most judges do not view policy propositions as generalizations that have to be proven true more often than not. Instead, most believe that the Government's plan represents one of many possible interpretations. This should not mean, however, that any Government case area that is topical, regardless of its significance, provides an adequate test of the proposition. Some topics even mandate that attention be paid to the significance of the change involved in the plan by including terms like "significantly alter" or "significantly change" in the proposition.

If you feel that the Government's case is an unreasonably limited representation of the proposition, you should present that argument to the judge. If there is language in the topic requiring that the plan represent a significant change, you should base your argument upon that language. Additionally, if the proposition includes the word "significant" and the plan does not represent that language, the Government has also violated topicality. You might also argue that an obviously insignificant plan does not provide an adequate test of the probable truth of the proposition and, as debaters, rigorously testing the proposition should be the goal. Finally, you might base your argument on the grounds that policy debate is usually modeled after some real world legislative forum (Congress, Parliament, etc.). Grossly insignificant case areas would, hopefully, not warrant their attention and should, therefore, not be the subject of an hour-long academic debate.

Arguing the Government's Criteria/Goal

If the Government has provided no criteria, the Opposition has greater authority to present reasonable criteria. If the Government attempts to limit the discussion by providing a specific goal/value, the Opposition can present a counter goal/value. Recall that you must first demonstrate what is wrong with the Government's criteria, and then offer counter criteria. (For a more detailed discussion of arguing counter values, see Chapter 6.)

The Opposition should be primarily concerned with whether or not the Government's criteria allows for a sufficiently broad discussion of the ramifications of its policy. The broadest possible criterion, and the criteria typically assumed in policy debates, is on balance. Under an on balance criterion, there are no limitations on the advantages and disadvantages that may be discussed in the debate. Broad criteria tend to favor the Opposition because they allow the Opposition to expand the debate beyond the discussion of the advantages produced by the Government's case. The Opposition may use the argument that a specific goal/value unreasonably limits the scope of the debate. It is true that policy makers in the "real world" may prioritize the goals that they are attempting to achieve. In crafting a domestic policy to combat terrorism, the Government might focus on public safety as its primary concern. It would probably be unrealistic, however, to suggest that only one goal (public safety) would be considered. In the "real world," policy makers would be forced to weigh the impacts of their anti-terrorism efforts on values such as privacy, justice, and freedom, as well as public safety.

Arguing the Government's Harms

Recall that one of the Government's burdens is to demonstrate that a significant problem exists that creates the need for the Government's plan. Typically, the problem area is the strongest part of the Government's case because it is fairly easy to demonstrate that problems exist in the status quo. If you were arguing against a proposition that supported restrictions on handguns, it would be difficult to claim that handguns are not associated with serious harms. Attempts to minimize the problem would sound pretty heartless: "The Government claims that 10,000 people a year are accidentally killed by handguns, but we believe the figure to be more like 8,000."

There are circumstances, however, when the Government's problem area is challengeable. For many, the phenomenon of global warming constitutes a real problem (e.g., Al Gore's book, *Earth in the Balance*). For others, warming trends are simply naturally occurring phenomena, and a few degrees of warming at either pole are irrelevant. Be open to challenging problems, particularly where researchers differ on their nature and severity. Politicians and others will frequently promote certain causes, creating the impression that the problems associated with those causes are universally accepted as real. Issues ranging from global warming to the harms of smoking in public have acquired a level of credibility with the American people. What that means to you is that if you choose to argue against public opinion, you will have presumption against you. That should not necessarily deter you from challenging conventional wisdom; it should, however, inspire you to thoroughly research the problem area. Be prepared to explain why your experts disagree with those cited by the Government.

Keep in mind that the Government has the burden of proof; you enjoy presumption. Press them to quantify the significance of their problem. If, for example, they argue that automobile emissions cause global warming, ask them to quantify the percentage of global warming caused by emissions from cars. If they argue that second hand smoke is hazardous, press them to quantify how much exposure must occur before disease is caused. The pathos associated with problems is often powerful; you can minimize its impact by forcing the Government to logically establish the significance of their problem.

Arguing the Government's Inherency

Recall that the Government has the burden of demonstrating that a barrier exists that prevents the status quo from being able to solve the problem. The intent of the inherency requirement is to force the Government to demonstrate that adoption of the proposition is necessary if the problem is to be solved. In responding to the Government's inherency, therefore, you might argue that there is movement in the status quo to address the problem so the Government's plan is not needed. One of the defense projects forwarded by the Bush administration has been the development of a national missile defense system. Though he has faced some opposition in Congress and elsewhere, his meetings with Russian President Putin seem to have laid the groundwork for setting aside part of the S.A.L.T. treaty that had been acting as a barrier to the development of a missile defense system. If a Government Team argued that we needed to develop a missile defense system and that S.A.L.T. was an inherent barrier to creating the system, the Opposition could argue that President Bush may already be setting aside the relevant portions of the treaty and is moving ahead with the missile defense system. Because the status quo is already moving to address the need, the Government's proposal is not required.

Minor Repairs

A strategic option that is open to the Opposition in the area of need and inherency is the *minor repair*. The Opposition does not have to defend the status quo as stagnant. If the problem presented by the Government can be fixed by small alterations in the status quo, the Opposition can argue that there is no inherent barrier to solving the problem and that the proposition is not needed. If, for example, the Government's plan is to ban handguns due to handgun violence, the Opposition might argue that all that is needed is enforcement of currently existing laws. When using the minor repair option, be careful not to suggest any repairs that are consistent with the proposition (that are topical). Additionally, drastic changes to the status quo are best handled in the form of a counter plan (which is described at the end of this Chapter). To be safe, the Opposition should limit minor repairs to increases in funding and enforcement of existing policies.

Limitation on Fiat

If the Government's inherent barrier seems too strong to overcome, it just may be. Government teams do have the power to *fiat* their proposal. *Fiat power allows the Government to hypothetically institute its policy and, therefore, alter any structural barrier associated with adoption of the proposition.* The intent of fiat is to move the debate from the question of *would* the policy be adopted to *should* the policy be adopted (Pfau, Thomas, and Ulrich, 1987). However, the language of the proposition limits the Government's fiat power to the agents and mandates implied. If the proposition is very broad, the Government has broader authority. While the Government can fiat the implementation of its plan over the inherent barrier they describe, they cannot fiat that their plan will work. Attitudinal barriers are very difficult to overcome. If a Government team claims that attitudes prevent the status quo from solving the problem, you may be able to argue that their plan will face similar challenges.

Solvency: Arguing That the Plan Won't Work

Solvency is probably the easiest of the stock issues for the Opposition to attack. It is easy to identify social problems. Politicians are famous for citing the need to address the "crisis" in schools, the problem of poverty, unemployment, etc. But being able to identify problems is one thing; being able to solve them requires substantially more skill. With careful analysis, it should be relatively easy for you to think of reasons why the Government's plan won't work.

The Government must solve for a substantial part of its problem (meet the need). Once again, most audiences would not require an advocate to prove that a solution will solve 100% of a problem. It must, however, solve enough of the problem to be worth its costs (something we will address in the next section). Furthermore, the Government must be able to solve for the advantages it claims. Two potential shortcomings of plans will prevent them from meeting their goals: inadequate resources and circumvention.

Inadequate Resources

Frequently, policies fail because resources needed to make them successful are missing. Some supporters of gun control argue that a society rid of guns would be safer. Opponents of gun control argue that even if you accept that premise, it would be impossible to enforce a ban on the possession of handguns. According to this view, a plan to ban handguns would almost certainly lack the resources necessary to enforce the ban. Assuming that law-abiding citizens turned in their firearms (unlikely, particularly in Texas), criminals would probably choose not to. How would the police enforce such a ban?

Plans requiring the utilization of new technologies are often subject to solvency challenges. Supporters of alternatives to fossil fuels frequently argue that solar and electric powered cars represent viable alternatives to the internal combustion engine. Skeptics, however, contend that these technologies are too costly and cannot, to date, adequately replace gasoline powered cars. Unless the Government can prove that the technologies needed to replace fossil fuels exist, its plan may be viewed as not workable.

Circumvention

Another reason that plans fail to solve involves the concept of *circumvention*. A plan is circumvented when either the agents assigned to implement the plan or the people it is intended to impact have the motive and the means to ignore the Government's policy. When the Government indicates that the inherent barrier to their policy is attitudinal, they have provided the motive for circumvention. Drug laws are prime examples of policies that are regularly circumvented by the people they are intended to protect. Critics of anti drug laws argue that unless you first deal with the causes of drug use, addicts will continue to seek drugs regardless of their legality. As mentioned earlier, criminals will likely circumvent handgun gun laws, having both the motive (guns make criminal activity easier) and the opportunity (criminals know many ways to acquire handguns).

When arguing that the Government's policy will be circumvented, you should indicate the motive that will cause the circumvention, the means by which the circumvention will be perpetrated, and the impact of the circumvention on the Government's solvency. The last requirement deserves further explanation. Solvency arguments do not necessarily imply that the Government will obtain no advantages from adoption of its policy. What solvency arguments generally attempt to do is to reduce the amount of solvency that the Government can claim. If, rather than replacing all gasoline powered automobiles, the Government's plan to implement electric cars would be workable only for wealthy drivers (who could afford the new technology), the Government's advantage would be greatly diminished. The Government could argue that any reduction in fossil fuel use is a good thing, but it would probably fail to meet the need it described in its problem area. When weighed against the possible disadvantages associated with its proposal, its advantages might not be sufficiently compelling. The following represents the structure of a solvency argument based in motive:

Observation: The Government will not solve

A. There is a motive to circumvent the plan (explain the motive)
B. There are means to circumvent the plan (explain the means)
C. Impact (describe the amount of solvency the Government will lose due to the circumvention)

Arguing the Disadvantages of the Government's Case

Disadvantages are the negative consequences of the Government's proposal. Explaining the disadvantages that are produced by the Government's plan is a critical part of the Opposition strategy. Solvency arguments alone are rarely enough to win the debate for the Opposition. Imagine that the Opposition successfully argues that the Government's plan will only be able to solve for a fraction of what it initially claimed. Absent a reason not to do the plan (a disadvantage), the Government can still claim that the plan is worth doing because, essentially, there is no reason not to do it.

There are a few things to be aware of when constructing disadvantages to the Government's plan. The first is that the disadvantage must be consistent with either the Government's criteria, the Opposition's criteria, or, ideally, both. If the criterion is simply "on balance," all possible disadvantages to the policy can be weighed against the advantages. If, however, a specific goal has been established, the disadvantages must relate to that goal. Suppose that the Government has suggested that the environment is the most important goal to pursue. If the Opposition has not provided a counter criterion, any disadvantages to the Government's plan must impact the environment.

The second concern is that the disadvantage must be unique to the Government's proposal. In other words, if the disadvantage was going to happen with or without the plan, it is not a reason for rejecting the plan. The exception to this is if the plan were to accelerate the development of the disadvantage, relative to its arrival in the status quo. Some smokers justify their behavior by saying that everyone dies someday. Indeed, death is not uniquely caused by smoking. On the other hand, smoking may well accelerate the arrival of the Grim Reaper.

In addition to uniqueness, the disadvantage must be clearly related, or *linked*, to the Government's plan. The Opposition should be able to articulate the element of the Government's policy that will cause the disadvantage to occur. Ideally, the Opposition will indicate the amount of Government action that must occur, sometimes referred to as a *threshold*, before the negative impacts will result. For example, some argue that retaliation against terrorism will result in further terrorist actions. To develop a solid link and threshold, the Opposition should be able to show the level of retaliation that must occur before terrorists will act again. Opposition teams are frequently tempted to simply say that any increase in X will produce the negative effect Y. This leaves the Opposition open to the Government's response that, if any retaliation will lead to more terrorism, why haven't past retaliations resulted in more immediate responses from the terrorists? Part of establishing the threshold also includes describing why current instability makes the plan particularly risky. Plans impacting the Middle East are unusually susceptible to disadvantages because the area is so frequently on the "brink" of all out war. The Opposition may be able to argue in such circumstances that the threshold for calamity is relatively low because, indeed, virtually any action may be viewed as offensive.

Once the link (and ideally the threshold) has been established, the Opposition must develop the impacts of the disadvantage. *Impacts* are the negative consequences of the Government's plan, described in the most vivid, specific terms possible. Rather than simply saying that the retaliation will lead to further terrorist activity, the Opposition should detail the types of activity that are likely to result. The impacts of the disadvantages are going to be weighed by the judge against the advantages of the Government's plan. The impacts that best meet any goal or criteria that have been established, and that are most clearly quantified, are likely to be the most persuasive.

Structure

Like any argument that cannot be applied specifically to a point on the Government's case structure, disadvantages are part of the Opposition's *off case* arguments. The disadvantage can utilize the following structure:

Disadvantage (Provide a name for the disadvantage)

  A. Link (Explain which part of the plan causes the impact to occur)
  B. Brink (Explain how much of the action must occur before the impact will occur—perhaps why instability makes the timing of the plan particularly risky)
  C. Impact (Explain in specific terms the negative consequences of the plan— there may be several impacts)

Providing a Counter Plan

So what if the Government has identified a legitimate problem that seems to call for a solution? One problem frequently discussed among educators in California involves the need to increase the representation of low-income students in the UC system. Advocates of increased representation contend that less privileged families lack the financial resources necessary to provide the educational opportunities that will prepare students for UC admission. SAT scores, they contend, reflect both the school systems that students attend, as well as additional preparatory course work; both of these factors are influenced by family income. To respond to this problem by simply saying something like, "there are alternatives to the UC system" would be viewed as callous. You might be able to minimize the problem by showing that there are low-income students who make it into the UC system. You might, however, opt to accept that the Government is at least partially correct in its assessment of the problem, but that you differ on the means for solving it. The Government's answer to the problem is the proposition as defined through its plan. The Opposition may attempt to solve the problem through a counter plan.

When offering a counter plan, the Opposition is granting that a problem exists. It may minimize the extent of the problem, but it would make no sense to offer an alternative solution to a problem that simply isn't there. The Opposition may, and should, argue that the Government's plan will not solve the problem and that the Government's plan produces disadvantages. You need to be careful, however, that your counter proposal does not have the same solvency problems and produce the same disadvantages as you have attributed to the Government's plan.

Before we continue, a word of caution: counter plan arguments are complicated. Debaters new to the game may wish to focus their energies on on case argument, solvency, and disadvantages.

The Counter Plan Can't Be Topical

There are a few requirements that you will need to adhere to if you opt for a counter plan strategy. The first is that the counter plan cannot be topical. Recall that the Government must be topical; it must provide a plan that upholds and is consistent with the language of the proposition. If the Opposition provides a plan that upholds and is consistent with the language of the proposition, they will have affirmed the truth of the proposition. If both sides support the proposition, the proposition carries and the side assigned to supporting it (the Government) wins.

To meet the non-topicality requirement, the Opposition must simply violate one or more of the key terms of the proposition (as interpreted through the definitions provided in the debate). Let's return to the example of low-income students not being fairly represented in the UC system. Suppose the proposition being supported was, "This House would abolish the SAT requirement for UC admission." To be topical, the Government's plan would obviously have to abolish the use of the SAT as an admission requirement. The Opposition's ground would be anything other than abolishing the SAT. If they modified the SAT, they would not be topical. If they retained the SAT, but provided a plan for helping low income students prepare to take the test, they would not be topical. What the Opposition cannot support, however, is any plan that calls for abolishing the SAT.

Where the proposition specifies an agent (the Federal Government, the United Nations, etc.), the Opposition can develop a counter plan using a different agent. The strategy can make a great deal of sense and is grounded in real world argument, because frequently we recognize that a problem must be addressed and that a series of actions would likely remedy the problem; we may differ, however, on who should be responsible for implementing the plan (the agent). For example, unilateral action on the part of the United States to manage foreign conflicts is regularly challenged on the grounds the United Nations or some other multi-national organization could better implement a solution to the conflict.

The Counter Plan Must Be Competitive

This standard mandates that the Opposition demonstrate that simultaneous adoption of the counter plan and the plan would be impossible, undesirable, or unnecessary. After all, the point of the counter plan is to demonstrate that the Government's plan should not be implemented. If both the plan and the counter plan can be adopted, the counter plan has not effectively discouraged the adoption of the Government's plan (and the proposition). Debate theorists have advanced three approaches to competitiveness. First, the Opposition can argue that the counter plan and the plan are *mutually exclusive*. The counter plan and the plan are mutually exclusive if they cannot be adopted at the same time. If the Government's plan is to increase taxes on cigarettes, a counter plan that called for decreased taxation on cigarettes could not be simultaneously adopted. A second theory, sometimes referred to as *net benefits*, contends that the counter plan is competitive if it would be undesirable to adopt both the plan and the counter plan. If, for example, the disadvantages associated with the Government's plan were substantial, it would be undesirable to adopt the plan with the counter plan. Finally, some theorists argue that the counter plan is competitive if it solves for the Government's problem. If the proposition requires that the Federal Government implement a health care system, a counter plan that argues that the States would more effectively solve the problem could be argued to be competitive.

Of the three paths to competition, mutual exclusivity represents the safest and most accepted theory. The net benefits standard is risky because it premises the competitiveness of the counter plan on the victory of the disadvantage. If the Opposition loses the disadvantage, is may no longer be undesirable to simultaneously adopt the counter plan and the plan. Additionally, merely solving the Government's problem area is also a risky standard for competition. In the real world, multiple solutions may be simultaneously adopted. The Federal Government and State Governments, for example, might institute redundant policies.

The Counter Plan Must Solve for the Government's Need

The point of the counter plan is to reject the proposition on the grounds that there is a better way to solve the problem. As a consequence, when offering a counter plan, the Opposition assumes the burden to prove that its counter plan will correct the problem. While the Opposition continues to enjoy the presumption against the proposition, under the counter plan model, both teams have a burden to prove the superiority of their plans.

The Counter Plan Must Be Equally Advantageous

The counter plan strategy requires a comparison of the advantages and disadvantages produced by both plans. The Opposition should reveal any disadvantages that the Government's plan will produce and be able to argue that their plan achieves the Government's goals, without suffering its flaws. Because the Opposition enjoys presumption, when comparing the advantages and disadvantages of both plans, the Opposition need only demonstrate that their plan is as desirable as the Government's. If both plans are of equal value, there is no unique reason to adopt the proposition, and the tie, theoretically, breaks for the Opposition. Ideally, however, the Opposition will be able to demonstrate that their plan is more beneficial than the Government's.

Structure

The counter plan is structured similarly to the Government's plan and advantages. Because the counter plan is solving for the Government's problem area, there is no need to reiterate the need for the plan. In addition to the plan and advantages, the counter plan needs to include sections addressing the issues of non-topicality and mutual exclusivity. The following represents a basic structure:

Observation One: Non-Topicality (explain why the counter plan is not topical)

Observation Two: Mutual Exclusivity (explain why the plan and counter plan cannot both be adopted)

Counter Plan

Plank One: Agency (Explain who will implement and oversee the mandates)

Plank Two: Mandates (Explain the actions that will be required by the counter plan)

Plank Three: Funding (Explain how much the counter plan will cost and where the funding will come from)

Plank Four: Enforcement (Explain what will happen to those who violate the mandates)

Advantages (Describe the advantages of the counter plan and explain why the counter plan produces greater advantages with fewer disadvantages than the Government's plan)

SUMMARY

Debates on propositions of policy are commonplace in academic debate and the "real world." When constructing its case, the Government team should think of the following burdens: 1) the plan must be topical, 2) goals and criteria should be established, 3) the problem must be significant, 4) the problem must be inherent, 5) the plan must solve for the problem, and 6) the plan must be advantageous.

When arguing policy propositions, the Opposition enjoys both a stipulated presumption against the proposition and a natural presumption against change. In addition to possibly arguing topicality and criteria, the Opposition's case will be a combination of arguing the Government's case point by point (direct refutation/on case argument) and presenting solvency arguments, disadvantages, and possibly a counter plan. The focus of the Opposition's strategy should be the stock issue burdens of the Government.

REFERENCES

Brownlee, Don and Mark Crossman. "Advocacy, Values, and Cost/Benefit Analysis." *CEDA Yearbook*. 1989.

Cox, J. Robert. "Attitudinal Inherency: Implications for Policy Debate." *The Southern Communication Journal*. 40 (Winter 1975).

Lewinski, John, Bruce R. Metzler, and Peter L. Settle. "The Goal Case Affirmative: An Alternative Approach to Academic Debate." *Journal of the American Forensic Association*. Spring 1973.

Pfau, Michael, David A. Thomas, and Walter Ulrich. *Debate and Argument*. Illinois: Scott, Foresman and Company, 1987.

EXERCISES

Chapter 7: Arguing Propositions of Policy

1. Develop a plan that would change any aspect of the foreign policy of the United States.

2. Describe the inherent barriers that would be faced by a policy that would substantially increase taxes.

3. Develop a counter plan to the elections results plan described in this chapter.

4. Using InfoTrac, research the search term "immigration policy." Describe an immigration policy that is under consideration.

5. Choose a policy proposition from those listed in the Appendix. Develop a plan that supports that proposition.

Chapter

8

Refutation: Defending Your Ideas throughout the Debate

SO WHAT IS REFUTATION?

So far, we have covered the essential responsibilities of the Government and the Opposition as they flow from the three types of propositions that are commonly debated. In Chapter 4, we briefly examined the duties associated with each of the six speeches that occur in the debate. It is time now to more closely examine the process of integrating the key issues in the debate into the duties of each of the speakers. The "connective tissue" that binds the individual arguments and speeches in a debate together is refutation. *Refutation is the process of defending your arguments by clashing with the objections of your opponent's.* Refutation takes many forms. You may advance your point by refuting your opponent's evidence. You may defend your case by refuting the reasoning advanced by your opponent. Even the Prime Minister's speech (the first speech in the debate) may include refutation in the form of preemptions to potential Opposition arguments. Through the process of refutation, individual arguments are shaped as they travel through the various speeches in a debate. Those arguments that are adequately emphasized by the debaters may play a role in forming the "big picture" that will determine the judge's decision. Because you have to be able to identify an argument to refute it, it is important that you take careful notes in the debate.

FLOWING: IF YOU CAN'T REMEMBER IT, YOU CAN'T ARGUE IT!

The process of taking down a record of the arguments in a debate is known as *flowing.* Flowing is arguably one of the most important skills you can develop because it involves the ability to accurately listen to, synthesize and record, and respond to your opponent's arguments. Flowing a debate is a challenge, particularly if you are one of the participants. You have to listen to what the other side is saying, write down their main points, and then, if you are the next speaker, write down what you will say in response when it is your turn to speak. A great benefit of learning to flow is that it forces you to focus on the task at hand. Public speaking can generate anxiety (see Chapter 9). When you're anxious, your ability to stay focused is challenged. If you can learn to concentrate on the arguments in the debate rather than your nerves, your anxiousness will decrease.

You clearly cannot write down everything that is said. Most people can talk much faster than they can write. Again, keep in mind that you will not only be writing down what your opposition says, you'll have to draft your responses to their arguments, as well. The only way to quickly get their main points down on paper is abbreviate and use symbols for commonly used words. For example, rather than writing out the word "increase," you might simply jot down:↗. "This House Believes That," can be abbreviated as THBT. There are no rules to guide your choice of abbreviations—you should simply develop a system that makes sense to you. Some people reason that if you write smaller, you can write faster. (It takes less time to write a small letter than it does to write a large one.) This tip makes some sense, but be careful not to write so small that you have difficulty reading what you have written. Furthermore, some debaters will flow the Government in red and the Opposition in blue. This practice is useful because having the contrasting colors may help keep you to quickly refer to the desired side's arguments.

Debates are typically flowed on a legal pad, divided into six columns (one for each of the speeches in the debate). One legal pad will keep track of the *on case* arguments: those arguments associated with the Government's case structure. A second legal pad, or a second sheet of paper, will be used to track the *off case* arguments: any arguments not directly related to a main point on the Government's case. Arguments, such as topicality, counter plans, and disadvantages, are typically flowed off case. Arrows are sometimes used to track arguments across columns when arguments have been dropped by one side and, therefore, "pulled across" to the next speech without refutation. The following represents the structure of a flow of a value debate. If you were actually flowing the debate, the generic headings (such as Def #1) would be replaced with abbreviations of the actual arguments. You will note that much of the strategy of refutation is based upon answering your opponent's arguments and reiterating your initial position. The redundancy inherent in this strategy helps to keep your story coherent.

On Case Flow Example

PMC	LOC	MGC	MOC	LOR	PMR
Defs					
Def#1	1. Attack Def	1. Response	1. Response	1. Summary	1. Response
	2. New Def	2. Reiterate	2. Reiterate		2. Reiterate
Def#2 ────────────→		1. Pull Across ────		──────→	1. Reiterate
Def#3 ────────────→		1. Pull Across ────		──────→	1. Reiterate
Crit					
A. Value	1. Attack V	1. Response	1. Response	1. Summary	1. Respond
B. Drule	2. New V	2. Reiterate	2. Reiterate		2. Reiterate
Contention					
A. Claim		1. Pull Across	1. Response	1. Summary	1. Respond
					2. Reiterate
B. Claim	1. Response	1. Response	1. Response	1. Summary	1. Respond
		2. Reiterate	2. Reiterate		2. Reiterate
C. Claim	1. Response	1. Response ────		──────→	1. Reiterate
		2. Reiterate ────		──────→	1. Reiterate

PMC=Prime Minister Constructive, LOC=Leader of Opposition Constructive, MGC=Member of Government Constructive, MOC=Member of Opposition Constructive, LOR=Leader of Opposition Rebuttal, PMR=Prime Minister Rebuttal, Defs=Definitions, Crit=Criteria, Drule=Decision Rule, Attack V=Attack Value, Pull Across=Argument was not answered.

Questions to Ponder

When you take notes in class, how much of what your instructor is saying are you actually writing down? To practice flowing, try to increase the accuracy of your note taking during classroom lectures.

APPLYING STRATEGY TO STRUCTURE

General Considerations

Before describing strategic issues that are relevant to the specific speeches in the debate, there are three considerations that should impact your issue selection throughout the contest. They are time, audience analysis, and the narrative.

Time

As you are putting together your case or selecting arguments for refutation, you must be conscious of time constraints. When developing arguments for the constructive speeches, avoid positions that are so complicated that they cannot be adequately explained in a relatively short speech. Government teams should be especially sensitive to time usage, because they have the burden to address each of the stock issues relevant to the proposition type. The Opposition has the luxury of being able to focus on a few key issues, because if they can win any of the stock issues, they will win the debate.

When selecting issues to argue, ask yourself whether or not the issue truly impacts anything major in the debate. In short: does the argument matter? The central turning points in a debate are referred to as points of *stasis*. By identifying points of stasis in the debate, debaters can increase the probability that their arguments will produce meaningful clash. When refuting arguments, you should allow yourself time to explain the impact of the argument. Keep the stock issues in mind when impacting arguments. Unless you explain how the argument fits into the big picture, the judge will almost surely miss the connection.

In addition to not allocating a lot of time to minor arguments, you can save time by looking for points of agreement. Acknowledging that you and your opponents agree on a particular point also helps reveal the stasis points in the debate. Be careful, however, not to grant issues that you have to win. If the Government, for example, admits out of spirit of collegiality that they are not topical, they will lose. Frequently, however, debaters get tangled up in small issues that do not matter, issues that either side could easily concede without suffering a strategic disadvantage. In fact, judges may grant more credibility (ethos) to a team that recognizes points of agreement. If you argue everything, it makes it sound like everything is of equal importance. By admitting areas of agreement, you will highlight the importance of those areas of contention.

Audience Analysis

Whenever possible, you should attempt to adapt your arguments to the perceived beliefs of your judge. Some debate theorists argue that judges and audiences of debates should take on a *tabula rasa*, or blank slate perspective, when judging. Such a perspective would require that judges and audiences lay aside all biases when evaluating the debate. While it is ideal for judges and audiences to attempt to be as objective as possible, it is highly unrealistic to assume that any audience has the capacity to totally ignore its predispositions. Further, there is no forum in the real world in which judges of argument set aside all preexisting beliefs. Juries are asked to set aside their personal biases that might be directed at a defendant, but they will be evaluating the facts of the case utilizing their value systems.

It is obviously not always feasible to know everything about your judge's/audience's preferences. Particularly when debating in front of a large group of people, it may seem nearly impossible to find common threads to appeal to. Begin by avoiding those arguments that are obviously *counter intuitive*. A counter intuitive argument is inconsistent with what the audience likely believes to be true. Thomas Malthus (1766-1834) was an economist who argued that disease and famine were God's tools for limiting population growth. Some debaters have argued that Malthus' theories should be used to justify denying inoculations and food aid to Third World countries on the grounds that such actions would merely increase their populations and prolong their suffering. While there may be some sense to this from a strictly economic perspective, many judges will view these arguments as morally bankrupt. It might be possible to overcome the judge's presumptions against such arguments, but why bother? If a legitimate case can be made for or against the proposition that is consistent with the judge's likely perspective, there is no strategically sound reason to risk counter-intuitive positions.

Occasionally, you will know something about your audience's beliefs. A judge who has indicated that he or she is conservative is likely to be supportive of policies that reduce the influence of the Government. Liberals tend to be supportive of Government programs. Unless a judge has disclosed specific information to you, be careful not to generalize based upon race or gender. There are, for example, many conservative women of color and a plethora of liberal Caucasian men. When you don't have specific knowledge of the judge's beliefs, appeal to the values that most people support.

In addition to the adaptations you may make when constructing arguments, you should be open to adapting your style and/or your arguments while debating. Audiences will almost always provide feedback to your arguments. That feedback may come in the form of a robust "here, here," or an equally enthusiastic "shame!" More frequently, the feedback is not so easily discernible, but it is still there; you simply have to look for it. The judge may nod his or her head in agreement on one point, or frown on another. That frown may mean you need to explain the point more, or it could mean that you should think about dropping that point altogether. When a judge is nodding in agreement, you probably need to spend less time explaining that. Emphasize those issues that the judge seemed to like in rebuttals. You will not be able to interpret feedback from your judge unless you look at him or her while you are speaking. As you will read in Chapter 9, eye contact is an important part of effective delivery.

Finally, adapt to your audience based upon their post debate feedback. When in class, listen to what the audience thought about your performance, and consider their recommendations for improvement. It is difficult, particularly after having the adrenalin rush of debating, to be open-minded to criticism. To be able to improve, however, you must be receptive to constructive criticism. Even if your debating technique is mechanically perfect (and it never will be—perfection in public speaking is not achievable), you can learn a lot about the way your audience thinks simply by listening to their feedback. At the completion of a trial, lawyers will often hire jury members to give them feedback on their style and arguments. As you will learn in Chapter 10, debaters at tournaments receive extensive feedback from a judge in the form of a ballot. Debaters can use that feedback to improve their general debate skills, and as a tool to adapt to the specific preferences of the judge in the future.

The Narrative

As was mentioned in Chapter 6, a well-constructed case will reflect those elements that make up a good story. Recall that the structure of the case should be conducive to clearly representing the arguer's position (coherence), and the arguments produced should be consistent with what the audience believes to be true (fidelity). Both sides in the argument should be sensitive to the need to tell their stories clearly. As the speeches progress in a debate, it is common for the stories presented to lose coherence. It is challenging, particularly for the Government, to present a clear story throughout the constructive and rebuttal period. Each speech must be clear, and there must be consistency between the stories told by the partners in the debate.

One tool that helps to develop a clear and coherent position is the use of a *central thesis*. As you probably already know, a central thesis is an important part of any speech or essay, and you will usually find it in the introduction of spoken or written prose. The central thesis is one sentence that summarizes the key philosophical objectives (Government) or objections (Opposition) held by the teams in the debate. The Government's central thesis should include its interpretation of the proposition and how it intends to support it. The Opposition's central thesis should include its interpretation of the proposition and which of the key stock issues the Government has failed to uphold. The central thesis should be one of the first things articulated by the speakers and should be reiterated in each of the key speeches in the debate.

There are multiple advantages to using a central thesis. From the perspective of the debaters, a central thesis allows them to focus their arguments under the umbrella of a coherent strategy. As previously mentioned, it is easy in a debate to get so focused on the individual arguments that you lose sight of the big picture. Additionally, without a unifying strategy, debaters are much more likely to contradict their partner. From the judge's perspective, a central thesis provides a "sign post" or preview of what to look for in the debate. Rather than having to guess which arguments are important to both sides and how those arguments fit into the debate, the judge can refer to the central thesis as their roadmap to the debate. The result for everyone is a much clearer, more coherent debate.

REFUTATION STRATEGIES AND SPEAKER RESPONSIBILITIES

In Chapter 4, we examined the primary responsibilities associated with each of the speeches in the debate. The goal of this section is to examine more specific responsibilities of each of the speakers and discuss a few of the strategic options available.

Prime Minister

Recall that the Prime Minister's speech will begin with a statement ingratiating to the audience, the other team, and his/her partner. Each of the constructive speeches in the debate should begin with such an ingratiation. The goal of the ingratiation is to emphasize that the debate is "nothing personal." As has been mentioned, people can and should engage in the critical refutation of ideas. In debates and elsewhere, however, argument gets ugly when refutation is turned against the person (see *Ad Hominem* fallacy in Chapter 3). Beginning with an ingratiation is a good way to remind all parties that good debaters are civil to each other.

Following the ingratiation statement, the Prime Minister will present the proposition to the audience. The proposition should be read verbatim. At this point in the speech, the Prime Minister should deliver the Government's thesis statement or its interpretation of the meaning of the topic and a preview of how they intend to support it. Once this has been done, the Government will define terms and provide criteria. The remainder of the case will follow the structures described in Chapters 6 and 7. Refutation in the Prime Minister's speech comes primarily in the form of arguments that preempt potential Opposition arguments.

LO (Leader of the Opposition) Constructive

The refutation responsibilities of the Leader of the Opposition depend, to some extent, on the type of proposition being debated. The LO needs to be flexible so that he/she can adapt to the case offered by the Government. The Prime Minister's case may have been entirely different than you expected it to be. It is important, therefore, that you not walk into the debate locked into any set strategy. Instead, your goal in preparation for the debate should be to develop several possible strategies.

The LO constructive speech should begin with an ingratiation. Following that, the LO should present a concise thesis statement that summarizes the Opposition's primary reasons for rejecting the proposition. With these introductory comments completed, the LO's strategy will depend upon the nature of the Government's case (policy, value, or fact). A few issues, however, should always be initiated by the LO.

These issues are often referred to as *a priori*, meaning that the judge will look at these issues before any other. Topicality and hasty generalization, because of their importance, must be initiated in the LO constructive speech. The only exception to this rule occurs when something that the Member of Government says reveals that the Government interpretation is not topical. The LO should also initiate any refutation of definitions and criteria. It is particularly important that the Leader and the Member of the Opposition communicate with each other prior to the debate with regard to the positions that the Member of the Opposition intends to argue (i.e., who will argue on case arguments, the criteria that the Leader intends to argue, etc.). Unless those arguments are consistent with the definitions and criteria that have been offered in the debate (either by the Government or by the Opposition), they will be irrelevant.

Refutation of Fact/Value

The LO's overriding strategy when arguing fact or value cases will be based upon the stock issues associated with debating such claims (see Chapter 6). The LO should utilize direct refutation (point by point refutation) of the Prime Minister's case. As the LO proceeds down the PM's case structure, they should first identify which argument they are addressing, and then number their responses. An example of the basic structure of the refutation would be, "The Prime Minster's second main point is that anti-terrorist measures have reduced our freedom. My first response to this is that freedom is meaningless if your survival is threatened. My second response is that most Americans are willing to trade convenience for security." Each of the LO's claims would be followed by support/explanation. But note that the basic structure of the LO's direct refutation is:

a. Identify the Prime Minister's argument.
b. Number and provide a counter claim.
c. Explain and support that counter claim.

The substance of the counter claim may take a variety of forms. The first counter claim should uncover any weaknesses in the Government's point in question. The standards described in Chapter 2 for evaluating inductive reasoning can provide a great foundation for your refutation. For example, perhaps the Government has provided a source to support their claim (Argument from Authority). The LO's first response might involve any of the tests of authority that we have discussed (expertise, bias, etc.). It is also common for the Prime Minister to support a fact/value case with arguments supported by examples. You can apply the test of argument from example and provide counter examples that are superior (at least in your mind) to the Government's.

Additional counter claims might attempt to reveal inconsistencies in the Government's case. Sometimes those inconsistencies result when a point on case fails to support the Government's own criteria. Other inconsistencies can occur between the Government's main claims. Revealing inconsistencies is a great way to undermine the Government's credibility and potentially weaken their case.

Where multiple points of your opponent's case are similar, it may not be necessary for you to individually address each point. You may *group* together arguments that are of essentially the same thesis. If, for example, the Government's (this strategy can be effective for both teams) first two arguments are the same, the LO could simply indicate that they are grouping those arguments together and will be addressing them as one central argument. You must be careful to only group together arguments that are truly similar. If you respond to arguments as if they are the same and your opponents can show that they are different, you may have failed to adequately respond to one or more of their arguments.

Once the main points of the Government's case have been argued, the LO, time permitting, can present off case arguments in the form of counter examples. Any counter examples must be consistent with either the Government's criteria, the Opposition's criteria, or, ideally, both. When criteria are contested, it is ideal to be able to argue that the Opposition's examples meet both teams' criteria, because you can never be sure which criteria will be victorious. If the LO's off case argumentation is based on the assumption that they carry their criteria and they lose it, their off case arguments will become irrelevant.

Refutation of Policy Cases

When refuting a plan-based policy case, the LO has some interesting strategic options. Generally, their speech should utilize the policy stock issues (described in Chapter 7). As when debating propositions of fact/value, it is the LO's responsibility to refute any of the *a priori* issues (definitions, hasty generalization, criteria, topicality) that may arise from deficiencies in the Government's case. Having addressed the *a priori* issues, the LO's refutation choices will depend on whether or not the Opposition will be presenting a counter plan.

If the Opposition does not present a counter plan, the LO should proceed through the case structure, utilizing direct refutation. The LO may attempt to undermine any of the key policy stock issues (significance, inherency, solvency, disadvantages). Ideally, the LO and the Member of the Opposition (MO) will have discussed a strategic division of duties. The LO may wish to discuss on case arguments such as inherency and significance and present off case disadvantages to the Government's plan. The MO may wish to attack any case arguments that the LO missed and concentrate their refutation on solvency arguments. The reason for this division is strategic. Disadvantages should be presented in the LO speech because they may be *turned* against the Opposition if the Government can successfully argue that the plan will actually solve for the disadvantage. For example, suppose the Government's plan called for tax credits to corporations that developed new job opportunities, and the Opposition presented a disadvantage to the Government's plan that contended that tax breaks will increase the budget deficit. The Government could *turn* this disadvantage by arguing that the new jobs created by the corporate tax incentives will increase tax revenues (new workers will be taxed on their income) and, therefore, reduce the deficit. There are responses to this *turn*, but if the Opposition waited until the MO speech to present the argument, the Prime Minister would have the last word on the issue in their rebuttal speech. *Turned* disadvantages are, essentially, new advantages to the Government's plan and can be independent reasons for voting for the Government.

If the Opposition Team decides to utilize a counter plan, the LO should present it. Following the refutation of *a priori* issues, the LO may minimize the significance of the Government's problem. As was discussed in the preceding chapter, presenting a counter plan assumes that the Opposition is granting the existence of a problem. They may, however, argue that the problem is not as severe as the Government claims. Next, the LO should present disadvantages to the Government's plan. Presenting the disadvantages before presenting the counter plan allows the LO to compare the disadvantages of the Government's plan to the advantages of the counter plan. Next, the LO will present the counter plan (see Chapter 7 for the counter plan structure). The LO should conclude by comparing the advantages of the counter plan to the Government's plan.

Member of Government (MG) Constructive

The basic job of the Member of Government is to rebuild the Prime Minister's case and answer any Opposition positions. Whether debating fact/value propositions or policies, the Member of Government will begin with an ingratiation, a thesis statement, and the refutation of any *a priori* issues (hasty generalization, topicality, definitions, and criteria). The overriding concern of the MG should be to keep the Prime Minister's case coherent in the judge's mind. The structure of the refutation is, therefore, important.

Fact/Value Cases

When rebuilding fact/value cases, the MG should simply follow the order of arguments in the Prime Minister's case. The MG should identify which point on the PM's case they are rebuilding, summarize the LO's argument against that point, and give their response to the LO argument. In this manner, the MG has "sandwiched" the LO's argument between the PM's argument and the MG's response. This is an effective rhetorical strategy because of the impact of the *primacy/recency* effect. The theory of primacy/recency posits that when a series of information is presented, an audience is most likely to remember the first and last thing presented. After refuting the LO's counter claim, the MG should provide additional support for the PM's initial claim. That support may come in the form of additional examples, analysis, or deferrals to authority.

As the MG proceeds through the PM's case, they may discover that the LO has neglected to argue a few points. These "dropped" arguments should be pointed out to the judge. Silence is consent in debate, and since no new arguments will be allowed in rebuttals, arguments that were initiated by the PM, LO, MG must be answered in the constructive period, or they will be viewed as dropped. Arguments presented by the MO may be answered by the Prime Minister's rebuttal, because that is the first opportunity the Government has to address those issues. In addition to identifying dropped arguments, the MG should explain why those issues matter. Finally, after rebuilding the PM's case, the MG should respond to any off case examples that the LO presented.

The MG's refutation should follow these basic steps:

1. Remind the judge of the PM's claim.
2. Briefly summarize the LO's counter claim.
3. Refute the LO's counter claim.
4. Provide additional support for the Government's case.

or

1. Remind the judge of the PM's claim.
2. Point out that the PM's argument was dropped by the LO.
3. Explain why the argument is important.

Policy Cases

With regard to policy cases, if no counter plan is offered, the MG's refutation should follow the same strategy recommended for fact/value cases. In addition to the rebuilding of the Government's case, the MG should be sure to argue any off case arguments presented by the LO (disadvantages, counter plan, etc.). After the LO's arguments have been refuted, the MG may choose to present additional advantages to the Government's plan.

When a counter plan has been offered, the MG must answer *a priori* issues first, proceed to any disadvantages, and conclude with refutation of the counter plan and any remaining Opposition arguments. The MG should allow sufficient time to summarize the main points of the PM's case. If all of the MG's time is devoted to arguing the LO's positions, the judge's attention will be drawn away from the

Government's case story. Because of the relationship between argument and narrative, the clearest story at the end of the debate will likely be victorious.

Member of the Opposition (MO) Constructive

Like each of the preceding constructive speeches, the MO's constructive should begin with an ingratiation, a thesis statement (consistent with LO's thesis), and refutation of any of the *a priori* issues. Beyond those issues, the MO's argumentation should not be duplicative of the LO's positions. Strategically, it makes more sense for the LO and MO to present different issues because more problems with the Government case can be exposed, forcing the PM to deal with a greater number of issues in their rebuttal. The MO strategies for propositions of fact/value and policy are similar. When debating either type of propositions, the MO should address any important argument that the LO has missed. Once that has been done, when debating claims of fact/value, the MO should present additional examples and analysis to support their case. When debating propositions of policy, the MO should present solvency arguments. As you read in the preceding chapter, solvency arguments reveal flaws in the Government's plan that make solving for their problem and/or advantages difficult.

LO Rebuttal

Because of the limited amount of time allocated to the LO rebuttal, he/she must focus only on those issues that are likely to influence the judge's decision. This is often a difficult task because most arguers think that all of their arguments are important. If you limit your issue selection to those arguments that impact one or more of the stock issues, you will have selected wisely. If the Opposition carries even one of the key issues (such as topicality, hasty generalization, significance, etc.), they will win.

Because the Member of the Opposition has just covered Opposition issues in his/her constructive, there is no need to extensively reiterate their positions. However, regardless of the type of proposition being debated, the LO must defend the key positions that they presented in the LO constructive. They should first remind the judge of their initial argument, then summarize the Government's response, and conclude by refuting that response. The LO may use new examples and analysis to support claims that were introduced in the constructives. They may not, however, introduce new issues into the debate.

After they have defended their constructive, the LO should *crystallize* (or narrow and summarize) the key voting issues in the debate. Because the LO has the penultimate speech in the debate, they are able to communicate the big picture to the judge. Opposition arguments that have been dropped should be emphasized, particularly if they involve one or more of the stock issues. Recall that no new arguments are allowed in the rebuttal period, so if the Government has dropped an argument that was raised in the LO constructive, that issue has been conceded to the Opposition by default. A useful strategy to use when organizing your summary is to number those issues that you view as the key voting issues in the debate. When numbering key voting issues, the LO should include the MO's most important issues. Finally, the LO should limit the total number of key issues (3-5, as a rule of thumb). If every argument is presented as a voting issue, it dilutes the importance of the true voting issues.

Prime Minister's Rebuttal (PMR)

The PMR should retell the Government's story and answer only the most important Opposition arguments. Because it is important that the Government's case story be prominent in the judge's mind, the PMR should focus first on any off case arguments that need to be addressed (counter examples, disadvantages, topicality, etc.), and then retell the Government's case from start to finish. As the case story is being retold, the PMR must answer any significant Opposition on case arguments.

Just as the LOR was able to capitalize on dropped arguments in their rebuttal, the PMR should attempt to do the same. Looking back on any key Government arguments that have been dropped, the PMR should emphasize those arguments to the judge and explain their impact in the debate. Because it is a rebuttal speech, no new arguments are allowed, with one exception. New arguments that were presented in the MO constructive may be answered with new arguments in the PMR. The new argument rule in rebuttals dictates that an argument is only new in rebuttal if a speaker (team) had *both* the reason and the opportunity to address it in an earlier speech. The PMR is the first opportunity that the Government has to respond to new arguments issued in the MO constructive.

Because the PM gets the last word in the debate and they can issue new responses to the MO constructive, the Government enjoys a huge strategic advantage. As mentioned earlier, disadvantages presented against policy cases in the MO constructive can be "turned" and argued to be advantages of the Government's plan. On propositions of fact/value, the PMR may also "turn" Opposition examples by showing that they support the Government's case. Even relatively weak argumentation will stand unchallenged because the Opposition has no opportunity for refutation. Ultimately, however, the judge will be left to evaluate the credibility of PMR answers to Opposition arguments, so specious turns are unwise.

POINTS OF INFORMATION, POINTS OF ORDER, POINTS OF PERSONAL PRIVILEGE

Points of Information, Points of Order, and Points of Personal Privilege are, as Dr. Robert Trapp has labeled them, the *interactive elements* in the debate. Points of Information often result in energetic, humorous, and interesting exchanges between the participants. Though they are brief, these questions and objections can impact the refutation of the major ideas and may actually introduce arguments and examples into the debate.

Points of Information (POI)

General Considerations

As you read in Chapter 4, Points of Information are questions posed or brief statements made by a member of the team that does not have the floor. Points of Information cannot be made during the first or last minute of a constructive speech and are prohibited entirely during the rebuttal speeches. To make a Point of Information, you must rise from your seat and be recognized by the person who is speaking. You should not interrupt the speaker in any way. After you have risen, the speaker has an obligation to recognize you and either yield the floor to the POI or indicate that they will not yield to the POI (typically by saying something like, "not at this time"). If you are recognized, your question or statement should be brief and concise (a statement should never exceed 15 seconds). The speaker may politely cut you off if you ramble on.

There are no rule-based limitations on the number of POI that you can introduce. POI are deducted from the speaker's time, and they may wish, therefore, to limit the number of POI that they accept. Some debaters will indicate to the other team that they allow a set number of POI (typically three). When recognizing the questioner for the first time, they might say, for example, "I will yield to the first of three points." It is a good idea for the speaker to take at least three POI. If the speaker regularly refuses to take a POI because they are "running out of time," or "have too much to get to," it creates the impression that the speaker is not in control of the debate.

On a general level, POI are useful to both the questioner and the answerer. The minimum strategic advantage for the questioner is the interruption of the flow of the speaker's speech. If a speaker is on a particularly strong point, a well-timed POI will cause an interruption in the persuasive impact of the message. Additionally, a well-asked question can enhance the asker's credibility. Questions, like statements, should be well-worded and clearly questions. In other words, do not make a statement if you intend to ask a question. Rambling or imprecise POI may actually reduce your credibility. From the perspective of the answerer, the POI can be useful because a witty or intelligent response may increase the speaker's credibility in the mind of the judge. To gain this boost in credibility, the speaker should answer the question or respond to the statement in as direct a fashion as possible. Questions attempting to elicit a yes or no answer may be best answered with a yes or no. Long rambling answers will give your opponents more ammunition to blast you with, will divert attention away from the point you were on, and will eat up your speaking time. Be on the lookout, however, for faulty dilemmas and *loaded questions* that condemn the speaker regardless of how they answer. As speaker, you control the floor and can point out the flaws in poorly asked questions.

Goals of the POI

The primary goals of POI are to *clarify issues* and *establish ground* for future argument. Sometimes POI simply seek to clarify meaning. If you don't understand something that the speaker has said, you should stand up and ask them to clarify the position. You are giving the speaker another opportunity to reiterate their point (which helps the judge better understand their point). If you don't clearly understand what they are saying, you run the risk of making inadequate responses to their arguments. You may also want to stand, be recognized, and make a brief statement that clarifies *your* position. If the speaker has misinterpreted your argument (either intentionally or accidentally), it may be wise to rise and clarify your argument. Be judicious in your use of statements that clarify your position; over use of this strategy can create the impression that you are "on the ropes" and have become defensive. You might want to save clarifying statements for only the most grievous misrepresentations of important issues.

The second broad strategic goal of POI is to establish ground for future argument. POI are part of the spoken record of the debate. Consequently, any statements made or answers given in the POI are part of the record of the debate. POI can result in very useful admissions that lay the groundwork for arguments that can be fully developed in a later speech. One great strategic use of POI is the revelation of contradictions. Suppose the Prime Minister argues that political correctness is detrimental because it reduces diversity in thought and expression, and the Member of Government extends on the PM's case by arguing that political correctness has detracted from the melting pot metaphor (the idea that all cultures come to America and blend into a more homogenous American culture). An observant member of the Opposition team could rise, be recognized, and point out that diversity of thought and the melting pot metaphor seem to contradict. The Opposition could then go on to develop an argument in one of its constructives based upon the response to this apparent contradiction.

Another avenue for establishing ground is by utilizing the test of arguments we discussed in Chapter 2 and by pointing out the fallacies of reasoning that were explained in Chapter 3. If, for example, a speaker utilizes a source to support a point that you believe is not an expert in the field of the claim, you may rise, be recognized, and probe the source's expertise. If you find the speaker's answer unsatisfactory, you may fully develop refutation of their argument from authority in your team's next constructive. When exposing fallacies, it is always better to base your question on the reasoning behind the fallacy, rather than simply asking if a particularly argument is fallacious. If, for example, you rise and ask if the speaker has created the *Post Hoc* fallacy, the speaker may simply say "no" and be done with you. It would be better to point out that the speaker seems to be reasoning that the first event caused the second, merely because it preceded it.

Points of Order

Points of Order are calls for the judge to rule on the potential violation of one of the "rules" of parliamentary debate. These rules only govern the practice of parliamentary debate as practiced at intercollegiate debate tournaments. Classroom debates may not utilize the same guidelines.

To make a Point of Order, you would rise, say "Point of Order," and briefly state which rule you believe has been violated. The judge will stop the clock and either rule immediately on the Point of Order or will "take it under consideration" and review the charge later.

There are not many rules in parliamentary debate. As a consequence, Points of Order tend to focus on a few key guidelines. The rule prohibiting new arguments in rebuttals is probably the most commonly cited. This rule is frequently misunderstood. First, an argument is new if the debater had both the reason *and* the opportunity to argue the point in question in an earlier speech. The PM may, therefore, make new arguments in response to the MO speech because the Prime Minister's rebuttal is the first opportunity that the Government has to respond. A more controversial application of this principle occurs when the MO does not respond to the MG's arguments against the LO constructive. The MO has no reason to respond to these arguments because the LO rebuttal follows immediately after the MO constructive. If the MO were forced to respond to the MG's arguments, the MO constructive and the LOR would be redundant. The new argument rule should generally not be interpreted to ban the introduction of new examples or analysis as backing to support old lines of argument, where those examples or analysis are merely backing for claims that were supported in the constructives. If, on the other hand, a team were to merely assert a point throughout the constructives and finally offer an example to support that point in the rebuttals, the judge might well rule that the example is a new argument in the rebuttal.

A second rule that generates Points of Order is the so-called "specific knowledge" prohibition. The NPDA guidelines prohibit the use of sources that are not available to the general public. Internal memos, unpublished diaries, classified documents, etc. may be ruled as illegitimate sources of information in the debate. The rule, however, only prohibits information that "no reasonable person could have access" to (NPDA, 23). The fact that a team may not be familiar with a source or an issue is not *prima facie* evidence that they did not "have access" to that information. Where information may be less than "common," yet is potentially accessible, the rule strongly encourages the debaters using the specific knowledge to clarify its meaning. Debaters who run cases that are particularly narrow/specific have an ethical obligation to make clear and thorough answers to Points of Information that are seeking clarification of their case.

Points of Personal Privilege

Like Points of Order, Points of Personal Privilege are directed to the judge. Points of Personal Privilege seek a remedy to a perceived decorum violation in the debate. *Ad hominem* attacks and insults, as well as sexist or racist speech, would clearly warrant intervention by the critic. It would be strange that a judge in a debate would not intervene if he/she noticed flagrant violations. A judge might, however, be preoccupied flowing the debate or considering an earlier argument. Points of personal privilege can point out abusive communication to the critic. To make a point of personal privilege, rise, say "point of personal privilege," and explain the problem to the judge. The judge will then decide whether the charge warrants a remedy. Where *ad hominem* attacks have been used, the remedy is typically an admonition against further name-calling. Serious violations could result in more severe sanctions. Like Points of Order, points of personal privilege should only be used for flagrant violations of propriety. Nerves sometimes get frayed in debates, and what is meant as a joke can come out as an attack. Debaters should be reluctant to make rude statements, quick to retract accidental slips of the tongue, and eager to promote an environment conducive to a rigorous and meaningful test of the proposition.

Questions to Ponder

If you were judging a debate, would multiple Points of Order and Points of Personal Privilege impact your impression of the speaker making the objections?

SUMMARY

Refutation is the process of defending your arguments by clashing with the objections of your opponent's. Flowing is an important tool in the refutation process. Because no new arguments are allowed in rebuttals, it is critical that you be able to take accurate notes on the debate. Each of the major speeches in the debate has specific responsibilities. The type of proposition being debated impacts those responsibilities, and debaters should base their strategic choices on the stock issues associated with those propositions. Points of Information are used to clarify issues and establish ground for future arguments. Points of Order help to maintain adherence to the rules of the debate. Points of Personal Privilege ensure that debaters are courteous to each other throughout the process.

REFERENCES

NPDA By-Laws. National Parliamentary Debate Association. January 2002. HTTP://www.bethel.edu/Majors/Communication/NPDA/.

Sonnenberg, Frank. "Presentations That Persuade." *The Journal of Business Strategy*, 55. September-October 1988.

Trapp, Robert. *Parliamentary Debate in Intercollegiate Forensics.* Ed. T.C. Winebrenner. Kendall/Hunt.

EXERCISES

Chapter 8: Refutation

1. Make a flow sheet of either an in-class or tournament debate. Based on the arguments on the flow, which team would you have awarded the decision to?

2. Using InfoTrac, research the beliefs of liberals and conservatives. Cite an article that discusses those differences and summarize its findings.

3. If you were asked to be a juror on murder trial, could you adopt a *tabula rasa* perspective? What biases do you think would be the most difficult to set aside?

4. Think of a controversial issue that you feel strongly about. Describe why you support your side of the issue. Describe points on the opposing side that you agree with.

Chapter

9

Presenting Your Argument

DELIVERY MATTERS

So you've prepared your arguments, predicted what your opponents are likely to say, and the day of your debate is rapidly approaching. Now that you have worked on what you are going to say, it is time to think about how you are going to say it. Perhaps in an ideal world, there would be no need to concern ourselves with the manner in which arguments are delivered. In such a world, substance would be valued over style. In the real world, however, delivery plays an essential role in the effective presentation of arguments. Gerry Spence is one of this country's most successful trial attorneys. In his book entitled, "How to Argue and Win Every Time," he observes:

> Think about the eternal languor of most company meetings. Who can listen to the reading of the auditor's reports? Think of the infuriating droning of the Sunday sermon. No wonder children would rather be whipped than go to church. Think of the lifeless, interminable palaver of the expert in court. No wonder jurors have begged to be jailed rather than to sit through a whole day of it. I tell you, to choke some boring blatherer to death rather than to listen to him another second might be successfully defended as justifiable homicide (154).

Indeed, the very thought of having to listen to a speech may be as frightening as the idea of having to give one. As Aristotle noted, speech making is an art. It seems that some people are born inherently artistic, while other must work on it. You probably know people who are able to play a musical instrument with very little training, while others must struggle to produce only average results. It is true that there are naturally gifted speakers. It is also true that anyone who can speak can become better at it. Sometimes dramatic results are possible! The trick is to understand the obstacles to effective speaking, the tools that you can use to improve your speaking ability, and the necessary role that practice plays in making real progress. One barrier that may block effective delivery, as well as the desire to improve, is speech anxiety.

SPEECH ANXIETY

Surveys that ask Americans to rank the things that they dread the most regularly find public speaking ranked above rattlesnakes in terms of pure ability to produce terror. Some surveys place public speaking over death (Walechinsky). Comedian Jerry Seinfeld has commented that most people attending a funeral would rather be in the casket than doing the eulogy. The bottom line is just about everyone feels some level of anxiety when confronted with the prospect of public speaking. Argumentative speech may be even more potentially nerve-racking, because the speaker knows that he or she will be facing an opponent who will challenge his/her ideas. Some may experience only mild nervousness or "stage fright." For others, however, fear of public speaking can become debilitating.

Questions to Ponder

Do you feel nervous when you speak?
What symptoms do you experience?

The Symptoms

Public speaking anxiety manifests in a number of ways. Most physical symptoms are a result of increased adrenalin in the bloodstream. People who are anxious about doing a speech or debate may notice an increase in heart rate, tingling or numbness in their toes or fingers, muscle tension, upset stomach, sweaty palms, dizziness, and hot flashes. Additionally, people suffering from speech anxiety may find it difficult to concentrate (particularly problematic when debating because listening is so important). Anxiety tends to be the greatest prior to the speech or debate and tends to abate once the speech has started. This fact should be somewhat comforting, because it indicates that we make the potential debate larger and scarier than the actual debate. Once the debate begins and we actually start speaking, we frequently find that it isn't nearly as scary as we imagined it would be.

The Thought-Symptom Relationship

There are times when a little fear is useful. Psychologists describe the phenomenon in which the mind interprets a threat and diverts blood to the large muscles as the *fight or flight response.* When confronted by a mugger, having a rush of adrenalin that prepares your body to fight or to run is useful. Getting the same physical response when thinking about doing a debate is neither fun nor productive.

Whether faced with a mugger or a debate, our physical response is a result of an *automatic thought* (Burns, 82). Unlike thoughts that we consciously generate, automatic thoughts come into our minds "automatically." We may not even be aware that we are having automatic thoughts. Sometimes, automatic thoughts are facilitative. If you are an experienced speaker and have taught yourself to enjoy the process, you may, when confronted with a potential speech or debate, send yourself an automatic thought that suggests you look forward to another opportunity to speak. When people are anxious about speaking, their automatic thoughts are negative and often debilitative. Some people will have automatic thoughts that involve catastrophic outcomes to the public speaking event. These thoughts fool our minds into believing that there is an actual threat (as opposed to a false/perceived threat), and the body then reacts by initiating the fight or flight response. This process happens so rapidly, and the thoughts can be so covert, that some people will simply think about researching their speech or debate and will become nervous for no apparent reason. The first step in confronting these thoughts is to become more aware of your negative self-talk.

Replace Fallacious Thoughts with Reason

The automatic thoughts that produce undesirable physical symptoms are associated with fallacious reasoning and beliefs. Once you are able to identify the automatic thought, you can begin to understand the irrational reasoning that is perpetuating it and find a more reasonable replacement thought. What follows is a discussion of common fallacies in reasoning that can cause speech anxiety. The list is not exhaustive, but the process of identifying the thought, understanding the flaws in reasoning, and replacing the thought can be utilized for any problematic automatic thoughts. If you sincerely utilize this approach, the replacement thoughts will eventually become automatic. You may wish to keep a journal that helps you to keep track of your automatic thoughts and the replacement thoughts that you devise. For a more thorough discussion of cognitive therapy, see *The Feeling Good Handbook* by David Burns, M.D.

All or Nothing Thinking (Perfectionism)

Do you remember someone telling you in your childhood that "if you can't do a job right, don't do it at all?" Establishing goals to accomplish can be useful. Our reasoning becomes fallacious when we start to believe that everything we do has to be perfect. This is particularly true in public speaking. Understand that there is no perfect speech or debate. Even the best debaters will have brilliant moments and moments that are, well, not so brilliant. To expect that everything you do will be perfect is to set yourself up for a truly stressful experience, because your expectation can never meet your perceived reality.

If you find yourself thinking that the speech or debate will fall short of some standard of perfectionism, replace those thoughts with the expectation that you will simply do your best. Releasing yourself from the need to be perfect does not free you from the need to work hard to prepare. In fact, you are more likely to succeed when you realize that your ability to honestly say that you have done "your best" requires that you work hard. The benefit of losing the expectation of perfectionism is that you can do the work and let it go knowing that you have prepared. If things don't go exactly as planned (and they almost never do), you will feel better about it knowing that there are no perfect debates.

Catastrophic Thinking

Have you ever found yourself imagining the worse possible outcome of some challenging task? A common worry among debaters and public speakers is that they will go blank and not be able to say anything. That thought then triggers the creation of a mental scenario in which the audience is laughing hysterically at the speaker's expense. You probably already have a sense of how counterproductive to a desirable outcome this type of thinking is. Athletes are often taught to visualize only the most positive outcomes to their efforts. Imagine the Olympic downhill skier who regularly visualizes catastrophe at the top of the run. How successful do you think he or she will be?

There are three general replacement thoughts for catastrophic thinking. The first is to realize that a debate or speech will generally not be as good or as bad as we imagine it will be. The best speech will probably not bring the audience to their feet in thunderous applause, and the worst speech will not cause the audience to break out in unsympathetic laughter. The truth is typically somewhere in the middle. Assuming that you have prepared, parts of your debate will be interesting and insightful, and parts of it will not be particularly deep. A second replacement thought involves testing the outcome of your imagined catastrophe. Suppose that your worst fears were realized and you forgot everything you were going to say, and the audience did cackle hysterically. Is your health threatened by this event? Is your economic well-being impacted? Even if a grade is attached to the debate, most instructors can recognize the difference between lack of preparation and a nervous speaker. In short, the consequences of our worst fears are usually not all that bad. Finally, if you have prepared and have good notes, you can tell yourself that you are ready. Even if you have a lapse in memory (we all do, debates can be intense), just move on to the next point. Continue to practice taking an accurate flow. Having accurate notes will increase your confidence and make it less likely that you will forget an important point. Your preparation and practice will increase your confidence and give you the ammunition you need to argue against thoughts that suggest that you will have nothing to say.

Mind Reading

While catastrophic thoughts may plague a speaker before a debate, the temptation to read minds may cause anxiety during the competition. When standing in front of an audience, it is tempting to read too much into its body language. It is a mistake to assume that an audience will look at you as if you are having a two-way conversation. Audiences typically simply sit and stare. A judge may have a pained look on his or her face. You may have caused this expression, or maybe the judge is tired or has a toothache. Some judges will give very clear feedback on arguments that they agree or disagree with. You should utilize this feedback and adapt. (Emphasize arguments they like, think about dropping arguments that they seem to disagree with.) Absent clear feedback, however, do not assume that an audience's reaction is a function of your speech. Once again, tell yourself that you are simply doing your best and you hope that the judge is enjoying the debate. Keep in mind, however, that it is unreasonable to expect that all audience members will be captivated by your speech. There are people who are bored by everything short of skydiving.

Fear of Conflict

Some would-be speakers have thoughts that make them reluctant to engage in argument. One belief that is common in people who are conflict phobic is the notion that they will not be liked if they assert their opinion. Because they believe that "likeable" people are passive, they may view argument as personal attack. When forced into conflict, they may become defensive and aggressive because they believe that they are being attacked personally. These beliefs can be crippling in both professional and personal relationships.

For some, these thoughts stem from cultural differences. In collectivist cultures, members are rewarded for collective, rather than individual, achievement. Women, in particular, may be discouraged from being assertive. The transition into Western culture, with its emphasis on individuality, can be challenging. The rewards for making the transition, however, are great.

The replacement thought to these beliefs is that, in Western culture, assertiveness is generally rewarded. In terms of being "liked," plenty of "likeable" people have the courage to express controversial ideas and argue with the opinions of others. In fact, Americans tend to admire those who do argue well. When was the last time a "passive" Presidential candidate was elected? Additionally, it is important to remember that debates should be about ideas. Four great friends can come together in a debate and rigorously test the probable truth of a topic and leave the debate friends. There is no reason why strangers who are engaged in argument should view each other in a less than amicable manner.

Just as individuals may be too passive, there are those who feel that how they express their ideas should not matter. We all have the right to convey ideas that are important to us and to contest ideas that we do not agree with. To do so in a manner that reflects respect for the other person, however, is a prerequisite for reciprocal respect. Society elevates and admires the advocates who vigorously and eloquently present their ideas. The loud, rude, and obnoxious are lonely.

Labeling

For some, an unpleasant past experience in public speaking has caused them to label themselves in a negative way. Typically, the experience was not objectively a total failure. Thinking in absolute terms, however, the speaker may view one previous lapse of memory (or similar problem) as representative of their public speaking experience. If they could view the totality of the speech from a more objective perspective, they would probably find that they are exaggerating their shortcomings. Without that perspective, however, when they are faced with the opportunity to debate or speak publicly, they tell themselves that they are not good at it. This label, while not initially accurate, can turn into a self-fulfilling prophecy. If you think you are not good at public speaking, you won't practice. Therefore, you will not improve and, consequently, will not be good at public speaking.

It is important to replace negative labels with more accurate perspectives. If a particular part of a past speech was a problem, reflect on ways to improve that area in the future. Instead of telling yourself that you are "no good" at debate, congratulate yourself for having the courage to try something new and challenging. No one is a "perfect speaker." Like golf, speech and debate is often frustrating because our progress can seem slow (frankly, golf is harder). Debaters (like golfers) learn to appreciate the one great argument (shot) that made the twenty mediocre arguments (shots) preceding it less memorable.

Additional Tips for Reducing Speech Anxiety

Don't Verbalize Anxiety

When you are anxious, your body will do strange things. Because anxiety makes you hyper-aware of physical symptoms, you will be much more likely than the audience to perceive a shaking hand or a tremble in your voice. Consequently, unless you tell everyone how nervous you are, they may never notice. Another downside to announcing that you are nervous is that the audience is encouraged to perceive you as nervous. Their focus then shifts from the content of your speech to any small physical symptom that they might have otherwise overlooked. If you find yourself getting nervous and you need a second to gather your thoughts, simply pause, look over your notes, and continue. There is no need to apologize. It is your speech; you can pause if you want to.

Breathe

Just about any book that you pick up on the subject of relaxation will have a chapter on breathing. When people get nervous, they tend to breathe and speak more rapidly. While it is highly unlikely that you will ever pass out while nervous (try to get to sleep when you are nervous!), you can make yourself really uncomfortable if you hyperventilate. Make a conscious effort during your debate to remind yourself to slow down and breathe. If you catch yourself stumbling over words, you are probably speaking too quickly and, therefore, not breathing properly. Forcing yourself to take deep breaths during the debate (while speaking and preparing) will help you feel more relaxed. You do not need to chant or perform elaborate breathing exercises. It is probably better if you do not.

Watch What You Eat

If we don't eat well, blood sugar has a way of making us feel uncomfortable. Meals that are protein rich will provide longer staying power than carbohydrates that will convert to sugar. If you find yourself debating at a tournament, you will notice that the schedule is demanding and food is often difficult to find. Bring good quality snacks with you. Avoid excessive caffeine. The good thing about being nervous is that you will not have a problem with sleepiness.

Practice and Perform

There is no substitute for preparation. If you research your debate and practice, you will greatly increase your comfort level. Because debates are mostly spontaneous, practice includes simply discussing the primary issues that you expect you will be debating. Talk about key issues with friends and associates who are knowledgeable about your topic area. Practice delivering speeches while standing. It is more challenging to deliver a speech while standing than while sitting. When you are standing, you will have to monitor your movement, your gestures, and your posture.

It is tempting to avoid opportunities to speak. People who are nervous about doing speeches will look for excuses to avoid public speaking. Eventually, however, they will have to do a speech. If you regularly practice and perform, you will not only become more comfortable, you will improve your speaking ability. You may even find that you enjoy it!

THE NONVERBAL ELEMENTS OF DELIVERY

We communicate with verbal communication (words) and nonverbal communication. The verbal part of the messages that we communicate comprises less than 10% of the total message (Mehrabian). Approximately 90% of the meaning that we communicate flows from the eye contact, gestures, posture, facial expression, vocal expression, clothing, and other elements of nonverbal communication. Understanding this is important, because when our verbal message contradicts the nonverbal, the audience will believe the nonverbal. Recall a circumstance when someone said that they were happy to see you, but something about the way they said it indicated that they were not. Did you believe their words or their nonverbal message? In debates, speakers may really be excited by what they are saying, but their nonverbal delivery may indicate that they are bored. A debater may be quite sincere about a particular point, but their delivery may indicate that they are being less than honest.

The good news is that debaters can greatly increase the impact of their verbal message by improving the nonverbal elements of their delivery. It makes no sense to work hard developing strong content only to undermine its effectiveness with weak delivery. Let us now examine some of the key nonverbal components of delivery and methods for optimizing your nonverbal message.

Make Consistent Eye Contact

Questions to Ponder

When someone avoids making eye contact with you, do you trust their message?

Eye contact is probably the most important nonverbal element of delivery. Lack of eye contact with a speaker may cause an audience to believe that the speaker is nervous, deceptive, or simply lacks interest in the audience's reaction. While the need or desirability of eye contact may vary across cultures, it is safe to say that most American audiences will be less than impressed with a speaker who does not look at them regularly.

When debating, vary your eye contact throughout the audience, paying particular attention to the person or persons designated as the judge(s). It is acceptable to look down from time to time to present a quotation (in classroom debates) or to refer to your flow. Looking at the judge will allow you to read their obvious nonverbal reactions and to see any time signals they might be giving you. More importantly, eye contact may create the impression that you are sincere about what you saying.

Make Facial Expressions That Sell Your Message

Think of the multitude of expressions that your face can communicate. In conversations with people whom we know well, we may be able to communicate our meaning with little more than a facial expression: a raised eyebrow, a smile, or a grimace. When we are nervous, we may lose the natural range of facial expressions that we commonly exhibit; our faces may tense up; we may simply frown. Audiences may think that we are angry or annoyed. Most audiences are naturally drawn to affable people. This does not mean that you need to be constantly smiling while speaking. On the contrary, when the topic that you are discussing is serious, your facial expression should communicate concern. When the subject matter lightens up, so should your facial expression. The bottom line is your facial expressions should be consistent with the message that you are verbally communicating. Where no clear message is apparent, it doesn't hurt to smile. Smiling will communicate that you are enjoying what you are doing and, if you are stressed, you may eventually fool yourself into actually having a good time.

Be Aware of Posture, Gestures, and Movement

Posture

It is more enjoyable to be relaxed when doing a debate. But the type of posture you may have when speaking to friends may not be appropriate for a debate. Speakers who lean on the podium or slouch at their desk create the impression that they do not care about how they appear. Additionally, there is some research that indicates that speaker height adds to credibility and communicates status (Knapp, 1980). While we all cannot be above average in height (the vertically challenged), we can maximize our credibility by standing straight when speaking.

Gestures

Gestures add energy to your speech. If you simply observe two people talking, you will usually notice that they enthusiastically "speak with their hands." We use gestures to illustrate and emphasize our ideas. For example, a speaker indicating that there are three arguments for an issue might hold up three fingers while they are previewing those arguments. These illustrations will generally come naturally. Sometimes, however, the anxiety associated with doing a speech makes people reluctant to use their hands to gesture. They will hold their hands behind their backs or in front of their bodies; they will cross their arms or stick their hands in their pockets. On the opposite end of the spectrum, nervous debaters may gesture so often and rapidly that their gestures become distracting. Each of these alternatives to poised, natural gesturing reduces the potential impact of your spoken message and may communicate that you are defensive. When not gesturing, simply allow your hands to rest at your sides. As you relax, they will naturally come up to emphasize your words. Make an effort to gesture gracefully, and take advantage of opportunities to use gestures to illustrate key ideas. Finally, if you must speak behind a podium, do not lean on it. This not only hurts your posture, it makes it nearly impossible to gesture.

Movement

With nerves and adrenalin comes the desire to move around and fidget. It may feel good to pace while you are talking (you do burn energy), but it is very distracting and may communicate that you are nervous. Furthermore, it is difficult to concentrate your eye contact on the audience/judge if you are busy pacing back and forth. If you are not speaking behind a podium, feel free to take an occasional step or two. Avoid so much movement that the audience feels as if they are watching a tennis match.

Work on Vocal Variety

To borrow a cliché, variety is the spice of life. Where there is no variety, boredom is soon to follow. As noted at the beginning of this chapter, Jerry Spence observed too many speakers seem more interested in putting an audience to sleep than communicating with them. A survey of top-level executives revealed that the majority of those polled had nodded off during important presentations (Lindstrom, 1981). Lack of enthusiasm in our vocal delivery may communicate that *we* are bored. We cannot expect the audience to be interested in our arguments if we cannot muster up the energy to at least pretend that we are excited by and committed to what we are saying. Vocal variety is made up of three factors: rate, volume, and tone.

Rate

Rate is simply how quickly we are speaking. There are people who speak too slowly. Their plodding rate is a sure cure for insomnia and creates the impression that they (and their message) lack personality. At the other end of the spectrum are the fast talkers. When people are nervous, there is a tendency to increase the rate of speech. In addition, debates, with their limited speaking time and emphasis on the need to answer all important arguments, would seem to encourage and reward rapid speech. The truth is that in academic debate, many judges have developed the ability to listen to arguments delivered at a higher rate of speed. For less experienced audiences and judges, however, speech that is too rapid makes it difficult to understand the arguments in the debate and creates the impression that the speaker is nervous and pressed for time. Additionally, rapid speech can harm your articulation, causing you to slur sounds and words.

The truth is, most debaters are somewhat nervous and are usually pressed for time. The trick is to deliver at a rate that allows the audience to understand you and that communicates a sense that you are absolutely in control of the debate. When you have many arguments to respond to, focus on word economy; do not repeat and belabor points. Forcing yourself to number your responses and give concise claims and support will allow you to cover more ground. Increasing the rate of delivery will not help you cover more arguments if you do not also reduce the number of words that you are saying. Another tip for saving time when arguing is to "group" together similar arguments and respond to them as a group rather than individually. This strategy is a great time-saver—just make sure the arguments you group together are really similar in thesis. If you group together and respond to arguments that are actually different, you will not have adequately responded and your opponents will be able to argue that you have essentially dropped those arguments.

A good delivery rate should reflect the fluctuations in rate that occur in normal conversations. When excited, people have a tendency to speed up a bit. When explaining complex material, such as technical information, speakers should slow down. It is this variety in rate that helps to produce a stimulating yet comprehensible message.

Volume

Just as there are fast and slow talkers, there are low and loud talkers. Low talkers mumble through parts of their sentences and drop their voices at the end of their sentences. Speaking too softly can create the impression that you are passive or unsure about what you are saying. Soft, passive speech robs speakers of their power, greatly diminishing their credibility. People who speak too loudly can be seen as overly aggressive and defensive. Where volume is consistently high, it is difficult to use volume for emphasis because there is no room to take it higher. It is also simply displeasing to listen to someone shout at you. Your volume should be loud enough throughout your sentences that the audience can hear you. Like rate, it should fluctuate as a result of the content of the speech. You may increase your volume to communicate enthusiasm for a particular point and reduce it to highlight an argument through volume.

Tone and Emphasis

It is difficult to think of great speakers and not recall their fantastic voices. Some speakers seem to be born with rich, melodic voices. Most of us have to work on it. Variety in tone, rate, and volume communicates warmth, interest, and excitement. Like the other aspects of verbal delivery, lack of variety in tone is associated with boring, monotonous speeches. Furthermore, variety in tone helps to shape the judge's perception of the speaker's charisma and personality. Nerves and excessive reading can have a negative impact on variety in tone. In preparations for in-class debates or other venues where written materials may be allowed, practice reading quoted material. Too many speakers read quotations as if they were reading the phone book. Try to make your voice reflect the emotions implied by the quotation. Your normal conversational voice probably reflects a great deal of variety in tone. If you concentrate on delivering your arguments with conviction, your natural vocal variety will emerge in your debate.

Another tone-related delivery issue is the problem of up-speak. You use "up-speak" when you raise the tone at the end of a declarative sentence, making it sound as if you are asking a question. Read the following out loud, raising the tone at the end of each sentence: "So global warming is really bad." "We should do something about it." Because up-speak confuses a declaration (a statement) with an interrogative (a question), it creates the impression that the speaker is not sure of the point they are making. Like other speaking habits that reduce the speaker's credibility, up-speak is a form of *powerless speech*. Debaters and anyone concerned with increasing the strength of their message should work on eliminating the up-speak habit.

In addition to variety in tone, rate, and volume, you should use pauses to emphasize key ideas. A pause before or after a word highlights that word and sets it apart from the rest of the sentence. The use of the pause is one of the most important elements in dramatic delivery. Imagine Hamlet's "To Be or Not To Be" soliloquy delivered without any pauses. When people get nervous, there is a tendency to forget to slow down and emphasize their ideas. However, if you force yourself to pause, you will both emphasize key points and give yourself an opportunity to breathe.

Pausing is also a cure for another element of powerless speech: *the verbal non-fluency*. Verbal non-fluencies are filler words and noises that speakers make when they need a second or two to think of their next word. Probably the most common verbal non-fluencies are "uhm," "like," and "y' know." Research has connected the use of verbal non-fluencies with audience perceptions of deception and decreased in speaker credibility (Mehrabian). You don't need to be obsessive about a few verbal non-fluencies in your speech; however, if you notice (or are told) that you are using so many non-fluencies it is becoming distracting, try to replace your "uhms" with pauses.

Check Your Appearance: If You Can't Judge a Book by Its Cover, Why Do Publishers Spend So Much on Book Covers?

A number of studies have found that dressing in a manner that is consistent with audience expectations will increase credibility. Clearly, the context in which you are speaking helps to establish the audiences' expectation. Within the context of a classroom debate, few audiences would expect you to dress up. It is, however, a good idea to avoid clothing that may reduce your credibility by distracting the audience (concert t-shirts, distracting slogans, etc.). At a debate tournament, most judges expect that you will dress professionally. A good rule of thumb is to dress as if you are going on a job interview. While judges understand the desire to rebel against norms by "dressing down," many judges will view such "rages against the machine" as disrespect for the activity. It is unlikely that a judge would give you a loss based entirely on appearance, but because credibility exists in the mind of the judge, it makes no sense to deliberately violate audience expectations and risk prejudicing the critic.

Questions to Ponder

Should our appearance influence our credibility?

Demeanor: Nothing Happens That You Did Not Expect

Your performance begins as soon as the audience/judge notices you. Even conversations that you have within earshot of the judge may influence the judge's impression of your demeanor. Good debaters are confident, but not arrogant. Be friendly to your opponents and the audience. We tend to find affable people charismatic and, therefore, credible.

As the debate progresses, your adrenalin may encourage you to abandon control over your demeanor. Someone may misstate your argument; you may find yourself pressed for time in a speech; you might even be offended by something that is said. Regardless of what happens, try to project the impression that everything is as you expected it to be. Avoid refusing to take questions because "you have too much to get through." This creates the impression that you are "on the ropes" and can't handle it. As you sit at your table and listen to your opponent's arguments, do not react by rolling your eyes or by making disapproving comments or sounds. During the 2000 Presidential election, Presidential candidate Al Gore was chastised for rolling his eyes and sighing repeatedly into the microphone during one his debates with President Bush. There is a great scene in the film "A Few Good Men," in which Demi Moore, frustrated over a judge's denial of an initial objection, "strenuously objects." Both the judge and Demi's co-council were unimpressed by this strategy. Like football games, debates have a palpable sense of momentum. Demeanor that seems defensive creates the impression that the momentum has shifted to the other team. You should appear composed even when the debate has concluded. The judge may not have made up his/her mind about the winner of the round. Even if the judge has decided the outcome of that debate, he/she will probably be judging you again soon.

VERBAL ELEMENTS OF DELIVERY

The specific issues and arguments generated by the topics that you debate will influence many of the verbal choices you make. There are, however, some general word choice strategies that you should consider.

Avoid Slang

Like verbal non-fluencies, slang use is habit forming. Over time, people become desensitized to the fact that they are constantly using slang. You might say "pissed-off" or "sucks" a lot around your friends and think nothing of it because you have grown accustomed to using objectionable language without being admonished for it. The problem is that if you regularly use slang and profanity, you increase the likelihood that you will use offensive language when you really don't want to. Slang terms that aren't particularly offensive remain imprecise and sophomoric. As a result, the use of even non-offensive slang will probably reduce your credibility. Good speakers don't use a lot of slang because they have found words that more professionally and precisely express their thoughts. Consequently, if you really want to improve your speaking ability, work on expanding your vocabulary, both in your private and professional life. While not all judges are bothered by the use of slang, many are. On the other hand, no judge or audience member will be offended by the use of precise, professional language.

Avoid Jargon

To persuade your audience, you must effectively communicate with them. Unfortunately, as subject matter becomes more complex, debaters have a tendency to demonstrate their mastery of the content by utilizing the jargon that is intrinsic to whatever field of endeavor they are discussing. Even experienced debate judges will admit (if they are honest) to hearing terms such as "WMD" bantered about in debates and not being entirely sure what the terms meant. Debaters should not assume that judges and audience members are repositories of the meanings of all possible terms and abbreviations related to the proposition. Had the debaters simply defined "WMD" as weapons of mass destruction, the judge would have been better able to follow the arguments. In addition to subject matter jargon, debaters may rely too much on technical language to describe debate concepts. Terms such as topicality, solvency, and mutual exclusivity may have meaning to audiences who are familiar with debate theory, but "lay" or inexperienced judges are less likely to be persuaded by debate jargon.

Jargon, however, can be useful because, unlike slang, jargon terms have precise meanings related to particular fields. Doctors and lawyers regularly use jargon. Jargon can help reduce the time needed to communicate an idea by allowing the speaker to use a few words to describe a broad concept. It is easier and faster to say WMD than to say weapons of mass destruction. Audience analysis can help you determine how much jargon you can get away with in a debate. If your debate judge is experienced, you probably have greater latitude in the use of jargon associated with debate theory. If you have doubts about their understanding of a particular term (perhaps they give you a puzzled look while you are speaking), be sure to define the term. Concepts associated with fields other than debate that may form the subject matter of your debate (issues associated with current events, medicine, law, etc.) should be clearly explained using language that is clear and easy to understand. When in doubt, define!

Using Humor: Everyone's a Comedian

There is ample research to support the notion that humor is persuasive. Humor can help maintain the audience's attention, which can be a challenge, particularly when discussing technical issues. People with a good sense of humor are often viewed as more charismatic and affable than their humorless peers. Imagine that you are judging a debate in which the Opposition has a great mastery of the facts but is, frankly, boring. The Government, on the other hand, also seems to know what they are talking about, but has made you laugh out loud during their speeches. Without knowing anything specific about the issues in the debate, which side do you think you would probably vote for?

Humor requires a combination of verbal and nonverbal strategies to be effective. In terms of verbal strategies, the most important thing to remember is not to offend. You should avoid any form of *ad hominem* attacks on your opponents. Even when you are all old friends, the judge may not be privy to those relationships and will have a lower threshold for what is abusive than you. Never make a joke based upon race, nationality, gender, religion, or ethnic heritage. There is a substantial risk that the judge will not appreciate remarks that could be viewed as even remotely disparaging of group affiliations. You may see this as political correctness run amok, and you may be right. There are, however, plenty of debaters who have lost debates, certain that they were "right."

The funniest humor seems unplanned. Simple jokes that have been told a lot are not typically the funniest. Judges appreciate seeing a debater who can generate wit and humor apparently spontaneously. While it is difficult to plan and execute effective humor, there are some humor strategies that can be effective:

Equivocation: Playing on the double meaning of words can be fun. In a debate on gun control, I once heard a debater from Texas quip, "In Texas, gun control means that you use both hands when you aim."

Observational Humor. Sometimes humor can be found in pointing out the ironies in everyday events. In a debate on legalizing prostitution, a debater observed that boxing, which is hitting someone in the face, is legal if you are paid for it in a public boxing match, but illegal if you do it for free (unsanctioned). Prostitution, on the other hand, involves a sexual act that is illegal if you are paid for it, but legal if done for free in private.

Self and Partner Deprecating Humor. While it's generally not a good idea to make jokes at the expense of your opponents, it can be funny to "poke" fun at yourself or your partner. Most great comedic duos have used this strategy (Burn/Alan, Ball/Arnez, Bill/Hillary). I once saw a debate on popular culture in which the Prime Minister blasted his partner for his Britney Spears collection (few thinking people over 15 years of age will actually admit to listening to Britney Spears). The judge was amused by this, and it loosened up the debate to the point that everyone was "having at" their partner.

Quick Wit

Points of Information often generate excellent opportunities to demonstrate quick wit. Before accepting a Point of Information, some speakers will conclude their thoughts by saying, "Wouldn't you agree?" The debater about to answer the question then has to quickly think of a response. "No, I do not," suffices, but isn't particularly creative. I have seen debaters have fun responses to being "shamed" by their opponent. (In Parliamentary Debate, debaters may say "shame" when they strongly disagree with a point.) After being "shamed," the speaker might say something like, "It is a shame that you don't agree with my point!"

Nonverbal Elements of Humor

Have you ever tried being funny by using sarcasm in an email only to find that you offended the recipient of the letter? Words alone can only rarely communicate humor effectively. Your timing (both when you use the humor and your pauses while using it) is critical. Your facial expressions (a raised eyebrow, a smirk, or even a deadpan) "sell" the joke. Some people have a natural sense for the nonverbal elements of humor. If you don't have a natural sense of comedic emphasis, spend some time observing comedians (tough homework). Notice how they use vocal and physical expression to accent their humor. Copy those elements that seem appropriate in the context of a speech or debate. Have someone videotape you while you are debating to see if your nonverbal communication is effectively accenting your verbal.

SUMMARY

While logicians might desire a society which values substance over style, the real world requires effective delivery. Speech anxiety can hinder optimal delivery, but it is treatable. By examining our automatic thoughts, the fallacies associated with those thoughts, and by developing facilitating replacement thoughts, we can greatly reduce our "stage fright." The verbal element of communication represents a small percentage of the total message. The nonverbal elements of delivery constitute at least 90% of that message. By working on key nonverbal elements, debaters can increase their credibility and the persuasiveness of their message. Body language, demeanor, and vocal emphasis are critical parts of the nonverbal tapestry. The verbal choices a debater makes will be influenced by the nature of the topic being debated. Arguers should avoid the use of slang and limit the use of jargon. Spontaneous humor can add interest and energy to the debate. Because humor makes us affable, it can greatly increase charisma and, therefore, credibility.

REFERENCES

Burns, David. *The Feeling Good Handbook*. New York: Plume, 1990.

Lindstron, Robert. "Podium." *Presentation Products Magazine*, November, 1990.

Knapp, Mark L. *Essentials of Nonverbal Communication*. New York: Holt, Rinehart and Winston.

Mehrabian, Albert. *Nonverbal Communication*. Chicago: Aldine-Atherton.

Mehrabian, Albert. *Silent Messages: Implicit Communication of Emotions and Attitudes*. 2nd ed. Belmont, CA: Wadsworth, 1981.

Seinfeld, Jerry. *SeinLanguage*. New York: Bantam, 1993.

Spence, Gerry. *How to Argue and Win Every Time*. St. Martin's Press, 1995.

Wallechinsky, David, Irving Wallace and Amy Wallace. *The Book of Lists*. New York: Morrow, 1977.

EXERCISES

Chapter 9: Delivery

1. Describe your most common public speaking-related worry. What automatic thoughts are associated with it? Describe the fallacy of reasoning associated with the automatic thought and the most effective replacement thought.

2. Using InfoTrac, research the search term "speech anxiety." Read an article on the topic and summarize its recommendations.

3. Using InfoTrac, research the search term "speaker credibility." Read an article that provides "tips" for successful speaking, and summarize its recommendations.

4. Attend or watch a public hearing on television (City Council, School Board, etc.). Describe delivery techniques that were utilized by at least two speakers. What did they do that maximized their message? How could they improve their delivery?

Chapter

Forensics: A Speaker's Playground

WHAT IS FORENSICS?

When you think about the word "forensics," dead bodies probably come to mind. The use of the term "forensics" to describe evidence in courtrooms and "forensics" as competitive speaking share a common origin. Aristotle identified three broad categories of speeches: deliberative (legislative speeches), epideictic (ceremonial speeches), and forensic (courtroom oratory). Today, forensics is the oldest academic subject still taught in our colleges and universities. Within the context of academic debate, we can think of forensics as "speaking for judgment" or competitive speaking.

Forensics has had, and continues to have, a tremendous influence in the United States. Presidents Kennedy, Johnson, Nixon, Carter, and Reagan were all involved in forensics. In a recent survey of Who's Who, forensics was chosen as the single most valuable class the people surveyed had taken in school. Whether you go to a forensics tournament to observe or actually end up on a forensics team, you will find the experience rewarding. From the perspective of the observer, you will have the opportunity to witness talented speakers honing their skills. Even if you do not feel that competitive speaking is your "thing," you can borrow techniques and styles from the contestants and utilize them in your public speaking experiences.

Forensic competition provides a forum for students who have excelled in speech classes (or a similar context) and need an environment in which they can further challenge and utilize their talents. The benefits of being on the forensics team reach far beyond just improving speaking skills and winning trophies, though granted, these are rewarding by-products. Students who compete on forensics teams and

171

participate in academic debate become knowledgeable of contemporary social and political issues, learn to manage their time, greatly enhance their public speaking confidence, develop strong critical thinking skills, learn to work in groups, and generate incredible resume material. Forensics changes lives. It regularly gives direction to students who, while talented at speech, may not have applied themselves in other areas of their academic and professional lives. They enter the activity thinking that it looks like fun and leave it (or end up coaching), completely changed by the experience. Students who have always had a sense of their academic and professional futures find the elite, competitive environment to be an ideal proving ground for their talents.

FORENSICS: IT'S MORE THAN JUST A DEBATE TEAM

Though debate remains an important centerpiece of forensics tournaments, forensics actually encompasses a variety of events, each emphasizing different skills and interests. Events are divided into team (events requiring more than one competitor) and individual (those you do by yourself) events. What follows is a description of each of the events that you might participate in if you were to join a forensics team.

EXPLANATION OF EVENTS

Limited Preparation Events

While these are called limited preparation events, the name is not entirely accurate. A great deal of preparation is necessary to be ready to compete in Impromptu and Extemporaneous Speaking. These events provide excellent preparation for Parliamentary Debate, because competitors must be well-versed in contemporary political and social issues, and they require the ability to make arguments with limited preparation time. Consequently, debaters will often choose to do one or both of these individual events.

Impromptu

In Impromptu, you are allowed two minutes to prepare a five-minute speech. Like the topics used in Parliamentary Debate, impromptu topics range from one-word abstracts (in some regions) to quotations (both famous and obscure). A good impromptu speaker has committed many examples of significant people, events, philosophies, and theories to memory. These examples can be used to illustrate the general themes that tend to be represented by impromptu quotations. Themes such as love, adversity, courage, failure, justice, and honor are common. The goal of the speech is to interpret the quotation and support or reject its validity through the use of supporting examples. Judges are looking for structure, content, and excellence in delivery. Humor is especially valued in impromptu speaking. The following represents a basic outline for an impromptu speech:

I. Introduction
    A. Attention Getter
    B. Presentation of the Quotation, and Your Interpretation (what it means and whether you agree or disagree with the quotation)
    C. Preview
II. Body
    A. First Example that Supports or Rejects the Quotation
    B. Second Example that Supports or Rejects the Quotation
    C. Third Example that Supports or Rejects the Quotation
III. Conclusion
    A. Summary
    B. Closure

Extemporaneous

In this event, you are allowed half an hour to prepare a 7-minute speech. You begin by choosing to answer one of three current event questions. The goal of the speech is to present a well-documented case, supporting your answer to that question. The questions are derived from the content of a story or stories found within the last three months of *Time*, *U.S. News and World Report*, and *Newsweek*. Contestants are expected to quote these, as well as other, periodicals throughout their speeches. Because Parliamentary Debate and Extemporaneous Speaking require extensive knowledge of current events, this event provides the best preparation for Parliamentary Debate. Successful contestants in Extemporaneous Speaking become masters of current events. Typically, forensic teams will develop extensive files (referred to as extemp files), cataloguing current event issues. Contestants will utilize these files while preparing for competition in Extemporaneous Speaking. Some tournaments allow Parliamentary Debaters to utilize their extemp files during preparation for debate, as well. While speakers may utilize a variety of different structures, the following is a basic structure for an Extemporaneous Speech:

I. Introduction
    A. Attention Getter
    B. Statement of Question and Brief Answer
    C. Preview
II. Body
    A. First Section: Background Information
    B. Second Section: First Reason for Your Answer
    C. Third Section: Second Reason for Your Answer

III. Conclusion
   A. Summary
   B. Closure

Platform Speeches

Platform speeches test the contestant's ability to write, memorize, and deliver a speech. The speech can be no longer than 10 minutes in length. In forensics, emphasis is placed on the creativity of the topic. Topics that are commonplace in Basic Speech classes (the death penalty, euthanasia, abortion, dreams, etc.) would not be viewed as creative enough to meet the challenge. There are four platform speeches: Informative, Persuasive, Communication Analysis, and Speech to Entertain.

Informative

Contestants in Informative must deliver a well-researched, memorized speech that attempts to inform the audience about a significant topic. Deference is given to innovative topics. Topics involving innovations in technology, medicine, and science are common and tend to do well. Visual aids are also common.

Persuasive

Persuasive Speaking requires contestants to present a well-researched, memorized speech that attempts to persuade the audience to do something about a significant social or political problem. One of the chief challenges of Persuasive Speaking is to find a topic that is significant, yet is not well-known. Like most of the events in forensics, there is an expectation that the speech will be supported by multiple, well-qualified sources. Judges will look for a clearly developed problem and a solution that offers some hope of solving that problem. Ideally, there is a clear action step that calls for the audience to get involved in enacting the solution.

Communication Analysis

Communication Analysis is, arguably, the most challenging of the individual events. The goal of the speech is to explain a communication artifact (a speech, an advertisement, a nonverbal icon, etc.). Communication scholars have developed "rhetorical" models that help to dissect and explain communication events. Contestants in Communication Analysis must explain a relevant rhetorical model and apply that model to the artifact.

Speech to Entertain

The goal of this speech is to amuse, while persuading or informing the audience about a significant social issue. Speech to Entertain is challenging because it is not simply a standup comedy routine; it requires both a significant social message and coherent structure. Contestants who succeed at this event have a good sense of comedic timing. Many of these speeches utilize informative or persuasive structures.

Interpretation of Literature

Interpretation of Literature is comprised of Prose, Poetry, Drama, Programmed Oral Interpretation, Duo Interpretation (a two-person event), and Reader's Theatre (a team event). The goal of interpretation is to bring the written text to "life." "Interpers" will research to find literature in their preferred genre (poetry, prose, etc.) and will "cut" or edit that materially artfully to produce a coherent program that supports a message or argument. While the Interpretation events are not debates, many judges believe that the programs presented must support a central argument. Interpretation shares with acting the need for nuance in facial and vocal expression. Unlike acting, there is limited movement in interpretation. The participants hold black binders containing their scripts to remind them and the audience of the centrality of the written work. To be competitive, the literature that is performed is typically obscure. Material must be from published sources. However, with the plethora of literary options now available on the Internet, some latitude is given to the definition of "published." All programs are ten minutes long.

Prose Interpretation

Prose Interpretation utilizes a cutting from a fiction or non-fiction book, short story, diary, or letter(s). The cutting should develop key characters well enough that the audience feels connected with them. While the goal of Prose Interpretation is not necessarily the revelation of the entire text, the story that emerges from the cutting must have coherence—a clear beginning and ending. We need to be able to understand everything that happens in the cutting. Ideally, there is emotional variety (humor, as well as drama) in the piece.

Poetry Interpretation

In Poetry Interpretation, contestants will typically weave together a variety of poetry around a central theme/argument. Occasionally, single pieces of poetry are used, but to be competitive they should have multiple voicings or characters. The use of verse distinguishes poetry from prose, although some poetry sounds like prose. Poetry, therefore, need not rhyme. In fact, most competitive poetry has cadence but does not rhyme. The event encourages competitors to experience talented new poets.

Dramatic Interpretation

Dramatic Interpretation requires a cutting from a play or screenplay. Contestants can, and are encouraged to, perform multiple characters. Like Prose, the cutting must be artistically crafted to allow sufficient character and scene development. Credit is also given for emotional variety and the student's choice of play. Well-known plays (*Death of a Salesman, Romeo and Juliet*, etc.) do not tend to appeal to the judges as much as newer and more obscure works and, consequently, are generally not competitive.

Programmed Oral Interpretation (POI)

In Programmed Oral Interpretation, contestants develop a program which communicates an argument by utilizing more than one of the three genres of interpretation (prose, poetry, drama). Rather than presenting the genres distinctly, it is popular to interlace or weave sections of each selection.

Duo Interpretation

Like Dramatic Interpretation, Duo utilizes a ten-minute cutting from a play. As the name implies, Duo consist of two performers. While the event is naturally suited for two person scripts, each performer may take on multiple characters or edit out non-essential characters. Some movement can enhance these performances, but the amount of movement allowed is controversial.

Team Events

Reader's Theatre

In Reader's Theatre, three or more performers present a program not more than 25 minutes long that uses a variety of material—poetry, prose, drama, newspaper clippings, song lyrics, etc.—to develop a complex argument/message. Unlike the interpretation individual events, movement is allowed (and encouraged). Performers wear ensemble dress (similar costumes), may sing songs that develop the theme, and will be involved in complicated blocking moves. This is an event that requires a great deal of rehearsal time and commitment on the part of the people doing it.

Parliamentary Debate

If you have read the preceding chapters, you should have a fairly good sense of what goes on in a Parliamentary Debate tournament. There are a few issues unique to the tournament experience that remains. After checking postings (see the next section), debate teams proceed to their assigned rooms. Once in the room, debaters will indicate on the board their school name and who will be debating the various positions in the debate. The following represents a sample listing:

GOV	EL CAMINO SJ		OPP	LONG BEACH RD
PM	David Smith		LO	Jane Rodriguez
MG	Sue Jones		MO	Bob Davidson

The judge will then read the topic and the debaters will have 15 minutes to prepare. It is customary for the Government to prepare in the room, while the Opposition prepares outside. The rules regarding the permissibility of coaching and the use of outside materials vary from tournament to tournament. Once the debate has begun, the judge will give time signals to indicate when the first minute of the Constructive Speeches has expired (recall that no questions may be asked during the first and last minute of Constructives) and indicate how much time is remaining in the speeches. When the debate is over, the judge will fill out his/her ballot, may make a few verbal comments, and the debaters will leave the room to check the postings for the next debate.

THE TOURNAMENT EXPERIENCE

Whether you are getting extra credit for observing a Speech Tournament or you are about to compete at one, it is important that you understand the unique environment you are about to enter. Speech tournaments defy linguistic descriptions. They must be experienced to be totally understood. However, here is a partial list of what happens at a tournament:

1) Anywhere between 20 and 70 colleges and universities meet on campus to compete.
2) The competition is divided into several categories, divisions, and events.
3) Speaking takes place in classrooms, usually in front of several fellow competitors and one judge.
4) You meet and become friends with students and coaches from the other schools.
5) You experience feelings of exhilaration, relief, inspiration, depression, fatigue, and tremendous accomplishment.

TOURNAMENT PROCEDURES

What Are Postings?

When you arrive at the tournament site, your school's coach will probably tell you which person or team they would like you to observe (assuming that you are there to watch) or will give you a code number for debate and individual events. Tournaments use codes to facilitate tournament administration and to provide school anonymity (reducing the impact of bias caused by school affiliation). If there are no coaches present, you can usually find this information on your own by checking the "postings area." Usually, a wall of a designated building will be covered with a number of sheets of paper referred to as postings. Because forensics competitors dress professionally at tournaments, if you simply look for a gathering of people who are uncharacteristically well-dressed (at least for a college environment), you should be able to easily locate the postings area.

The good people who run the tournament will post a decoder sheet for all of the participants, an individual listing for each of the events, and a schedule listing the times of all of the events in the tournament. The event postings will indicate who is in the event, the room in which they are competing, the order in which they speak (in individual events), the team they are debating (assuming they are debating), the time the round starts, and who is assigned to judge the round.

At many tournaments there are three divisions—novice for true beginners, junior for those with one year of experience, and open or senior division for those with more experience. If you are observing, think about going to both a novice and a senior level event. This will allow you to see the contrast between the two different levels of experience. If you are competing, your coach will enter you in the appropriate division. All tournaments have different rules for who is allowed to be entered in which division, but usually after you have received a first, second, or third place in an event, you move from novice to junior.

You Know Where You Are Going. Now What?

Always arrive a few minutes early to the round you are observing or competing in. Often the round begins a few minutes late, but it is impolite for you to arrive late. Before going into the room, turn off any communication devices (beepers, cell phones, etc.). Having your cell phone ring in class is bad enough; having it happen at a speech tournament is unpardonable. It would be the equivalent of using an air horn while Tiger Woods is putting. If for some reason you are a bit late and the door is closed, listen carefully before opening the door. *Never walk in while another student is giving a speech.* Once inside, sit quietly and avoid any distracting noises or movements. If you are observing and want to quietly take notes, have your notebook ready before the round begins. Again, you are trying to minimize any potential distractions in the round. The preceding may sound a bit harsh, but you have to be aware that, particularly in the senior division, even the slightest flaw in a speech may be the difference between first and second. Consequently, judges have an extremely low tolerance level for any form of distraction.

Once the debate or speech has begun, be a good audience member. If you are competing, simply try to do your best. Remember why you are there—to learn and enjoy. If you are competing and make a mistake, blank out, or in general are not satisfied with your performance, don't get discouraged! Keep in mind that nobody is perfect. Make a note of how you can correct the mistake in the future, but above all, be positive.

After the Speech or Debate

Typically after the last speech in a round of individual events or after the PMR, everyone simply leaves the room to go to their next round. Once in awhile, a judge may make a comment or ask a question about a speech or debate. If you are competing, listen to the comments and answer the question very politely, never defensively. Judges usually don't make comments after rounds, but some feel they can communicate their decisions better verbally than in writing on the ballot. Always let the judge decide whether or not they will offer verbal comments.

So How Many Rounds Do I Have to Go to?

After your first round, check postings for information on your second round of competition. Most tournaments have three rounds of preliminary competition in each individual event and six preliminary rounds of debate. This means competitors will receive feedback from three judges and compete against three different panels of contestants in individual events. If they debate, they will be heard by six judges and compete against six teams during the course of debate prelims.

It is a good idea to highlight the activities that you wish to watch or that you are competing in on your copy of the schedule. You can do this before you get to the tournament. Your school's coach almost always receives a time schedule before the actual tournament. Occasionally, changes are made to the original schedule, so be sure to double check your copy against the copy posted at the tournament.

A sample schedule from a past tournament is provided for your information:

Sample Schedule

September 11, 2002

8:00-9:00	Registration, Lecture Hall 333
9:00-10:00	Round I Pattern A (Impromptu, Persuasion, Expository)
10:00-11:15	Round I Pattern B (Extemp., CA, Poetry, STE)
11:15-12:30	Round I Parliamentary Debate
12:30-1:30	Round II Pattern A
1:30-2:45	Round II Pattern B
2:45-4:00	Round II Parliamentary Debate
4:00-5:45	Round III Parliamentary Debate
5:45-7:00	Round III Pattern A

CHAPTER 10

September 12, 2002

8:00-9:00	Round III Pattern B
9:00-10:15	Round IV Parliamentary Debate
10:15-11:30	Round V Parliamentary Debate
11:30-12:30	Finals Pattern A
12:30-1:45	Round VI Parliamentary Debate
1:45-3:00	Finals Pattern B
3:00-4:15	Quarterfinals in Parliamentary Debate
4:30-5:45	Semi-Finals in Parliamentary Debate
6:00-7:15	Finals in Parliamentary Debate and AWARDS

As you look over this sample schedule, notice there are several events going on at the same time. This is called a conflict pattern. At some tournaments, you may enter two events in the same pattern. It is ideal to enter one event in each pattern, but at different tournaments, different events conflict. Also notice that debate runs independently of the individual events, so it is possible to enter both. It is always your responsibility to check postings for yourself and get to the round on time!

How Are the Speakers Evaluated?

In individual events, judges write comments on small cards called ballots. On these ballots, the judge(s) will rank the speeches in the round (1, 2, 3, 4) and rate them according to college speakers in general (superior, excellent, good, fair, poor, unprepared). In debate, judges fill out a ballot that indicates which team won the debate, and they rate each speaker on a scale from 0-30. The ballots are then taken to the tournament headquarters where they are tallied and recorded. Each school receives a packet of their ballots after the awards assembly at the conclusion of the tournament.

"Breaking" into Elimination Rounds

After round III of individual events and round VI of debate is completed, the speakers/teams advancing to elimination rounds (debate may cut to octo-finals, quarter finals, semi-finals, and finals, depending on tournament size) are notified. Contestants are notified by postings in the same location as the preliminary round postings. Contestants find this time to be really exciting and perhaps a bit nerve-racking. Most speakers feel a tremendous sense of accomplishment when they see their code on the posting of elimination round participants. Of course, this can also be a disappointing time, particularly if you think you performed well and did not advance to elimination rounds. If you do not make it to elims, keep in mind that experience and hard work are typically, eventually, rewarded. It is not at all uncommon for individual events contestants or debate teams to miss breaking at a few tournaments before they finally make it into elimination rounds.

If you do not advance to the elimination rounds, make sure that you watch the competitors who did. This may be difficult for you, because your ego may tell you that you should be competing, not watching. Don't go in to be a critic; rather, try to see what they may be doing that you might emulate. Tremendous amounts of learning can take place in a final round, especially if you aren't in it! If one of your school's teams or individual event competitors is in an elimination round, show your support by watching them. Elimination rounds can be a bit intimidating, and it's good to see familiar, supportive faces in the audience.

Awards

Awards assemblies are typically a blast (particularly if you have won). While it is sometimes difficult to accept a result that did not meet your expectation, most competitors do a great job of masking disappointment and gracefully acknowledging achievement. Trophies are awarded to individual competitors and debate teams, and sweepstakes awards are awarded to schools based upon the total awards won by their squad members. Results of Parliamentary Debate are forwarded to the Secretary of the NPDA, who compiles a record of all sanctioned debate tournaments. The NPDA generates a National Sweepstakes ranking based upon the record of each school's best four tournaments.

The table below represents the final ranks for the top fifteen schools during the 2002-2003 academic year. 377 schools were included in the rankings. The NPDA system awards points for wins in novice, junior, and senior division. Consequently, even new debate teams may contribute to a squad's national ranking.

NPDA Tournament Rankings
2002-2003 Season

Rank	School	Total	#1	#2	#3	#4
1	Point Loma Nazarene	88	24	24	21	19
2	Truman State University	88	24	23	21	20
3	South Orange County	86	23	23	21	19
4	El Camino	85	24	22	20	19
5	Pacific Lutheran Univ	84	24	22	20	18
6	Univ of Oregon	84	23	23	20	18
7	Univ of California - Berkeley	82	22	21	20	19
8	Notre Dame	79	26	21	16	16
9	Rice University	79	22	22	18	17
10	Lewis & Clark College	77	22	20	19	16
11	Univ of Florida	75	21	20	17	17
12	California State Univ - Long Beach	75	23	19	17	16
13	Colorado College	74	21	20	17	16
14	Wyoming	72½	23	17	16½	17
15	Asuza Pacific	72	24	20	14	14

Finally, it is important to keep awards in perspective. While trophies and national standings are fun, most "retired" forensics competitors will look back upon their competitive experiences and reflect that the friendships they made, and the skills that they developed were the most valuable outcomes of their forensics experience.

SUMMARY

Forensics is competitive speech and debate. In addition to debate, forensics competitors compete in a rich variety of events, each emphasizing different skills. Forensics events include Debate, Reader's Theatre, Platform Speeches, Oral Interpretation of Literature, and Limited-Preparation Events. Forensics tournaments provide wonderful opportunities for students seeking more than the traditional speech course can offer. Whether observing or competing, students will come away from speech tournaments impressed and enriched by what they have encountered.

REFERENCES

National Parliamentary Debate Association Home Page:
    http://www.bethel.edu/Majors/Communication/npda/home.html.

EXERCISES

Chapter 10: Forensics

1. Attend a forensics tournament. Watch at least four rounds of debate. Flow the debate. Indicate which side you would have voted for and why.

2. Interview a member of your school's forensics team. Try to determine why they compete in forensics. Do they have any tips that might help your classroom competitions?

3. Attend a forensics tournament and watch a round of Persuasive, Impromptu, and Extemporaneous Speaking. What similarities did you notice? What were the differences?

4. Attend a rehearsal for your school's forensics team. Watch a practice round of debate and practice flowing the debate.

Chapter

Advanced Strategies for
Tournament Debaters

OVERVIEW

The primary purpose of this textbook is to give beginning argumentation students and potential tournament debaters a strong foundation in argumentation theory and parliamentary debate. Mastery of the simple theories described thus far will undoubtedly make you a better arguer in the "real world" and will also serve you well in tournament competition. As they advance in their debate careers, however, tournament debaters will notice that many parliamentary debates involve theories more advanced than those described in the previous chapters of this text. This chapter seeks to provide a sampling of theories that more advanced debaters may encounter in tournament competition. Because of the subjective nature of advanced theories and strategies, this chapter is not intended to imply a definitive or normative perspective on any of the theories discussed. The author's hope is that this chapter might serve as part of the discussions that should be taking place in debate squad rooms regarding the validity and strategic use of controversial strategies.

THE ORIGIN AND NATURE OF DEBATE
THEORY

Many of the theories described in this chapter are controversial; no clear consensus exists as to whether or not they are legitimate. This lack of consensus stems both from the origin of parliamentary debate theory and the very nature of debate theory in general. Undeniably, contemporary parliamentary debate theory represents a mixture of parli as it was intended to be debated and theories "sampled" from CEDA/NDT debate. Recall, however, that the popularity of parliamentary debate can be attributed in part to, what some saw as, growing inadequacies in those activities (see Chapter 4). Consequently, there are judges and coaches who wish to maintain theoretical and practical distinctions between CEDA/NDT and parliamentary debate. However, there are also many coaches, judges, and competitors who are supportive of the utilization of CEDA/NDT-based theories in parliamentary debate. The competing philosophies of these two camps undoubtedly influence the theories utilized in parliamentary debate.

Another substantial influence on the development of debate theory is obviously the debaters who often invent new theories, and, perhaps more frequently, rename previously existing theories and strategies. A debater at the Community College State Championships was overheard describing what he called a "terminal solvency takeout." When queried as to the meaning of this impressive-sounding term, he indicated that it was an Opposition argument that demonstrated that the Government plan gained no solvency. Debaters enjoy the mystification that occurs when they coin names for theories such as "prefiat kritik and "artificial permutation." As debaters experiment with new theories, or old ones with new packaging, their ideas are often adopted by their colleagues, and a trend begins.

Debate theory is, therefore, constantly evolving, and practices that may be persuasive to one judge may be offensive to another. There are some theories and practices that are generally accepted. Topicality is a voting issue, for example. It is difficult, however, to articulate any universally accepted theories. Some judges will not vote against the Government based on a topicality argument. It is important, therefore, for you to distinguish between "rules" and "theories." Rules are established by the NPDA in its constitution and cover matters such as speaker order and the use of written evidence in the "debating chamber." There are very few rules in parliamentary debate. Theories, by contrast, are arguable. If, for example, someone tells you in a debate that the Government's plan must include a funding plank, they need to tell you why because there is no "rule" that dictates plan content.

Justifying Theory

Given that there are a variety of different sources for debate theories, how will you decide which theories and strategies are valuable? For some coaches and debaters, a theory is valuable if it helps you win. Others look beyond simple utility to more complex standards for theory justification. As you justify, and hear others justifying the strategies that they use in debates, you will probably notice a few reoccurring criteria. Keep in mind that, like the theories they attempt to justify, criteria for good theories are equally arguable. Many theorists would contend, however, that good debate theories should accomplish at least four things: they should facilitate the examination of the proposition, encourage clash, contribute to fairness, and be conducive to the longevity of the activity.

Good Theories Facilitate the Examination of the Proposition

For many judges, the proposition plays a central role in the debate. They assume that the topic has meaning that should be explored. A well-written topic warrants such an assumption. Topics such as "freedom is more important than security," or "the United States should forgive the debt of developing nations," can provide the starting point for significant and contemporary discussions. They deserve to be thoughtfully debated. It is true that not all topics would seem to warrant such deference, but many coaches and backroom personnel try diligently to create interesting and important topics. The fact that some propositions are poorly crafted should not be viewed as an excuse to generally dismiss the primacy of the proposition.

This criterion is particularly controversial because many judges would argue that the focus of clash in the debate should be negotiable. Some would contend that the Government's case should be the focus of the debate, regardless of whether or not the case is objectively probative of the resolution. Others would entertain strategies such as language critiques that often have very little to do with either the resolution or the case thesis.

Good Theories Encourage Clash

As Chapter 4 observed, clash is really the animating force in a debate. Clash can be viewed as both a means and an end. As a means, clash is important because it promotes the rigorous examination of the proposition and the variety of sub-issues that are part of that process. Absent clash, debate speeches become little more than dueling persuasive speeches in which neither side truly engages the other. Debaters often justify theories and strategies premised on the notion that they promote clash. Clash, therefore, can be viewed as an end, or a desired outcome of valuable theories and strategies.

Good Theories Contribute to the Fairness of the Contest

Debate can be viewed as a game with a variety of desired educational outcomes. Like all games, rules and practices should contribute to fair play. Fairness mandates that debaters be given equal speaking time, and that resolutions not be so grossly truistic that the Opposition cannot win. The criterion of fairness demands that critics attempt to set aside their ideological biases when judging the debate. While most would agree that debate contests should be fair, it is not as easy to reach agreement on what is and what isn't fair. Should, for example, the Government have exactly the same chance of winning as the Opposition, or does presumption require that the scales be initially tipped in favor of the Opposition? If all teams in the tournament have the opportunity to debate the same number of Government and Opposition rounds, does that help to mitigate the challenges created by assigning presumption to the Opposition?

Good Theories Contribute to the Longevity of the Activity

From the perspective of the debater, it is tempting to advocate theories based primarily on whether they are fun and successful. It is important, however, for coaches, judges, and enlightened competitors to share the responsibility of stewardship of the activity. In addition to their coaching obligations, directors of forensics typically allocate a great deal of time to marketing the activity to administrators. As a general rule, administrators like to know that debate is contributing to the education of students. They tend to value the positive effects that debate can have on the critical thinking and delivery skills of participants. When debate deviates from those goals, when it becomes less "real world," it makes it difficult to justify debate to those who aren't impressed by game playing. Long-serving debate coaches can share stories of CEDA/NDT debate programs that were cancelled after an administrator visited a practice round or a tournament. Even in the relatively short period of time that parliamentary debate has existed, a number of nationally ranked parli programs have been cancelled, for no clear reason other than apparent funding priorities. It is critical that directors of forensics have the ability to defend their programs on the grounds that they are important vehicles for teaching critical thinking and effective communication. Practices that deter from those goals increase the vulnerability of the activity to charges that it is not worth funding.

Because of the controversial nature of many debate theories and practices, you will undoubtedly encounter coaches and judges who have very differing views concerning the ideas that we are about to examine. Your ability to successfully utilize these theories will be greatly influenced by your willingness to adapt your arguments to each judge's preferences. This is sometimes difficult, especially when tournaments utilize a mass announcement format that precludes any discussion with the judge prior to preparation time. When in doubt, however, your odds of winning are greater with the utilization of more conservative theoretical positions.

CRITIQUE ARGUMENTS: SEARCHING FOR HIDDEN PREMISES OR AVOIDING CASE CLASH?

Kritik/critique arguments originated in CEDA/NDT and are becoming popular, particularly in open division competition in parli. Critique arguments may question the underlying assumptions behind the topic, the arguments in the debate, or the language used by the debaters. Critiques are generally initiated by the Opposition, but can be used by the Government as well. While on their face, many critiques would appear to be simple disadvantages to the Government's plan (they are typically structured with links and impacts), they are generally impacted as absolute voting issues (like topicality). As a consequence, even if you choose not to utilize the critique as an offensive strategy, it is important that you understand the argument well enough to successfully answer it. What follows is an overview of the most common forms of critiques. Because debaters frequently improvise and create new critiques, it is important that you use points of information to clarify the links and impacts of the critiques that you will encounter in tournament debate. Keep in mind that debaters will invent new names to describe old arguments, but if it walks like a duck...etc.

Language Critiques: Political Correctness or Enlightened Sensitivity?

The language critique is generally premised in the argument that because no actual policy is implemented if the judge votes for the Government (fiat is illusory), our attention should be on more meaningful issues, such as the language used by the debaters. These arguments are sometimes referred to as pre-fiat in orientation because the impacts of the critique do not stem from the implementation of the Government's plan. Often the language critique is grounded in communication theories that contend that language creates reality. Language use, it is therefore argued, may impact the mindset of the judge and the other participants in the debate, who may then influence others. Like the punishment paradigms that came into vogue in CEDA debate in the 1980's, the language critique contends that debaters should be punished for their language choice, or the language of the proposition, and that the only way the judge can produce a lasting impression is to assign a loss to the offending team. Often, language that may "trigger" this form of critique is argued to be disparaging to minorities and/or women. Because these arguments attempt to deconstruct the common meaning of terms to test their underlying assumptions, even words that the average person might find innocuous may be argued to be offensive. Gender-specific pronouns and expressions that may reflect a gender bias (he, she, human, "all men are created equal," "common man standard," etc.) may provide the link to a language critique. Similarly, words that may attempt to classify groups of people, such as "terrorist," may trigger the critique. When argued in front of critics who enjoy critique arguments, especially those who are interested in the relationships between language, race, gender, and social construction, the language critique can be very effective. On the other hand, there are many critics who believe that the proposition ought to be the central focus of the debate and that critique arguments, especially language critiques, are tangential to that focus.

Potential Responses to Language Critiques

There are several potentially effective responses to the language critique. Many critiques rely on theories that, while interesting in a graduate course, do not apply well to a debate. It is appropriate, therefore, for you to question the applicability of the theory that the critique is premised on to the context in which it is being used. The works of philosophers such as Michel Foucault, or linguists such as Edward Sapir and Benjamin Whorf are regularly quoted to support critique positions. Clearly these authors did not assume the artificial environment of an academic debate context, in which the actions of participants are generally influenced by the desire to win the contest. Further, you should feel free to question the validity of the theory. Does language create reality? Was there no reality before there was language? Another common argument against language critiques is that they trivialize the very causes that they are supposedly advocating. The debate context involves many elements of game playing, including strategies, competitors, and trophies. It seems somewhat disingenuous to use issues as serious as race and gender discrimination to attempt to win a game. In responding to language critics, some debaters argue that simply apologizing for language that the other team finds offensive ought to be enough to satisfy them (unless, of course, they are interested primarily in who wins the debate). If the judge believes that a sanction is in order, why not simply reduce the offending speaker's points rather than assigning a loss to the team? You may also be able to effectively argue that language critiques unjustly limit freedom of expression. Courts have long held that the protection of the right to free speech is nearly absolute, especially within the context of higher education. First Amendment advocates have argued that policies that attempt to restrict speech may chill the free expression of ideas as speakers attempt to avoid topics and language that may be deemed offensive. Finally, another common strategy is to permute the critique. As we will find in this chapter's discussion on counter plans, a permutation is a hypothetical alteration of a plan. In the case of permuting a plan to defeat a critique, the Government (generally) is attempting to show that the plan can function substantially the same with or without the offensive language or concept. In the case of a language critique, the Government could simply agree to retract any offensive language in the plan.

Assumption and Reasoning-Based Critiques: Value Objections, Disadvantages, or Voting Issues?

In addition to the language used in the debate or the proposition, critiques may question the assumptions underlying the arguments in the round. This form of critique may closely resemble a disadvantage, in that the Opposition will generally contend that some key assumption the Government is making is likely to produce devastating results. A Government plan to liberalize the immigration policy of the United States might be critiqued on the grounds that it further entrenches the mindset of national borders. The critique advocate would then go on to explain the problems associated with national borders. A Government case on a value proposition that utilized the value of national security might prompt a critique that questions the wisdom of upholding national security in a world that seems to be increasingly interconnected. The impacts of utilizing national security as a value might include everything from war mongering to assaults on personal liberties.

A close cousin of the assumption-based critique is the reasoning critique. The reasoning critique calls into question assumptions made about the legitimacy of the underlying reasoning processes used in the debate. A case premised in scientific knowledge, for example, might be challenged on the grounds that scientific knowledge precludes the use of more intuitive forms of reasoning. Some debaters argue that certain types of reasoning are inherently more masculine and patriarchal. They impact that analysis by contending patriarchal reasoning leads to increases in aggressive actions, such as war, hegemony, and environmental destruction. The arguer might go on to show the negative consequences of strictly adhering to scientific reasoning.

These critiques may be viewed by some judges as more legitimate than language-based critiques because they tend to stem from the core assumptions in the Government's case (as opposed to what may be the accidental use of language, or slips of the tongue). Indeed, debate should teach us to question the underlying assumptions in our arguments. In addition, some argue that assumption and reasoning-based critiques are valuable because they provide a vehicle that allows for the exploration of alternative worldviews (Schnurer, 1997). Because of their similarity to disadvantages, many judges seem to have an easier time understanding and, therefore, voting for assumption and reasoning-based critiques. As a consequence, you should be especially careful when addressing these arguments.

Potential Responses to Assumption and Reasoning Critiques

There are many potential responses to assumption and reasoning critiques (note that some of these responses apply equally well to language critiques). First, challenge the notion that the critique should be weighed as an absolute voting issue (like topicality). Your goal is to persuade the critic to weigh the critique like a disadvantage. If the critique is suggesting that disadvantages will occur if we follow the Government's reasoning, it is reasonable to compare the advantages versus the disadvantages of utilizing that reasoning. Even if there are negative consequences to the Government's reasoning, if the positive effects outweigh the negative, the Government should still prevail.

A strategy that can be effective against many different types of critiques (including language critiques) involves revealing any contradictions between the theory of the critique and the other arguments used by the Opposition. Debaters have come to refer to these inconsistencies as *performative contradictions*. Against a case that advocates the legalization and regulation of marijuana, the Opposition might offer a critique based in the notion that regulation, as a tool in the hand of the state, is counterproductive. If the Opposition were to offer a counter plan that included any form of regulation, the Government could argue that the counter plan contradicted the critique. This example points to yet another critique response. Many judges want to hear the Opposition provide an alternative to the Government's case that won't violate the theory of the critique. An Opposition critique that any level of regulation is wrong could be challenged on the grounds that some state-based regulation is necessary. How could a modern society function without any regulation? Requiring the Opposition to provide an alternative policy or way of thought that is consistent with the theory of the critique is a great way of revealing that while the critique may be based in interesting theories, the real world could not operate utilizing its apparently utopian assumptions.

THE COUNTER PLAN REVISTED

The Counter Plan as an Opportunity Cost: When the Counter Plan Becomes a Disadvantage

In Chapter 8, we discussed the counter plan and noted that it was a policy offered by the Opposition that would compete with the Government's plan. Like virtually all theoretical positions, there are at least two views of the counter plan. Some theorists view the counter plan as actual advocacy. In other words, just as the Government is advocating the adoption of their plan through fiat, the actual advocacy view of counter plans contends that the Opposition is advocating the adoption of their counter plan. Another school of thought that is growing in popularity in parliamentary debate involves the notion that the counter plan should be viewed as an opportunity cost of the Government's plan. Under this perspective, the counter plan is used to reveal policy options that would be lost as a result of the Government's plan. The opportunity cost perspective views the counter plan as a disadvantage to the plan. If the plan precludes adoption of a more advantageous alternative, the loss of that alternative is a disadvantage to be weighed against the advantages of the plan. The opportunity cost perspective does not necessarily assume that the Opposition is actually advocating the counter plan. It may be simply pointing out that the plan precludes alternative policies that could be superior to the plan. This hypothetical approach to the counter plan can come in handy, particularly when dealing with topics that are bi-directional. Suppose, for example, that the topic was that the FCC should substantially alter its policy regarding the regulation of the public airwaves. The Government could topically argue either an increase in regulations or a decrease. Assuming that the Opposition does not want to risk running an arguably topical counter plan, it can't actually advocate a counter plan that is an alternative regulation. But by pointing out the potential policies that would be precluded by adoption of the Government's plan, it can demonstrate that the plan creates opportunity costs.

Because the opportunity cost model views the counter plan as a disadvantage to the plan, it raises interesting theoretical opportunities. If the Government is able to demonstrate that what the alternative plan precludes would produce more ill than good, the Government could then claim that the precluded counter plan is actually another advantage of the Government's plan. To do this, the Government would simply grant the counter plan and the plan are mutually exclusive, and proceed to argue disadvantages to the counter plan. The counter plan, therefore, would simply be viewed as a disadvantage "turned" to warrant the adoption of the proposition.

While accepted by many debate theorists, there are critics who reject the opportunity cost model. These judges view the hypothetical counter plan advocacy as unfair to the Government because it does not require that the Opposition actually commit to the counter plan. They prefer the traditional model of the counter plan in which the counter plan, like the Government's plan, is offered as actual advocacy.

Topical Counter Plans: When the Opposition Becomes the Government

In Chapter 7, we discussed the standards for running a counter plan. Among those requirements was the notion that the Opposition cannot present a topical counter plan. This requirement can get tricky depending on the manner in which the Government defines terms. In traditional policy debate, the plan is presented as an operational definition of the resolution/proposition. Effectively, the plan becomes the proposition and anything that is not the plan, is not the proposition. The Opposition's counter plan ground is, therefore, anything other than the Government's plan. While theoretically defendable, this approach may seem counterintuitive to many judges (particularly those without extensive theoretical backgrounds). Suppose, in support of the proposition, that, "This house would leave no child behind," the Government team runs a plan to mandate music curriculum in public elementary schools. The Opposition offers a counter plan calling for the adoption of new teaching methodologies, and incentives for teacher recruitment and retention. They argue that the counter plan is mutually exclusive based on funding. Both sides are supporting the proposition that no child should be left behind and only the technicality that the plan is an operational interpretation of the topic justifies the Opposition's perspective on topicality. Because this strategy is somewhat controversial, Opposition teams determined to run counter plans that appear topical must carefully analyze their audience.

Another theoretical implication of the topical counter plan stems from the notion that some believe topical counter plans do not have to capture the Government's advantages. On the topic, "The United States should protect the environment," the Government might present a policy to protect the national parks, and the Opposition could present a topical counter plan that would protect the water supply. Assuming that the plans were mutually exclusive, the Opposition could contend that their counter plan was superior to the Government plan because it solved for more significant harms and produced greater advantages.

Another view of the relationship between the Government's plan and the proposition posits that the Government team is not required to claim that the plan is an operational definition of the proposition. This alternate view contends that the plan is only one of many possible interpretations of the topic. Under this strategy, the Government is warranting the proposition through argument from example. To establish this relationship, the Government would define terms and transition into the plan with a claim that they are offering the following plan as one interpretation of the proposition. If the Opposition presents a counter plan that does not violate one or more of the key concepts in the proposition, the counter plan would be topical. While this approach offers some protection against the topical counter plan, it leaves open the question of hasty generalization. When the Government claims that its interpretation is an operational definition of the proposition, many judges will grant the Government broad discretion over the breadth of its case area. If, however, the Government claim is that the case is an example of the proposition, drawn from many possible examples, the Opposition should have more ground to question the significance of the Government's case area.

It is important that the Opposition understand the relationship between the Government's plan and the proposition before they present the counter plan in the Leader of the Opposition speech. It would be appropriate to utilize a point of information to ask the Prime Minister about that relationship.

Permutation: Because it Sounds Better than Alteration

Within the context of counter plan refutation, a permutation is either an actual or hypothetical (sometimes referred to as *artificial*) alteration of the Government's plan that attempts to demonstrate that the plan and the counter plan are not mutually exclusive. It is, essentially, a test of the competitiveness of the counter plan. If the plan can be altered in such a manner that it subsumes the counter plan, capturing its advantages, then the counter plan may not compete with the plan.

Some critics prefer that permutations be actual advocacy. This school of thought significantly restricts the ability of the Government to capture portions of the counter plan because the Government can only advocate actions that are topical. This is a particularly problematic restriction if one views the Government plan as the operational definition of the proposition because no action other than the plan would be topical, meaning no permutation of a non-topical counter plan provision could be legitimately advocated. Assuming that the Government plan is one of many possible interpretations of the proposition, it could permute topical portions of the counter plan. Suppose the topic was that the "United States should increase aid to the African continent." The Government's plan called for substantial increases in HIV medication to the continent. Further assume that the counter plan called for a similar policy to be performed by the United Nations with a specific plan plank on HIV education. The Government could, in theory, permute the education plank of the counter plan by arguing that the U.S. agents in the plan could provide the needed education, thus capturing any advantages associated with HIV education. Because of topicality constraints, however, the Government could not permute its plan to mandate that the United States and the United Nations. act in unison.

A contrasting (and perhaps majority) view contends that while permutations can be actual alterations of the plan, they can also be hypothetical (sometimes referred to as *artificial*) alterations that simply seek to test the mutual exclusivity of the counter plan. Because of their hypothetical nature, many judges will allow the Government to "perm" portions of the counter plan to reveal that the counter plan and plan could, hypothetically, be done at the same time. In this regard, the permutation becomes a test of competitiveness (Herbeck, Katsulas, 1986). Because the permutation is hypothetical, there is no requirement that the permutation be topical. One limitation of the hypothetical/artificial permutation is that if the permuted portion of the counter plan is not topical (portions of counter plans are often topical, while the counter plan remains non-topical because it violates one or more of the key terms in the topic), the Government cannot claim that the permutation represents an actual change in the Government plan and, therefore, cannot claim advantages from the permutation. Finally, for many judges, permutations should not represent major shifts in Government advocacy. If, for example, the Government argued that the United States has a moral imperative to immediately remove its troops from Iraq, it would be a shift in advocacy for the Government to attempt to perm a counter plan that advocated a delayed withdrawal of troops.

Opposition Fiat: Are There Any Limitations?

Recall that *fiat* power gives debaters the ability to debate the desirability of their plan/counter plan, excusing them from being obliged to argue the likelihood that the policy would be adopted. The question in a policy debate is not whether a policy *would or will* be adopted, but whether it *should* be adopted (consider the potential confusion created when topic framers use the word "would" in policy topics). The Government's fiat ability is limited to the actions and actors implied by the proposition (when the proposition is a metaphor, there is obviously more room for interpretation).

While there is some agreement as to the nature of Government fiat, the waters get muddier as we turn our attention to Opposition fiat. For some judges, the Opposition has fiat ability over anything other than the Government's plan. This view of fiat is simply an extension of the perspective that views Opposition ground as anything other than the plan (McGee, Romanelli, 1997). This perspective gives the Opposition limitless counter plan ground. The *utopian counter plan* in which the Opposition contends that nations switch their entire way of governing is grounded in this approach to fiat. Other critics favor limitations on the Opposition's counter plan ground (Herbeck, Katsulas, Panetta, 1987). They may limit the agent to a realistic national or international organization. They may also limit the mandates of the counter plan to reasonably feasible actions. Some will go so far as to limit the Opposition's fiat ability to that enjoyed by the Government (*reciprocal fiat*).

Opposition fiat preferences are obviously influenced by the arguer's view of the role of the counter plan. If the counter plan is viewed as an opportunity cost, it could be argued that no fiat is necessary because no actual counter plan advocacy is assumed. If the counter plan is viewed from the traditional perspective in which it is advocated as an alternative to the plan, it seems reasonable that the Opposition would be limited to the same levels of realism assumed by the Government's fiat. If the Government is obliged by the topic to defend the United States as the agent of action, reasonable counter plan ground would include other countries and non-governmental organizations. Worldwide anarchy would not be a counter plan option because it assumes a different level of realism. If, however, the counter plan is viewed as simply another strategy within a game, utopian fiat would be defendable as a potentially interesting part of that game.

ANOTHER LOOK AT TOPICALITY

Revisiting Jurisdiction, Ground, and Reasonability

This text has assumed that topicality is a stock issue when debating propositions of fact, value, and policy. Topicality, in its various manifestations, has played an important role in debate theory from the early days of NDT, through CEDA. Now, parliamentary debaters find themselves struggling with the concept. The NPDA rules for debating (see Appendix B) seem to suggest that topicality is a voting issue: "The proposition team must affirm the resolution by presenting and defending a sufficient case for that resolution." Yet, despite its history as generally recognized "rule" of debate, advanced debaters have undoubtedly come to the realization that not all critics will vote for topicality arguments, and many others are reluctant to do so. It is important that you understand why topicality is controversial, so that you can argue topicality in a manner that both increases your individual chances of winning topicality arguments and fosters a positive view of topicality arguments within the debate community.

Parliamentary debaters frequently justify topicality on two levels: jurisdiction and ground. Jurisdiction borrows from the legal analogy that suggests that the Speaker of the House, like a judge in a court room, only has jurisdiction to vote on the topic as worded. Understand that simply asserting topicality is a jurisdictional issue does not help to clarify the question of how to determine that jurisdiction. To establish jurisdiction, debaters will generally provide definitions that attempt to sketch out the parameters of the topic. Standards are simply criteria for determining which definitions are superior. The most commonly used standard is reasonability. Unfortunately, debaters rarely provide clear criteria for interpreting reasonability.

Like the term "jurisdiction," reasonability requires definition. What is reasonable to one critic may not be reasonable to the next. In a defense of the reasonability standard as it applied to NDT/CEDA debate, Herbeck and Katsulas (1985) argued that definitions were reasonable if they maintained the grammatical integrity of the topic and were consistent with the meaning established by experts in the field. The grammatical standard can easily be applied to parliamentary debate. Drawing again from Herbeck and Katsulas, suppose the proposition required that the United States significantly strengthen the regulation of print media. A Government interpretation that defined "to regulate" as "to protect" could allow the Government to run a plan that protected offensive publications. Their interpretation would violate the grammatical standard, however, because regulation functions as a noun in the proposition. "To regulate," on the other hand, is the verb form of regulation. As parli debaters scramble through a Webster's Dictionary to define terms, it is easy to confuse the various meanings of the terms in the proposition. Because grammatical integrity serves as an operational definition of reasonability, it can function as a check on potential definitional errors and deliberate attempts at manipulating the meaning of the topic.

The field context standard is more problematic in parliamentary debate. Parli's ban on written evidence, coupled with the fact that parli debaters do not know the topic before coming to the tournament, creates challenges for debaters seeking to offer field-specific definitions. Parli debaters frequently define terms using their own sense of the meaning of the words, or from common usage dictionaries such as Webster's. These sources of definitions give a sense of how the individual terms may be commonly used, but they generally do not assume the denotative meaning of the terms when viewed within the context of the proposition.

The lack of expert definitions in parli is one of the reasons that some judges reject topicality arguments. Because topicality is an all or nothing issue for the Government, some judges find it difficult to vote against the Government based solely on the Opposition's assertion of the meaning of the topic. One partial solution to the challenge presented by the field context standard is to encourage debaters to defer to specialized dictionaries. Many parli topics are related, at least in part, to the law. Black's Law Dictionary is an excellent source of field-specific definitions.

In addition to jurisdiction, parli debaters often base their topicality arguments in the need to fairly divide ground. It would be difficult to argue that the Government's interpretation is legitimate only if it provides equal ground for the Opposition. To the extent that, in any given debate, it is difficult to objectively define all possible ground, a standard requiring equal division of ground cannot be adequately defined or met. It is also important to remember that while providing ground for the Opposition may be a necessary test of the Government's interpretation, it is not a sufficient test of topicality. The Government's interpretation may be very arguable (provide adequate ground), but it may not pass the test of jurisdiction.

Despite potential pitfalls in ground as justification for topicality, a reasonable approach to ground division is justified. When the topic wording clearly establishes the central controversy of the proposition, both teams have the opportunity to make meaningful use of preparation time. The Opposition should attempt to prepare and advance arguments that are objectively within their argumentative ground. A Government interpretation that encroaches on that ground would probably violate the jurisdiction standard, but would also be unfair because it essentially robbed the Opposition of meaningful preparation time. This is problematic because a basic defining characteristic of debate is equal time allocation. Finally, restricting the Government interpretation to a position that provides for reasonable Opposition responses is consistent with parli's history of rejecting truistic interpretations. If ground division is not a criterion for a fair interpretation, there is no reason to uphold parli's opposition to truisms.

Taylor and Anderson (2003) took the issue of ground and truistic interpretations one step further when they argued that the Government interpretation must be controversial. Many canned cases attempt to force the Opposition into arguing seemingly heinous positions (don't give food to starving children, don't allow equal rights to all people, etc.). While these cases might meet the jurisdiction standard, it could be argued that they excessively limit Opposition arguments. The extent to which the Government must limit its interpretation and its strategic options is controversial. Opposition teams who contend that their strategic options have been excessively limited should be able to provide a clear bright line for what constitutes reasonable argumentative options. That, unfortunately, is easier said than done.

Because there seems to be no limit to the number and nature of topicality standards that debaters will invent, it is clearly impossible for any source to present them all to you. You are well advised, however, to utilize Points of Information to clarify the meaning of standards. Do not assume that you share your opponent's meaning of the terms used in the topicality argument. As was discussed earlier, even commonly used terms such as "reasonability" mean different things to different people.

Adapting to Judges Who Don't Love Topicality

If topicality arguments have been utilized for decades in academic debate, why is it often difficult to get critics in parli to vote on topicality? One answer stems from the fact that many judges dislike topicality arguments because they are frequently grounded in trivial standards that are easily met by the Member of Government's refutation. Suppose the topic required the Government to argue that standardized tests in K-12 education are detrimental. The Government selected the Stanford 9 tests, which measure achievement at a variety of grade levels. If the Opposition argued that the Stanford 9 is only one test, and the proposition requires "tests" to be the focus, many critics would view this as a trivial topicality argument. It is easily met by arguing that the test is administered at various grade levels, to various students. It is clearly a significant enough case area to give the Opposition ample ground to debate. The odds of the Opposition winning this argument, even with a critic who favors topicality arguments, are extremely low.

Many critics oppose topicality and other "procedural" arguments on the grounds that they distract from clash with the case. Case clash can be sacrificed in debates in which topicality becomes a central issue. This is particularly true when the topicality battle degenerates into arguments over multiple standards and counterstandards, some legitimate and some more creative than realistic. Critics without extensive debate backgrounds are reluctant to award a win to the

Opposition based on a rules-based issue when they are unfamiliar with the "rules."

When faced with a clearly non-topical case and a critic who has indicated a disdain for topicality, you have to decide if making the topicality argument is worth losing credibility with the critic. If you choose to argue topicality, it may be helpful to introduce the position by recognizing the critic's philosophy, to ensure him/her that you are not ignoring his/her preferences. If your critic is not an experienced debate judge, consider explaining the need for topicality by drawing analogies to other events the critic may have more experience judging. Judges of impromptu and extemporaneous speaking understand the need for competitors to choose examples and analysis that uphold the assigned topic. Judges of interpretation events regularly require that the pieces selected for a program support a central argument or thesis. By likening the topicality position to the requirement to support the topic in other events, explaining the commonsense meaning of the proposition, and by showing how the case violates that meaning, you may increase your chances of winning the topicality argument.

If your critic is an experienced debate judge who disfavors topicality, it may be prudent to avoid excessive use of standards and multiple violations. Again, many experienced critics have grown weary of so-called "time suck" topicality in which the Opposition presents highly detailed topicality arguments, hoping that the Government will fail to address an obscure sub-point or two. Keep standards and violations to a minimum. Your credibility and the clarity of the position will be enhanced by focusing on the exact problem with the Government's interpretation. Finally, limit the amount of time spent on topicality and do your best to argue the case. You may want to transition into the case argument by suggesting that your ability to argue the case is not a sign of it being topical. Recall that ground may be viewed as a necessary test of a fair interpretation, but not a sufficient test of topicality. You could have plenty to say about the case, and the case may still fail to support the topic.

PLAN VAGUENESS: CAPITALIZING ON AMBIGUITY

In Chapter 7, we discussed a model of plan construction that included the agent, the mandates, enforcement, and funding. This has been the basic model for plan construction in CEDA and NDT debate for decades. When debating hypothetical policies, it seems reasonable that the Government be obliged to indicate who will enact and oversee the policy (agent), what they will be required to do (mandates), the consequences for those who would violate the policy (enforcement), and how the policy might be paid for (funding). Once again, however, there are no "rules" that require the presence of each of these elements in the plan. Consequently, Government plans in parli range from fairly specific to very general. Some teams will omit any discussion of funding and enforcement.

Plan vagueness positions are one way that Opposition teams have been attacking underdeveloped Government plans. The plan vagueness argument contends that certain aspects of plan construction are mandatory, and that the Government has either failed to adequately develop those areas of the plan, or that they have simply left them out altogether. The position is generally impacted as a violation of the Government's responsibility to present a *prima facie* case. Clarification of the plan planks in the Member of Government speech would come too late to meet the *prima facie* requirement. Further, if the Government is permitted to provide substantial clarification of the plan after the Prime Minister's speech, they could abuse that license to shift out of their implied original position to avoid disadvantages, solvency arguments, etc.

Government teams will generally argue that the plan text is clear enough and that the Opposition could have used Points of Information to clarify anything that they did not understand. The POI answer, while common, is problematic because it assumes that it is the Opposition's burden to help the Government articulate the necessary parts of their plan. However, from the Government's perspective (and ultimately the judge's) it is challenging to clearly define what must be in the plan text to meet the *prima facie* burden. Government teams will generally respond that plan vagueness arguments are infinitely regressive, in that the Opposition can always assert a new and more rigorous test of the plan's specificity. If, for example, the Government indicates that it will fund the plan through "normal means," the Opposition can argue that normal means is not sufficiently clear. If they specify that funding will come through the federal budget, they can then question how much funding will be required. Additionally, if the Government becomes overly specific in its plan language, it risks being extra topical. Suppose, for example, the topic required that the U.S. Government change its foreign policy toward Africa. If the Government plan involved using troops to combat genocide in Africa, the Opposition might argue that U.S. forces are over-deployed now. To preempt that objection, the Government might include a plank in plan that called for a withdrawal of U.S. forces from Iraq. While specific, this plank would be extra topical. Additionally, very intricate plans might trigger objections from judges who are predisposed against canned cases.

It is reasonable to expect that the Government provide the basic framework of their policy. It is unreasonable to expect that, in fifteen minutes of preparation time, the Government provide extensive details of funding sources, methods of enforcement, etc. Given that the Government's plan is generally viewed as an operational definition of the topic, the judge and the Opposition should be able to listen to the plan and understand what is meant by the topic and what the Government intends to advocate or defend in the debate.

In terms of Opposition strategy, it may make more sense to create arguments that capitalize on the ambiguity of the Government's plan, rather than spending a lot of time trying to convince the judge that the plan is not sufficiently specific. Many judges view vagueness positions as attempts at an easy win. It is much more effective to provide, for example, a number of solvency arguments, pointing out that nothing in the plan language addresses those solvency challenges. In this manner, a judge that may be reluctant to vote on plan vagueness as a *prima facie* issue can now base his/her decision on more tangible and familiar solvency arguments. If the Government attempts to provide additional plan content in the Member of Government speech that was not in the Prime Minister's speech, the Member of Opposition can then argue that the lack of specificity in the plan has made it a moving target. Rather than being viewed as avoiding clash through the use of procedural arguments, the Opposition will be seen as the team that attempted to initiate clash through plan attacks.

SPLITTING THE OPPOSITION BLOCK

Splitting the Opposition block is one of the most controversial strategies available to the Opposition. At the outset, it is important for you to understand that a very small percentage of parli judges will accept this strategy. When splitting the block, the Leader of the Opposition is responsible for answering the Member of Government arguments in the Leader of the Opposition Rebuttal. Rather than responding to the Member of Government, the Member of the Opposition presents a number of new Opposition arguments. The goal of this strategy is to minimize redundancy between the Leader and Member of the Opposition, thereby placing the Prime Minister in the unenviable position of answering twelve minutes of Opposition arguments in his/her five minute rebuttal.

Supporters of the strategy often point out that CEDA/NDT debate do not require the second negative constructive speaker to cover the arguments of the second affirmative constructive. The first negative rebuttal is allowed to argue the second affirmative constructive positions, despite the fact that their partner did not address them in his/her constructive. One of the principles guiding this approach to speaker responsibilities is that an argument is only new in rebuttals if the team in question had both the reason and the opportunity to address the issue in an earlier speech (note that the "reason and opportunity" principle can also be used to justify topicality or other jurisdictional arguments in speeches past the Leader of the Opposition Constructive if the Member of Government explains a position in a manner that provides a "reason" for the jurisdictional argument). In CEDA/NDT, the second negative constructive speaker clearly has the opportunity to address the arguments made by the second affirmative. Arguably, however, there is no reason for him/her to address those arguments because the first negative rebuttal immediately follows the second negative constructive. If the second negative constructive was required to address the second affirmative constructive, the first negative rebuttal would become redundant and superfluous. Supporters of applying the block strategy in parli argue, therefore, that the Leader of the Opposition should be allowed to respond to the Member of Government constructive, regardless of whether or not the Member of the Opposition chose to do so. As in CEDA/NDT, these arguments should not be viewed as new because there is no reason for the Member of the Opposition to respond given that his/her partner delivers the next speech and may be better suited to defending the arguments that he/she made in the Leader of the Opposition constructive.

Opponents of the block strategy frequently point out that the comparison between Parli and CEDA/NDT is flawed because Parli has two rebuttals, while CEDA/NDT have four. The last two rebuttals in CEDA/NDT (the second negative rebuttal and the second affirmative rebuttal) are often used to summarize or "crystallize" the key issues. Because the Opposition is limited to one rebuttal period, it makes sense that it should be utilized for closing arguments and summaries. Opponents of the block position also argue that redundancy between the Member of the Opposition and the Leader of the Opposition rebuttal can be reduced if the LOR is diligent about using the speech to explain how the arguments made in the debate fit into the "big picture." By applying the arguments to the criteria/decision rule and other stock issues, the LOR has the opportunity to show the critic why the arguments matters. Furthermore, our goal should only be to limit excessive redundancy. Reviewing the key issues is crucial for retention. Debaters may remember the fourth argument they made in their constructive, but the critic may view it as simply another bit of scribble on their flow. A well-executed LOR will not simply reiterate that argument (ineffective redundancy), rather he/she will explain why that argument matters given the totality of the arguments made in the debate. Finally, opponents of the block strategy argue that allowing the Leader of the Opposition to respond for the first time to the Member of Government's constructive will put an undue burden on the Prime Minister's rebuttal. In CEDA/NDT, the need to cover all potentially damaging arguments caused the first affirmative rebuttal to be one of the fastest speeches in the activity. Opponents argue that Parli should emphasize eloquent delivery, and practices that encourage rapid delivery undermine that goal.

DEFENDING FACT/VALUE PROPOSITIONS WITH POLICIES

In Chapter 4, you read that parliamentary debate topics are propositions of fact, value, or policy. While this text, as well as many others, assumes there are three relatively distinct proposition types, it has become increasingly common to encounter Government teams that utilize policy debate structures to support propositions of fact and value. This practice is substantially less controversial when the proposition does not clearly fit into a particular category. Consider the proposition, "The best course of action is the fastest." This proposition includes evaluative language (best course), as well as quasi-policy implications. While it would be possible to prove the topic empirically (through the use of historical examples and analysis), it would be within the Government's topical mandate to test the truth of proposition by presenting a plan that attempted to rapidly solve some problem. Existing on the periphery of policy and value, this topic gives the Government the ability to draw from the stock issues of either policy or value propositions. Of greater controversy is the practice of using a plan to support a proposition that fits neatly into the fact/value category. The proposition "Recreation is undervalued in America," is probably best classified as a proposition of value. The legitimacy of utilizing a plan to support this proposition would be questioned by many critics.

Those who support utilizing policy stock issues on what are objectively fact or value proposition often argue that policy analysis is superior to simple criteria/example-based reasoning. They contend that the policy stock issues promote greater depth of analysis and that fact/value debates often devolve into example wars in which one side claims victory because they have presented the most examples. Values, being subjective, are more difficult to argue than the more tangible results of policies. The Government team also argues that if the critic votes for a plan that, say, increases recreation, they have thereby proven the resolution true (of course they haven't-they've only proven the specific plan more advantageous than not).

From the Government's perspective, there are potential strategic advantages to interpreting fact/value propositions as policy. Fact/value propositions are often worded and regarded as generalizations. The Government burden on a generalization is to demonstrate that it is true most of the time. This burden exposes the Government to the risk of under-supporting the topic and committing the fallacy of hasty generalization. When allowed to interpret the proposition as a policy, the Government captures the advantage of being able to operationally define the topic through the plan. The topic is, therefore, simply viewed as a parameter from which the Government can choose any plan, thus immunizing the Government from claims of hasty generalization. Additionally, because it is more difficult to prepare fact/value cases in advance of a tournament (to "can" them), the option of running a policy on a fact/value proposition can be seductive to a Government team with a healthy canned case file.

Opponents of the practice often ground their arguments in both authority and tradition. A cursory examination of argumentation and debate texts (see, for example, Freeley and Steinberg, Patterson and Zarefsky, Rybacki and Rybacki, Rieke and Sillars) reveals that, since at least the beginning of CEDA debate in the early 1970's, debate theorists have discussed distinctions between the three proposition types and have generally advocated stock issue burdens unique to those proposition types. Outside of the context of academic debate, the three proposition types have long been recognized as three types of declarative (as opposed to interrogatives or imperative) claims in the English language. Additionally, there are a variety of contexts in which propositions of fact and value are argued with few policy implications. For example, in a court room, guilt or innocence is determined based on the applications of fact to the law (criteria). Even where policy formulation is the ultimate goal, debates over facts and values are often important precursors. Before arguing the policy ramifications of euthanasia, for example, there are a number of questions of both fact and value that ought to be examined. Is there a constitutional basis for a "right to die"? Does a persistent vegetative state necessarily imply that there is no hope for recovery? Is suffering an important part of the human condition? These questions of fact and value are difficult to answer, and when advanced as claims they demand skillful debate. Because these types of propositions are part of "real world" advocacy, it is important that debaters understand how to argue them. The fact that value propositions are necessarily subjective and, therefore, difficult to argue does not provide adequate justification for ignoring the wording of the proposition and defending it with stock issue burdens that simply do not fit.

An additional objection to confounding policy and fact/value is that the plan and its advantages are extra-topical when utilized to support fact/value propositions. Generally, only the harms area of the case is required to prove the topic true. Even if the plan is a desirable part of the discussion, if there is nothing in the topic that implies a policy, the Government enjoys no fiat power. Essentially, everything in the case after the harms section is extra-topical. Returning to the topic, "Recreation is undervalued in America," if the Government opted to interpret this proposition as a policy, it might first demonstrate that there is a problem with the American emphasis on work over family. It might then proceed to provide a plan that mandates a four-day work week, and advantages to the shorter work week. The Opposition could argue that the plan and its advantages are extra-topical because the proposition does not require that the Government solve for the problem of undervalued recreation, rather it only requires that the Government demonstrate that recreation is undervalued.

The fact that the plan is really beyond what the Government is required and empowered to do leads to a final question on this section. Does it really make good strategic sense for the Government to assume all of the policy stock issues when it is not required to? To win a debate on a fact/value proposition, the basic Government responsibility is to articulate a reasonable criteria and do a better job than the Opposition of meeting the burdens established in that criteria. By comparison, the policy stock issues require that the Government prove harms, inherency, solvency, and net benefits. A loss of any one of these issues should, in theory, result in a Government loss. In sum, the strategic advantage the Government gains from being able to run a "canned" policy case may be outweighed by the additional burdens they assume in so doing.

SUMMARY

Debate theories are the result of a mixture of tradition, well-established methods of argument, and the experimentation of debaters and coaches. Good debate theories advance the participant's understanding of the proposition, promote clash, contribute to fairness, and help promote the longevity of the activity. From critique theory to alternative views of speaker responsibilities and resolutional burdens, the constantly evolving nature of debate theory requires that advanced debaters remain vigilant. Even if you choose to concentrate on more conservative strategies, success in advanced divisions of competition will demand that you know how to effectively respond to the more controversial approaches to parliamentary debate.

REFERENCES

Freeley, Austin J. and David L. Steinberg. *Argumentation and Debate*. 10th Ed. California: Wadsworth, 1993.

Herbeck, Dale A. "A Permutation Standard of Competitiveness." *Journal of the Ameican Forensic Association.* 22 (Summer 1985): 12-19.

Herbeck, Dale A. and John P. Katsulas. "The Affirmative Topicality Burden: Any Reasonable Example of the Resolution." *Journal of the American Forensic Association.* 21 (Winter 1985): 133-145.

Herbeck, Dale A. and John P. Katsulas. "In Response to Rowland on 'Realism and Debatability in Policy Advocacy'." *Journal of the American Forensic Association.* 23 (Fall 1986): 102-107.

Katsulas, John A. and Dale A. Herbeck, and Edward M. Panetta. "Fiating Utopia: A Negative View of the Examined: Implications for Counterplan Theory." *Journal of the American Forensics Association.* 25 (Winter 1989): 150-164.

McGee, Brian R. and David Romanelli. "Policy Debate as Fiction: In Defense of Utopian Fiat." *Contemporary Argumentation and Debate.* 18 (1997): 23-25.

Patterson J.W. and David Zarefsky. *Contemporary Debate.* Boston: Houghton Mifflin, 1983.

Rieke, Richard D. and Malcolm O. Sillars. *Argumentation and Critical Decision Making.* New York, Longman, 2001.

Rybacki, Karyn C. and Donald J. Rybacki. *Advocacy and Opposition.* 4th Ed. Boston: Allyn and Bacon, 2000.

Schnurer, M. "Conservative Critiquing," Paper Presented at the 1997 National Communication Association Convention, Chicago IL, p.np.

Taylor, M. and Joseph Anderson. "From Jurisdiction to Narration: Standards for Topicality in Parliamentary Debate." *The Journal of the National Parliamentary Debate Association.* 8 (2003): 81-91

Exercises

Chapter 11: Advanced Strategies for Tournament Debaters

1. Develop five arguments for and against topicality as a Government burden.

2. Develop responses to each of the answers to language and assumption critiques discussed in this chapter.

3. Participate in a practice debate in which the Opposition utilizes the block strategy outlined in this chapter. After the debate, discuss the advantages and disadvantages of the strategy with your coach.

4. Develop a critique on the topic, "Military intervention is in the best interest of the United States." Develop potential responses to your critique, and then create answers to those responses.

5. Utilizing the criteria for justifying theory discussed in this chapter, defend the language critique as a legitimate debate strategy.

.

CHAPTER 11

APPENDIX A: SAMPLE TOPICS

Tournament administrators throughout the nation wrote the following topics. The capitalization of terms and grammar are as they were presented on the National Parliamentary Debate Association's homepage.

Democracy is not for everyone.
The use of grades to evaluate student performance should be abolished.
Resolved: Presidential supremacy in the area of international treaties is desirable.
Resolved: That gender segregation improves the quality of education.
This House would open adoption records.
There is no place like home.
Tax dollars should not support bad art.
This house would hold parents responsible.
America deserves Professional Wrestling.
Be it resolved that national comprehensive health care would fail.
Be it resolved that the government that governs least governs best.
This house would reform the United States welfare system.
This house would embrace its feminine side.
Resolved: That when in conflict, the preservation of endangered species is more
    important than the protection of indigenous culture.
Resolved: That the United States should significantly increase humanitarian
    assistance to foreign nations.
Resolved: that the quality of life does not matter.
This House should give every species equal protection.
This House would change it foreign policy with the United States.
Education vouchers should not be used to fund private education.
The US should ratify the nuclear test ban treaty.
The US judicial system dispenses inadequate justice.
This house believes that it is more important to give than it is to receive.
This house would support radical redistribution.
Be it resolved: that hate speech ought to be banned.
The right to die must be protected.
The US Government owes its native peoples an apology.
This House believes that the IRS should be abolished.
This House believes that civil litigation should have the same requirements as
    criminal litigation.
This House would take from the rich and give to the poor.
This House believes that the government has forgotten its role.
This House would kill all the lawyers.
This House would change its locks.
This House believes that justice is blind.

This House supports the power of labor unions.

This House supports radical feminism.

This House would rock the Boat.

This House would rather be East than West.

The United States Federal Government should provide employment to all employable U.S. citizens living in poverty.

The U.S. Supreme Court should overturn one or more decisions that limit freedom of speech or press.

It is better to sing than to speak.

The United States should significantly curtail its arms sales to one or more foreign countries.

This House values a history of political service over a history of political service.

This House values nationalism over internationalism.

The best is yet to come.

This House would turn down the volume.

Peace has had its chance.

This House would increase the minimum wage.

This House would significantly increase environmental protection in the United States.

This House supports comprehensive reform of the nation's health care system.

This House believes the process of science should not be constrained by politics.

The United States should significantly increase support for the U.S. Armed Forces.

This House values Walmart.

The United States should significantly reduce its foreign military commitments.

Significantly increasing gas prices are good for America.

The United States Federal Government should significantly change its foreign policy toward one or more Asian countries.

This House would disregard its moral compass.

This House needs a spiritual re-awakening.

Support of athletics by higher education harms the educational process.

Congress should be given the power to reverse decisions of the Supreme Court.

Patriotism is misguided.

The United States should elect its President by popular vote.

The United States should substantially increase its border security.

This House would reject the lesser evil.

This House would remake others in its own image.

The United States should pay reparations for slavery.

This House prefers to root for the underdog.

Resolved: the music industry has gone too far.

This house values the community over the individual.

This house supports the doctrine of military preemption.

The terror alert system does more harm than good.

Term limits are not beneficial.
The war on terrorism has failed.
This house would wait for the Great Pumpkin.
Let nature take its course.
The jury system should be tampered with.
The United States should substantially expand the right to vote.
The United States should sign and ratify one or more international treaties.
In international relations, pragmatism is preferable to idealism.
This house would strengthen entitlement programs.
This house would protect American jobs.
This house should be forgiven for its past sins.
Media ethics need overhauling.
The tail is wagging the dog.
Science needs a stronger conscience.

APPENDIX

APPENDIX B: NPDA RULES OF DEBATING

The purpose of these rules is to define some goals and procedures of the debates so that, to the extent possible, everyone will enter the debates with a shared set of expectations. These rules are designed to apply to the goals and procedures of debate rather than the substance. They are framed in ways that attempt to allow many degrees of freedom in regard to debaters' creativity.

These Rules apply to the NPDA Championship Tournament. They also shall be considered to apply to any NPDA sanctioned tournament unless the director of that tournament publishes changes or alterations to these Rules in the tournament invitation.

Sanctions for violation of Section 4 of Rules of Debating and Judging (rules that apply during the debate) shall be province of the judge. In the case of a dispute regarding a judge's interpretation of the rules, enforcement of the rules, or adhering to the procedures of the tournament, one or both debate teams may appeal a judge's decision regarding sanctions to the tournament director for a final decision.

Charges of violations of any rules other than those in Section 4, including violations of rules before and after the debate, should be taken to the Tournament Director. In the case of serious violations of these Rules other than those in Section 4, the Tournament Director if supported by a 2/3 vote of the Tournament Committee may impose a penalties ranging from reprimand, to changing of a decision or speaker points, to withdrawal of a team or judge from the tournament.

RULES OF DEBATING AND JUDGING

1. Resolutions

1A. A different resolution for each round will be presented to the debaters at a specified time prior to the beginning of each debate. The specified time will be determined by adding fifteen minutes to the amount of time needed to walk to the most distant building in which debates are to occur.

1B. The topic of each round will be about current affairs or philosophy. The resolutions will be general enough that a well-educated college student can debate them. They may be phrased in literal or metaphorical language.

2. Objective of the debate

The proposition team must affirm the resolution by presenting and defending a sufficient case for that resolution. The opposition team must oppose the resolution and/or the proposition team's case. If, at the end of the debate, the judge believes that the proposition team has supported and successfully defended the resolution, they will be declared the winner; otherwise the opposition will be declared the winner.

3. Before the debate

The proposition team, if they wish, may use the room assigned for debate for their preparation. If the proposition team uses the debating room for preparation, both the judge and the opposition must vacate the room until the time for the debate to begin.

4. During the debate

4A. Any published information (dictionaries, magazines, etc) which may have been consulted before the debate cannot be brought into the debating chambers for use during the debate. Except for notes made during preparation time and a copy of the "NPDA Rules for Debating and Judging," no published materials, prepared arguments, or resources for the debater's use in the debate may be brought into the debating chambers.

4B. Debaters may refer to any information which is within the realm of knowledge of liberally educated and informed citizens. If they believe some cited information to be too specific, debaters may request that their opponent explain specific information with which they are unfamiliar. In the event further explanation of specific information is requested, the debater should provide details sufficient to allow the debater to understand the connection between the information and the claim. Judges will disallow specific information only in the event that no reasonable person could have access to the information: e.g.. information that is from the debater's personal family history.

4C. Format of the debate

First Proposition Constructive 7 minutes
First Opposition Constructive 8 minutes
Second Proposition Constructive 8 minutes
Second Opposition Constructive 8 minutes
Opposition Rebuttal 4 minutes
Proposition Rebuttal 5 minutes

4D. Constructive and Rebuttal Speeches

Introduction of new arguments is appropriate during all constructive speeches. However, debaters may not introduce new arguments in rebuttal speeches except that the proposition rebuttalist may introduce new arguments in his or her rebuttal to refute arguments that were first raised in the Second Opposition Constructive. New examples, analysis, analogies, etc. which support previously introduced arguments are permitted in rebuttal speeches.

4E. Points of Information

A debater may request a point of information--either verbally or by rising--at any time after the first minute and before the last minute of any constructive speech. The debater holding the floor has the discretion to accept or refuse points of information. If accepted, the debater requesting the point of information has a maximum of fifteen seconds to make a statement or ask a question. The speaking time of the debater with the floor continues during the point of information.

4F. Points of Order

Points of order can be raised for no reason other than those specified in these Rules of Debating and Judging. If at any time during the debate, a debater believes that his or her opponent has violated one of these Rules of Debating and Judging, he or she may address the Speaker of the House with a point of order. Once recognized by the Speaker of the House, the debater must state, but may not argue for, the point of order. At the discretion of the Speaker of the House, the accused may briefly respond to the point of order. The Speaker of the House will then rule immediately on the point of order in one of three ways: point well taken, point not well taken, or point taken under consideration. The time used to state and address a point of order will not be deducted from the speaking time of the debater with the floor. A point of order is a serious charge and should not be raised for minor violations.

4G. Points of Personal Privilege

At any time during the debate, a debater may rise to a point of personal privilege when he or she believes that an opponent has personally insulted one of the debaters, has made an offensive or tasteless comment, or has grievously misconstrued another's words or arguments. The Speaker will then rule on whether or not the comments were acceptable. The time used to state and address a point of personal privilege will not be deducted from the speaking time of the debater with the floor. Like a point of order, a point of personal privilege is a serious charge and should not be raised for minor transgressions.

Debaters may be penalized for raising spurious points of personal privilege.

5. After the debate

5A. After the final rebuttal, the Speaker of the House will dismiss the teams, complete the ballot and return it to the tournament director. The judges should not give oral comments before the ballot is completed and returned to the tournament director.

5B. A running update of all teams' records will be publicly posted in a "warm room" or common area accessible to all participants. After returning the ballot, the judge may, at his or her discretion, give brief constructive comments to the debaters. Such conversations should, if possible, take place in the established "warm room" area. No one may be required to enter the "warm room" area or participate in discussions. Judges should refrain from checking the records of teams they are about to judge should such information be available.

5C. Debaters or coaches will refrain from requesting that judges reveal decisions. Debaters or coaches who harass judges for information may be withdrawn from the tournament on a two-thirds vote of the Championship Tournament Committee.

Index

INDEX